CAMBRIDGE LIBRARY COLLECTION

Books of enduring scholarly value

Medieval History

This series includes pioneering editions of medieval historical accounts by
eye-witnesses and contemporaries, collections of source materials such as
charters and letters, and works that applied new historiographical methods
to the interpretation of the European middle ages. The nineteenth century
saw an upsurge of interest in medieval manuscripts, texts and artefacts, and
the enthusiastic efforts of scholars and antiquaries made a large body of
material available in print for the first time. Although many of the analyses
have been superseded, they provide fascinating evidence of the academic
practices of their time, while a considerable number of texts have still not
been re-edited and are still widely consulted.

Historical Memorials of Canterbury

Arthur Penrhyn Stanley (1815–81), later Dean of Westminster, was a canon
of Canterbury when he published this work, consisting of four essays on
the history of the cathedral, in 1854. It was reprinted almost immediately,
and the 1855 printing is reissued here. Stanley described the work as 'an
endeavour to connect topics of local interest with the general course of
history', and he takes four events associated with Canterbury – the arrival
of Augustine, the murder of Becket, the death of the Black Prince, and
the development of the shrine of Becket – and puts them in a historical
context, while also describing the locations in which scenes of historical
importance were enacted, and fascinating details from his literary sources,
such as Becket's hair shirt, discovered after his murder to be alive with
vermin. Other works by Dean Stanley, including his *Historical Memorials
of Westminster*, are also reissued in this series.

T0381752

Cambridge University Press has long been a pioneer in the reissuing of out-of-print titles from its own backlist, producing digital reprints of books that are still sought after by scholars and students but could not be reprinted economically using traditional technology. The Cambridge Library Collection extends this activity to a wider range of books which are still of importance to researchers and professionals, either for the source material they contain, or as landmarks in the history of their academic discipline.

Drawing from the world-renowned collections in the Cambridge University Library and other partner libraries, and guided by the advice of experts in each subject area, Cambridge University Press is using state-of-the-art scanning machines in its own Printing House to capture the content of each book selected for inclusion. The files are processed to give a consistently clear, crisp image, and the books finished to the high quality standard for which the Press is recognised around the world. The latest print-on-demand technology ensures that the books will remain available indefinitely, and that orders for single or multiple copies can quickly be supplied.

The Cambridge Library Collection brings back to life books of enduring scholarly value (including out-of-copyright works originally issued by other publishers) across a wide range of disciplines in the humanities and social sciences and in science and technology.

Historical Memorials
of Canterbury

The Landing of Augustine; The Murder of Becket;
Edward the Black Prince; Becket's Shrine

ARTHUR PENRHYN STANLEY

CAMBRIDGE
UNIVERSITY PRESS

CAMBRIDGE
UNIVERSITY PRESS

University Printing House, Cambridge, CB2 8BS, United Kingdom

Cambridge University Press is part of the University of Cambridge.
It furthers the University's mission by disseminating knowledge in the pursuit of
education, learning and research at the highest international levels of excellence.

www.cambridge.org
Information on this title: www.cambridge.org/9781108078726

© in this compilation Cambridge University Press 2018

This edition first published 1855
This digitally printed version 2018

ISBN 978-1-108-07872-6 Paperback

This book reproduces the text of the original edition. The content and language reflect
the beliefs, practices and terminology of their time, and have not been updated.

Cambridge University Press wishes to make clear that the book, unless originally published
by Cambridge, is not being republished by, in association or collaboration with,
or with the endorsement or approval of, the original publisher or its successors in title.

The original edition of this book contains a number of colour plates,
which have been reproduced in black and white. Colour versions of these
images can be found online at www.cambridge.org/9781108078726

The original edition of this book contains a number of oversize plates
which it has not been possible to reproduce to scale in this edition.
The can be found online at www.cambridge.org/9781108078726

HISTORICAL

MEMORIALS OF CANTERBURY.

THE TRANSEPT OF THE MARTYRDOM, CANTERBURY CATHEDRAL.

HISTORICAL

MEMORIALS OF CANTERBURY.

THE LANDING OF AUGUSTINE,
THE MURDER OF BECKET,
EDWARD THE BLACK PRINCE,
BECKET'S SHRINE.

By ARTHUR P. STANLEY, M.A.,

CANON OF CANTERBURY.

WITH ILLUSTRATIONS.

SECOND EDITION.

LONDON:
JOHN MURRAY, ALBEMARLE STREET.
1855.

TO THE VENERABLE

BENJAMIN HARRISON,

ARCHDEACON OF MAIDSTONE AND CANON OF CANTERBURY CATHEDRAL,

IN GRATEFUL REMEMBRANCE OF MUCH KINDNESS,

THESE SLIGHT MEMORIALS OF THE CITY AND CATHEDRAL
WHICH HE HAS SO FAITHFULLY SERVED

ARE INSCRIBED WITH SINCERE RESPECT,

BY THE AUTHOR.

CONTENTS.

I.—LANDING OF AUGUSTINE AND CONVERSION OF ETHELBERT.

The five landings, 3; Gregory the Great, 5—7; Dialogue with the Anglo-Saxon slaves, 7—10; Mission of Augustine, 11; Landing at Ebbe's-fleet, 12—14.

Ethelbert and Bertha, 14; St. Martin's church, 14; Interview of Ethelbert and Augustine, 15—17; Arrival of Augustine at Canterbury, 17; Stable-gate, 18; Baptism of Ethelbert and of the Kentish people, 19; Worship in the church of St. Pancras, 20; First endowment in the grant of the Cathedral of Canterbury, 21; Monastery, library, and burial-ground of St. Augustine's Abbey, 24; Foundation of the Sees of Rochester and London, 25; Death of Augustine, 26; Reculver, 27; Death of Ethelbert, 27.

Effects of Augustine's mission: Primacy of Canterbury, 28; Extent of English dioceses, 29; Toleration of Christian diversities, 30; Toleration of heathen customs, 31; Great results from small beginnings, 33.

II.—MURDER OF BECKET.

Variety of judgments on the event, 38; Sources of information, 39, 40.

Return of Becket from France; Controversy with the Archbishop of York on the right of coronation, 41, 42; Parting with the Abbot of St. Albans at Harrow, 43; Insults from the Brocs of Saltwood, 44; Scene in the Cathedral on Christmas day, 45.

Fury of the King, 47; The four knights, 48; Their arrival at Saltwood, 50; at St. Augustine's Abbey, 50; The fatal Tuesday, 51; The entrance of the knights into the Palace, 52.

Appearance of Becket, 53; Interview with the knights, 54—57; Their assault on the Palace, 58.

Retreat of Becket to the Cathedral, 59; Miracle of the lock, 60; Scene in the Cathedral, 61; Entrance of the knights, 62; The transept of "The Martyrdom," 63—65.

Meeting of the knights and the Archbishop, 66; Struggle, 67; The murder, 68, 69; Plunder of the Palace, 70; The storm, 71.

The dead body, 71; The watching in the choir, 72; The discovery of the haircloth, 73; The aurora borealis, 74.

The morning, 74; Unwrapping of the corpse and discovery of the vermin, 75, 76; Burial in the crypt, 77; Desecration and re-consecration of the Cathedral, 77; Canonisation, 78.

Escape of the murderers, 78; Turning-table at South Malling, 79; Legend of their deaths, 79; Their real history, 80; Moreville, Fitzurse, Bret, Fitzranulph, 81; Tracy, 82, 83; Pictorial representations of the murder, 85, 86.

The King's remorse, 86; Penance at Argenton, Gorham, and Avranches, 88; Ride from Southampton, 90; Entrance into Canterbury, 91; Penance in the crypt, 91; Absolution, 92; Conclusion, 94.

III.—EDWARD THE BLACK PRINCE.

Historical Lessons of Canterbury Cathedral, 100; The tombs, 101.

Birth of the Black Prince, 102; Union of hereditary qualities, 102; Education at Queen's College, Oxford, 102; Wycliffe, 103.

Battle of Cressy, 104—106; Name of "Black Prince," 107; Battle of Poitiers, 108, 109.

Visit to Canterbury, 110; "Black Prince's Well" at Harbledown, 111; "King John's Prison," 111.

Marriage—Chantry in the crypt, 112; Fawkes' hall, 112; Spanish campaign, 112; Return—sickness, 113; Appearance in Parliament, 113; Death-bed, 114; Exorcism by the Bishop of Bangor, 115; Death, 116.

Mourning, 117; Funeral, 118, 119; Tomb, 120; Effects of the Prince's life: (1) English and French wars, 122; (2) Chivalry—sack of Limoges, 123; (3) First great English captain, and first English gentleman, 125.

APPENDIX.

1. ORDINANCE FOR THE TWO CHANTRIES FOUNDED BY THE BLACK PRINCE IN THE UNDERCROFT OF CHRIST CHURCH, CANTERBURY, 127.

2. THE WILL OF THE BLACK PRINCE, 132.

Notes by Mr. Albert Way, 138.

IV.—THE SHRINE OF BECKET.

Comparative insignificance of Canterbury Cathedral before the murder of Becket, 147.

Relative position of Christ Church and St. Augustine's, 148; Change effected by Archbishop Cuthbert, 151.

Effect of the "Martyrdom," 152; Spread of the worship of St. Thomas, in Italy, France, Syria, 153; In Scotland and England, 154; In London, 155.

Altar of the Sword's Point, 156; Plunder by Roger and Benedict, 156.

The Tomb in the crypt, 157; Henry II., Louis VII., Richard I., John, 157.

Erection of the SHRINE, 157; The fire of 1174, 158; William of Sens and William the Englishman, 158; Enlargement of the eastern end, 160; The watching chamber, 160.

The Translation of the Relics in 1220, 161; Henry III., Langton, 161—163.

Pilgrimages, 164; Approach from Sandwich, 164; The Bohemian embassy, 165; Approach from Southampton, 165; "The Pilgrims' Road," 165; Approach from London, 166; CHAUCER'S CANTERBURY TALES, 166—170.

Entrance into Canterbury, 171; Jubilees, 172; The Inns, 173; The Chequers, 174; The Convents, 175.

Entrance into the Cathedral, 176.

The Nave, 177; The "Martyrdom," 177; The Crypt, 178; The Steps, 179; The Crown, 180; THE SHRINE, 181; The Regale of France, 183.

The Well and the Pilgrims' signs, 185; The Dinner, 187; The Town 187; The Return, 187.

Greater pilgrims, 188; Edward I., 188; Isabella, 188; John of France, 188.

Reaction against pilgrimage, 189; The Lollards, 189; Simon of Sudbury, 190; Erasmus and Colet, 191; Scene at Harbledown, 193.

Visit of Henry VIII. and Charles V., 195.

The Reformation, 196; Abolition of the festival, 196; Cranmer's banquet, 197; Trial of Becket, 198; Visit of Madame de Montreuil, 200; DESTRUCTION OF THE SHRINE, 201; Proclamation, 202.

Conclusion, 203—206.

Note A.—Extracts from the "Polistoire" of Canterbury Cathedral, 208.

Note B.—Extracts from the Travels of the Bohemian Embassy, in 1465, 211.

Note C.—Extracts from the "Pelerino Inglese," 215.

Note D.—The Pilgrims' Road, by Mr. Albert Way, 216.

Note E.—The Pilgrimage of John of France, by the same, 221.

Note F.—Documents from the Treasury in Canterbury Cathedral, relating to the Shrine of Becket, with Notes, by the same, 223.

     I.—Grants of William de Tracy, and of Amicia de la More, 223.
     II.—The 'Corona' of S. Thomas, 227.
     III.—Miraculous Cures at the Shrine of S. Thomas, 230.

Note G.—The Crescent on the Roof of the Trinity Chapel, 236.

Note H.—The Painted Windows commemorating the Miracles of Becket, 238.

Note I.—Becket's Shrine in Painted Window, Canterbury, 243.

ILLUSTRATIONS.

Page.

THE TRANSEPT OF THE MARTYRDOM, CANTERBURY CATHEDRAL
Frontispiece

PLAN OF THE CATHEDRAL, *at the time of the Murder of Becket* . . 64

THE CRYPT, CANTERBURY CATHEDRAL 92

THE TOMB OF THE BLACK PRINCE IN CANTERBURY CATHEDRAL 120

Relics of the Black Prince Suspended over his Tomb 120

Enamelled Escutcheons on the Tomb of the Black Prince 141

Representation of the Black Prince, illustrating the Canopy over the Tomb . 141

CANOPY OF THE BLACK PRINCE'S TOMB IN CANTERBURY
CATHEDRAL 121

BECKET'S SHRINE 181

REPRESENTATION OF BECKET'S SHRINE IN A PAINTED
WINDOW IN CANTERBURY CATHEDRAL 243

INTRODUCTION.

THE following pages, written in intervals of leisure, taken from subjects of greater importance, have nothing to recommend them, except such instruction as may arise from an endeavour to connect topics of local interest with the general course of history. It appeared to me, on the one hand, that some additional details might be contributed to some of the most remarkable events in English history, by an almost necessary familiarity with the scenes on which those events took place ; and, on the other hand, it seemed possible that a comparative stranger, fresh from other places and pursuits, might throw some new light on local antiquities even when they have been as well explored as those of Canterbury.

To these points I have endeavoured, as nearly as possible, to limit myself. Each of the four subjects which are here treated opens into much wider fields than can be entered upon, unless as parts of the general history of England. Each, also, if followed out in all their details, would require a more minute research than I am able to afford. But in each, I trust, something will be found which may not be altogether useless either to the antiquary or to the historian, who may wish to examine these events fully under their several aspects.

Other similar subjects might be added; and, if time and opportunity should be granted, may perhaps be added at some future period. But the four here selected are so indisputably the most important in themselves, as well as the most closely connected with the history of Canterbury Cathedral, that I have not scrupled thus to bring them together apart from any topics of kindred but subordinate interest.

The first Essay is the substance of a lecture delivered before an institution at Canterbury in the present year, and necessarily partakes of a more popular character than so grave a subject as the conversion of England would naturally require. For the reasons above stated, I have abstained from entering on the more general questions which the event suggests,—the character and position of Gregory the Great,—the relation of the Anglo-Saxon to the British Church; and the gradual spread of Christianity through the northern tribes of England. It is sufficient for my purpose if I have exhibited, in fuller detail than is usually found, the earliest tradition which England and Canterbury possessed on the origin of the mission of Augustine, and the successive steps by which that mission was established in Kent. And I have, in so doing, endeavoured to point out how forcibly these details illustrate the remote position which Britain then occupied in relation to the rest of the civilised world, and the traces which Roman civilisation then for the first time planted among our rude Saxon forefathers left in the country.

The second Essay, which originally appeared in the " Quarterly Review," September 1853, has been since considerably enlarged by additional information, contributed chiefly through the kindness of friends. Here again the general merits of the controversy between Henry II. and Becket have been avoided ; and my object was simply to give the facts of its closing scene. For this, my residence at Canterbury provided special advantages ; and the narrative purposes to embrace every detail which tends to place the transaction in a more perspicuous light. In order to simplify the number of references to the numerous authorities I have sometimes contented myself with giving the chief authorities when they seemed sufficiently to guarantee the facts. Of the substantial correctness of the whole story, the remarkable coincidences between the several narratives, and again between the narratives and the actual localities, appear to me decisive proofs.

The third Essay was delivered as a lecture at Canterbury, in July, 1852. Although in point of time, it preceded the others, and was in part intended as an introduction to any future addresses or essays of a similar kind, I have removed it to a later place for the sake of harmonising it with the chronological order of the volume. The lecture stands nearly as it was delivered ; nor have I altered some allusions to our own time, which later events have rendered, strictly speaking, inapplicable, though, perhaps, in another point of view, more intelligible than when first written. Poitiers is not less interesting when seen in the light of Inkermann, and the French and English wars receive a fresh and happy illustration from the French and English alliance. There is, of course, little new that can be said of the Black Prince ; and my

chief concern was with the incidents which form his connexion with Canterbury. But, in the case of so remarkable
a monument as his tomb and effigy in the Cathedral, a
general sketch of the man was almost unavoidable. The
account of his death and funeral has not, to my knowledge,
been put together before.

The fourth Essay is the substance of two lectures
delivered at Canterbury. The story of the Shrine of
Becket was an almost necessary complement to the story
of his murder; its connection with Chaucer's poem gives
it a more than local interest; and it brings the history of
the Cathedral down to the period of the Reformation.
Some few particulars are new, and I have endeavoured to
represent in this, most conspicuous instance, the rise,
decline, and fall of a state of belief and practice now
extinct in England, and only seen in modified forms on
the Continent.

In the Appendix to the two last lectures will be found
various original documents, most of them now published
for the first time, from the archives of the Chapter of
Canterbury. For this labour, as well as for much
assistance and information in other parts of the volume, I
am indebted to the kindness of my friend and relative,
Mr. Albert Way. He is responsible only for his own
contributions, but without his able and ready co-opera-
tion, I should hardly have ventured on a publication
requiring more antiquarian knowledge and research than
I could bestow upon it; and the valuable Notes which he
has appended to supply this defect will, I trust, serve to
perpetuate many pleasant recollections of his pilgrimages
to Canterbury Cathedral.

THE LANDING OF AUGUSTINE,

AND

CONVERSION OF ETHELBERT.

B

THE authentic materials for the story of the Mission of Augustine are almost entirely comprised in the first and second books of Bede's "Ecclesiastical History," written in the beginning of the eighth century. A few additional touches are given by Paul the Deacon and John the Deacon, in their Lives of Gregory the Great, respectively at the close of the eighth, and the close of the ninth century; and in Ælfric's "Homily on the Death of Gregory" (A.D. 990—995), translated by Mrs. Elstob. Some local details may be gained from "The Chronicles of St. Augustine's Abbey," by Thorn, and "The Life of St. Augustine," in the *Acta Sanctorum* of May 26, by Gocelin, both monks of St Augustine's Abbey, one in the fourteenth, and the other in the eleventh century, but the latter written in so rhetorical a strain as to be of comparatively little use, except for the posthumous legends.

LANDING OF AUGUSTINE,

CONVERSION OF ETHELBERT.

———◆———

THERE are five great landings in English history, each of vast importance,—the landing of Julius Cæsar, which first revealed us to the civilised world, and the civilised world to us ; the landing of Hengist and Horsa, which gave us our English forefathers, and our English characters ; the landing of Augustine, which gave us our English Christianity ; the landing of William the Conqueror, which gave us our Norman aristocracy ; the landing of William III., which gave us our free Constitution.

Of these five landings, the three first and most important were formerly all supposed to have taken place in Kent. It is true that the claims of Deal to be the scene of Cæsar's landing, though capable of a strong, probably of a successful, defence, are not quite what they were before the elaborate argument of the present Astronomer Royal in favour of Pevensey. And, so much doubt has been lately thrown on the historical existence of Hengist and Horsa, that this too must be received with some hesitation. Still, whatever may be said for or against these earlier landings, there is no doubt of the close connection of the landing of St. Augustine, not only with Kent, but with Canterbury.

It is a great advantage to consider the circumstances of this memorable event in our local history, because it takes us immediately into the consideration of events which are far removed from us both by space and time—events too of universal interest, which lie at the beginning of the history, not only of this country, but of all the countries of Europe,—the invasion of the Northern tribes into the Roman Empire, and their conversion to Christianity.

We cannot understand who Augustine was, or why he came, without understanding something of the whole state of Europe at that time. It was, we must remember, hardly more than an hundred years since the Roman Empire had been destroyed, and every country was like a seething caldron, just settling itself after the invasion of the wild barbarians who had burst in upon the civilised world, and trampled down the proud fabric, which had so long sheltered the arts of peace, and the security of law. One of these countries was our own. The fierce Saxon tribes, by whomsoever led, were to the Romans in Britain what the Goths had been in Italy, what the Vandals had been in Africa, what the Franks had been in France ; and under them England had again become a savage nation, cut off from the rest of the world, almost as much as it had been before the landing of Julius Cæsar. In this great convulsion it was natural that the civilisation and religion of the old world should keep the firmest hold on the country and the city, which had so long been its chief seat. That country, as we all know, was Italy, and that city was Rome. And it is to Rome that we must now transport ourselves, if we wish to know how and from whence it was that Augustine came—by what means, under God, our fathers received the light of the Gospel.

In the general crash of all the civil institutions of the Empire, when the last of the Cæsars had been put down, when the Roman armies were no longer able to maintain their hold on the world, it was natural that the Christian clergy of Rome, with the Bishop at their head, should have been invested with a new and unusual importance. They retained the only sparks of religious or of civilised life, which the wild German tribes had not destroyed, and they accordingly remained still erect amidst the ruins of almost all besides.

It is to one of these clergy, to one of these Bishops of

Rome, that we have now to be introduced ; and, if in the
story we are about to hear, it shall appear that we
derived the greatest of all the blessings we now enjoy from
one who filled the office of Pope of Rome, it will not be
without its advantage, for two good reasons: First,
because, according to the old proverb, every one, even the
Pope, must have his due—and it is as ungenerous to
deny him the gratitude which he really deserves, as it is
unwise to give him the honour to which he has no
claim ; and, secondly, because it is useful to see how
different were all the circumstances which formed our
relations to him then and now ; how, although bearing
the same name, yet in reality the position of the man and
the office, his duties towards Christendom, and the duties
of Christendom towards him, were as different from
what they are now, as almost any two things are one from
the other.

It is then on Gregory the Great that we are to fix our
attention. At the time we are first to meet him, he was
not yet Pope. He was still a monk in the great monastery
of St. Andrew, which he had himself founded, and which
still exists, on the Cælian Mount at Rome, standing conspicuous amongst the Seven Hills—marked by its crown of
pines—rising immediately behind the vast walls of the
Colosseum, which we may still see, and which Gregory
must have seen every day that he looked from his convent
windows.

This is not the place to discuss at length the good and
evil of his extraordinary character, or the position
which he occupied in European history, almost as
the founder of Western Christendom. I will now
only touch on those points which are necessary to make
us understand what he did for us and our fathers. He
was remarkable amongst his contemporaries for his bene-
volence and tenderness of heart. Many proofs of it are
given in the stories which are told about him. The long
marble table is still shown at Rome where he used to feed
twelve beggars every day. There is a legend that on one
occasion a thirteenth appeared among them, an unbidden
guest—an angel, whom he had thus entertained unawares.

There is also a true story, which tells the same lesson—that
he was so much grieved on hearing of the death of a poor
man, who, in some great scarcity in Rome, had been
starved to death, that he inflicted on himself the severest
punishment, as if he had been responsible for it. He also
showed his active charity in one of those seasons,
which give opportunity to all faithful pastors, and all
good men, for showing what they are really made of,
during one of the great pestilences which ravaged Rome
immediately before his elevation to the pontificate. All
travellers who have been at Rome will remember the
famous legend, describing how, as he approached at the
head of a procession, chanting the Litany, to the great
mausoleum of the Emperor Hadrian, he saw in a vision
the Destroying Angel on the top of the tower sheathing
his sword ; and from this vision, the tower, when it afterwards was turned into the Papal fortress, derived the name
of the Castle of St. Angelo.   Nor was his charity confined
to this world.   His heart yearned towards those old Pagan
heroes or sages who had been gathered to their fathers
without hearing of the name of Christ.   He could not bear
to think, with the belief that prevailed at that time, that
they had been consigned to destruction.   One especially
there was, of whom he was constantly reminded in his
walks through Rome—the great Emperor Trajan, whose
statue he always saw rising above him at the top of the
tall column which stood in the market-place, called from
him the Forum of Trajan.   It is said, that he was so
impressed with the thought of the justice and goodness
of this heathen sovereign, that he earnestly prayed in
St. Peter's Church, that God would even now give him
grace to know the name of Christ and be converted.   And
it is believed, that from the veneration which he entertained for Trajan's memory, this column remained when
all around it was shattered to pieces ; and so it still remains,
a monument both of the goodness of Trajan, and the true
Christian charity of Gregory.   Lastly, like many, perhaps
like most remarkable men, he took a deep interest in
children.   He instructed the choristers of his convent
himself in those famous chants which bear his name.   The

book from which he taught them, the couch on which he reclined during the lesson, even the rod with which he kept the boys in order, were long preserved at Rome ; and in memory of this part of his life, a children's festival was held on his day as late as the 17th century.[1]

I may seem to have detained you a long time in describing these general features of Gregory's character. But they are necessary to illustrate the well-known story[2] which follows, and which was preserved, not, as it would seem, at Rome, but amongst the grateful descendants of those who owed their conversion to the incident recorded. There was one evil of the time—from which we are now happily free—which especially touched his generous heart, —the vast slave-trade which then went on through all parts of Europe. It was not only as it once was in the British empire, from the remote wilds of Africa, that children were carried off and sold as slaves, but from every country in Europe. The wicked traffic was chiefly carried on by Jews and Samaritans;[3] and it afterwards was one especial object of Gregory's legislation to check so vast an evil. He was, in fact, to that age what Wilberforce and Clarkson, by their noble Christian zeal, have been to ours. And it may be mentioned, as a proof both of his enlightened goodness, and of his interest in this particular cause, that he even allowed and urged the sale of sacred vessels, and of the property of the Church, for the purpose of redeeming captives. With this feeling in his mind he one day went with the usual crowd that thronged to the market-place at Rome, when they heard, as they did on

[1] Lappenberg's Hist. of England (Eng. Tr.), i. 130.

[2] The story is told in Bede, II. i. § 89, and from him is copied, with very slight variations, by all other ancient mediæval writers. It has been told by most modern historians, but in no instance that I have seen with perfect accuracy, or with the full force of all the expressions employed. As Bede speaks of knowing it by tradition, "traditione majorum," he may, as a Northumbrian, have heard it from the families of the Northumbrian slaves. But most probably it was preserved in St. Augustine's monastery at Canterbury, and as the earliest of "Canterbury Tales," it seemed worthy of being here repeated with all the illustrations it could receive. There is nothing in the story intrinsically improbable ; and, although Gregory may have been actuated by many motives of a more general character, such as are ably imagined by Mr. Kemble, in the interesting chapter on this subject in his "Saxons in England," yet perhaps we learn as much by considering in detail what in England at least was believed to be the origin of the mission.

[3] See Milman's "History of the Jews," iii. 208.

this occasion, that new cargoes of merchandise had been imported from foreign parts. It was possibly in that very market-place, of which I have before spoken, where the statue of his favourite Trajan was looking down upon him from the summit of his lofty pillar. To and fro, before him, amongst the bales of merchandise, passed the gangs of slaves, torn from their several homes, to be sold amongst the great families of the nobles and gentry of Italy—a sight such as may still be seen (happily nowhere else) in the remote East, or in the southern states of North America. These gangs were doubtless from various parts ; there were the swarthy hues of Africa ; there were the dark-haired and dark-eyed inhabitants of Greece and Sicily ; there were the tawny natives of Syria and Egypt. But amongst these, one group arrested the attention of Gregory beyond all others. It was a group of three [1] boys, distinguished from the rest by their fair complexion and white flesh, the beautiful expression of their countenances, and their light flaxen hair, which, by the side of the dark captives of the south, seemed to him almost of dazzling brightness,[2] and which, by its long curls, showed that they were of noble origin.

Nothing gives us a stronger notion of the total separation of the northern and southern races of Europe at that time, than the emotion which these peculiarities, to us so familiar, excited. He stood and looked at them ; his fondness for children of itself would have led him to pity them ; that they should be sold for slaves struck (as we have seen) on another tender chord in his heart ; and he asked from what part of the world they had been brought. The slave merchant, probably a Jew, answered, "From Britain, and there all the inhabitants have this bright complexion."[3]

---

[1] Thorn, 1737. "Tres pueros." He alone gives the number.

[2] "Candidi corporis," BEDE; "lactei corporis," PAUL THE DEACON, c. 17; "venusti vultûs, capillorum nitore," JOHN THE DEACON; "crine rutilâ," GOCELIN; "Capillos præcipui candoris," PAULUS DIAC.; "capillum formâ egregiâ," BEDE; "noble (æthelice) heads of hair," ÆLFRIC. It is from these last expressions, that it may be inferred that the hair was unshorn, and therefore indicated that the children were of noble birth.—See Palgrave's "History of the Anglo-Saxons," p. 58 ; Lappenberg's Hist. of England, i. 136.

[3] "De Britanniæ insulâ, cujus incolarum omnis facies simili candore fulgescit." (Acta Sanct. p. 141, JOHN THE DEACON, i. 21.)

It would almost seem as if this was the first time that Gregory had ever heard of Britain. It was indeed to Rome nearly what New Zealand is now to England, and one can imagine that fifty years ago, even here, there may have been many, even of the educated classes, who had a very dim conception of where New Zealand was, or what were its inhabitants. The first question which he asked about this strange country, was what we might have expected. The same deep feeling of compassion that he had already shown for the fate of the good Trajan, now made him anxious to know whether these beautiful children—so innocent, so interesting—were Pagans or Christians. "They are Pagans," was the reply. The good Gregory heaved a deep sigh[1] from the bottom of his heart, and broke out into a loud lamentation expressed with a mixture of playfulness, which partly was in accordance with the custom of the time,[2] partly perhaps was suggested by the thought that it was children of whom he was speaking. " Alas! more is the pity, that faces so full of light and brightness should be in the hands of the Prince of Darkness, that such grace of outward appearance should accompany minds without the grace of God within!"[3] He went on to ask what was the name of their nation, and was told that they were called " Angles " or " English." It is not without a thrill of interest that we hear the proud name which now is heard with respect and awe from the rising to the setting sun, thus uttered for the first time in the metropolis of the world—thus awaking for the first time a response in a Christian heart. " Well said," replied Gregory, still following out his play on the words—"rightly are they called Angles, for they have the face of angels, and they ought to be fellow-heirs of angels in Heaven." Once more he asked, " What is the name of the province from which they were brought ? " He was told that they were " Deirans,"

---

[1] "Intimo ex corde longa trahens suspiria," BEDE.

[2] The anonymous biographer of Gregory in the *Acta Sanctorum*, March 12, p. 130, rejoices in the Pope's own name of good omen, "Gregorius," quasi "Vigilantius."

[3] "Tam lucidi vultus . . . . auctor tenebrarum . . . . gratiâ frontis . . . . gratiâ Dei," BEDE ; " Black Devil," ÆLFRIC.

that is to say, that they were from Deira[1] (the land of
"wild beasts," or "wild *deer*,") the name then given to
the tract of country between the Tyne and the Humber,
including Durham and Yorkshire. "Well said, again,"
answered Gregory, with a play on the word that can only
be seen in Latin,—"rightly are they called Deirans,
plucked as they are from God's ire (de irâ Dei), and called
to the mercy of Christ." Once again he asked, "And who
is the king of that province?" "Ella," was the reply.
Every one who has ever heard of Gregory, has heard
of his Gregorian chants, and of his interest in sacred
music; the name of Ella reminded him of the Hebrew
words of praise which he had introduced into the Roman
service,[2] and he answered, "Allelujah! the praise of
God their Creator shall be sung in those parts."[3]

So ended this dialogue—doubly interesting because
its very strangeness shows us the character of the man
and the character of his age. This mixture of the playful
and the serious—this curious distortion of words from
their original meaning—was to him and his times the
natural mode of expressing their own feelings and of
instructing others. But it was no passing emotion which
the sight of the three Yorkshire boys had awakened in
the mind of Gregory. He went from the market-place to
the Pope, and obtained from him at once permission to go
and fulfil the design of his heart, and convert the English
nation to the Christian faith.

He was so much beloved in Rome, that great opposition (it was felt) would be made to his going; and therefore
he started from his convent with a small band of his
companions in the strictest secrecy. But it was one of
the many cases that we see in human life, where even
the best men are prevented from accomplishing the objects
they have most at heart. He had advanced three days
along the great northern road, which leads through the
Flaminian gate from Rome to the Alps. When[4] they

[1] Deore—Thier—deer.—See Soames'
"Anglo-Saxon Church," 31.
[2] See Fleury, H. E. xxxvi. 18.
[3] See the account of Gregory's own

Commentary on Job, as shortly given
in Milman's "Hist. of Latin Christianity," vol. i. 435.
[4] "Vit. S. Greg."—PAUL THE DEACON.

halted as usual to rest at noon—they were lying down
in a meadow, and Gregory was reading; suddenly a locust
leapt upon his book, and sat motionless on the page. In
the same spirit that had dictated his playful speeches to the
three children, he began to draw morals from the name
and act of the locust. " Rightly is it called Locusta," he
said, " because it seems to say to us 'Loco Sta,' " that is,
" stay in your place. I see that we shall not be able to
finish our journey. But rise, load the mules, and let us
get on as far as we can." It was whilst they were in the
act of discussing this incident that there gallopped to the
spot messengers, on jaded horses, bathed in sweat, who had
ridden after him at full speed from the Pope, to command
his instant return. A furious mob had attacked the Pope
in St. Peter's Church, and demanded the instant recall of
Gregory. To Rome he returned; and it is this interrup-
tion, humanly speaking, which prevented us from having
Gregory the Great for the first Archbishop of Canterbury
and founder of the English Church.

Years rolled away[1] from the time of the conversation in
the market-place, before Gregory could do anything for
the fulfilment of his wishes. But he never forgot it, and
when he was at last elected Pope, he employed an agent
in France to buy English Christian youths of seventeen or
eighteen years of age, sold as slaves, to be brought up in
monasteries. But before this plan had led to any result,
he received intelligence which determined him to adopt a
more direct course. What this intelligence was, we shall
see as we proceed. Whatever it might be, he turned
once more to his old convent on the Cælian hill, and
from its walls sent forth the Prior, Augustine, with forty
monks as missionaries to England. In one of the
chapels of that convent there is still a picture of their
departure.

I will not detain you with his journey through
France; it is chiefly curious as showing how very remote
England seemed to be.[2] He and his companions were

---

[1] The mention of "Ella" in the
dialogue fixes the date to be before

A.D. 588. Augustine was sent, A.D. 597.
[2] Greg. Epp. v. 10.

so terrified by the rumours they heard, that they sent him back to Rome to beg that they might be excused. Gregory would hear of no retreat from dangers, which he had himself been prepared to face. At last they came on, and landed at Ebbe's Fleet,[1] in the Isle of Thanet.

Let us look for a moment on the scene of this important event as it now is, and as it was then. You all remember the high ground where the white chalk cliffs of Ramsgate suddenly end in Pegwell Bay. Look from that high ground over the level flat which lies between these cliffs and the point where they begin again in St. Margaret's cliffs, beyond Walmer. Even as it is, you see why it must always have invited a landing from the continent of Europe. The wide opening between the two steep cliffs must always have afforded the easiest approach to any invaders or any settlers. But it was still more so at the time of which we are now speaking. The level ground which stretches between the two cliffs, was then in great part covered with water; the sea spread much further inland from Pegwell Bay, and the Stour, or Wensome[2] (as that part was then called), instead of being a scanty stream that hardly makes any division between the meadows on one side and the other, was then a broad river, making the Isle of Thanet really an island, nearly as much as the Isle of Sheppey is now, and stretching at its mouth into a wide estuary, which formed the port of Richborough. Moreover, at that remote age, Sandwich haven was not yet choked up, so that all the ships which came from France and Germany on their way to London, sailed up into this large port, and through the river, out at the other side by Reculver: or, if they were going to land in Kent, at

---

[1] It is called variously *Hypwine, Epwine, Hiped, Hepe, Epped, Wipped,* Fleet; and the name has been variously derived from *Whipped,* (a Saxon chief, killed in the first battle of Hengist,) *Hope* (a haven), *Abbet* (from its being afterwards the port of the Abbey of St. Augustine). *Fleet* is "Port."

[2] The "Boarded Groin" which Lewis (Isle of Thanet, p. 83) fixes as the spot, still remains, a little beyond the coast-guard station, at the point marked in the Ordnance Survey as the landing-place of the Saxons. "Cotmansfeld" seems to be the high ground running at the back of the level: the only vestige of the name now preserved is "Cottington." But no tradition marks this spot, and it must then have been covered by the sea.

Richborough on the mainland, or at Ebbe's Fleet, in the Isle of Thanet.

Ebbe's Fleet is still the name of a farm-house on a strip of a high ground rising out of Minster marsh, which can be distinguished from a distance by its line of trees, and on a near approach you see at a glance that it must once have been a headland or promontory running out into the sea between the two inlets of the estuary of the Stour on one side, and Pegwell Bay, on the other. What are now the broad green fields, were then the waters of the sea. The tradition, that "some landing" took place there, is still preserved at the farm, and the field of clover which rises immediately on its north side is shown as the spot.

Here it was that, according to the story preserved in the Saxon Chronicle, Hengist and Horsa had sailed in with their three ships and the band of warriors who conquered Vortigern. And here now Augustine came with his monks, his choristers, and the interpreters they had brought with them from France. The Saxon conquerors, like Augustine, are described as having landed, not at Richborough, but at Ebbe's Fleet, because they were to have the Isle of Thanet for their first possession, apart from the mainland,—and Augustine landed there, that he might remain safe on that side the broad river, till he knew the mind of the king. The rock was long preserved on which he set foot, and which according to a superstition found in almost every country, was supposed to have received the impression of his footmark. In later times it became an object of pilgrimage, and a little chapel was built over it : though it was afterwards called the footmark of St. Mildred, and the rock, even till the beginning of the last century, was called "St. Mildred's rock,"[1] from the later saint of that name, whose fame in the Isle of Thanet then eclipsed that of Augustine himself. There they landed "in the ends," "in the

[1] "Not many years ago," says Hasted (iv. 325), writing in 1799. "A few years ago," says Lewis (Isle of Thanet, 58) writing in 1723. Compare, for a similar transference of names in more sacred localities, the foot-mark of Mahomet in the Mosque of Omar, called during the Crusades the footmark of Christ,— and the footmark of Mahomet's mule on Sinai, now called the footmark of the dromedary of Moses. The stone was thought to be gifted with the power of flying back to its original place if ever removed.—(Lambard's "Kent," p. 104.)

corner of the world,"[1] as it was then thought, and waited
secure in their island retreat, till they heard how the
announcement of their arrival was received by Ethelbert,
King of Kent.

To Ethelbert we must now turn.[2] He was, it was
believed, great-grandson of Eric, son of Hengist, surnamed
" the Ash,"[3] and father of the dynasty of the " Ashings,"
or "sons of the Ashtree," the name by which the kings
of Kent were known. He had besides acquired a kind of
imperial authority over the other Saxon kings as far as
the Humber. To consolidate his power, he had married
Bertha, a French princess, daughter of the king of Paris.
It was on this marriage that all the subsequent fate of
England turned. Ethelbert was like all the Saxons, a
heathen ; but Bertha, like all the rest of the French royal
family from Clovis downwards, was a Christian. She had
her Christian chaplain with her, Luidhard, a French bishop,
and a little chapel[4] outside the town, which had once been
used as a place of British Christian worship, was given up
to her use. That little chapel, " on the east of the city,"
as Bede tells us, stood on the gentle slope now occupied
by the venerable Church of St. Martin, itself of a far later
date, but possibly retaining in its walls some of the original
Roman bricks of Bertha's chapel ; and, in all probability,
deriving from Bertha's use of it the name by which it has
ever since been known.[5] Of all the great Christian saints
of whom she had heard in France before she came to

---

[1] "Fines mundi—gens *Anglo*rum in
mundi *angulo* posita," Greg. Epp. v.,
158, 159. Observe the play on the
word, as in p. 9.

[2] Ethelbert is the same name as
Adalbert and Albert (as Adalfuns =
Alfons, Uodelrich = Ulrich), meaning
" Noble-bright."

[3] "Ashing" (Bede, ii. 5, § 101) was
probably a general name for *hero*, in
allusion to the primeval man of Teutonic mythology, who was believed to
have sprung from the sacred Ash tree,
Ygdrasil. (Grimm's "Deutsche Myth.,
i. 324, 531, 617.) Compare the venerable Ash which gives its name to the
village of Donau-Eschingen, "the Ashes
of the Danube," by the source of that
river.

[4] The postern-gate of the Precincts
opposite St. Augustine's gateway, is on
the site of *Quenengate,* a name derived
—but by a very doubtful etymology—
from the tradition that through it
Bertha passed from Ethelbert's palace
to St. Martin's. (Battely's " Canterbury," 16.)

[5] It is possible, though hardly probable, that the name of St. Martin may
have been given to the church of the
British Christians before. Bede's expression is ambiguous, and rather leans
to the earlier origin of the name.
"Erat .... ecclesia in honorem Sancti
Martini antiquitus facta dum adhuc
Romani Britanniam incolerent." Hasted (Hist. of Kent, iv. 496) states
(but without giving any authority),

England, the most famous was St. Martin of Tours, and thus the name which is now so familiar to us that we hardly think of asking why the church is so called, is a memorial of the recollections which the French princess still cherished of her own native country, now that she was settled in a land of strangers.

To her it would be no new thought that possibly she might be the means of converting her husband. Her own great ancestor, Clovis, had become a Christian through the influence of his wife Clotilda, and many other instances had occurred in like manner elsewhere. It is no new story ; it is the same that has often been enacted in humbler spheres, of a careless or unbelieving husband converted by a believing wife. But it is a striking sight to see planted in the very beginning of our history, with the most important consequences to the whole world, the same fact which every one must have especially witnessed in the domestic history of families, high and low, throughout the land.

It is probable that Ethelbert had heard enough from Bertha to dispose him favourably towards the new religion ; and Gregory's letters show that it was the tidings of this predisposition which had induced him to send Augustine. But Ethelbert's conduct on hearing that the strangers were actually arrived was still hesitating. He would not suffer them to come to Canterbury ; they were to remain in the Isle of Thanet, with the Stour flowing between himself and them ; and he also stipulated that on no account should they hold their first interview under a roof—it must be in the open air, for fear of the charms and spells which he feared they might exercise over him. It was exactly the savage's notion of religion, that it exercises influence, not by moral and spiritual, but by magical means. This was the first feeling ; this it was that caused the meeting to be held, not at Canterbury, but in the Isle of Thanet, in the wide open space— possibly at Ebbe's Fleet—possibly, according to another

that it was originally dedicated to the Virgin, and was dedicated to St. Martin by Luidhard. The legendary origin of the church, as of that in the Castle of Dover; of St. Peter's, Cornhill; of Westminster Abbey, and of Winchester Cathedral, is traced to King Lucius. (Ussher, Brit. Eccl. Ant. pp. 129, 130.)

account, under an ancient oak on the high upland ground
in the centre of the island,[1] then dotted with woods
which have long since vanished.[2]

The meeting must have been remarkable. The Saxon
king, "the Son of the Ash-tree," with his wild soldiers
round, seated on the bare ground on one side—on the
other side, with a huge silver cross borne before him
(crucifixes were not yet introduced), and beside it a large
picture of Christ painted and gilded,[3] after the fashion of
those times, on an upright board, came up from the
shore Augustine and his companions ; chanting, as they
advanced, a solemn Litany, for themselves and for those to
whom they came. He, as we are told, was a man of almost
gigantic stature,[4] head and shoulders taller than any one
else ; with him were Lawrence, who afterwards succeeded
him as Archbishop of Canterbury, and Peter who became
the first Abbot of St. Augustine's. They and their
companions, amounting altogether to forty, sat down
at the King's command, and the interview began.

Neither, we must remember, could understand the
other's language. Augustine could not understand a word
of Anglo-Saxon, and Ethelbert, we may be tolerably
sure, could not speak a word of Latin. But the priests
whom Augustine had brought from France, as knowing
both German and Latin, now stepped forward as interpreters ; and thus the dialogue which followed was carried on,
much as all communications are carried on in the East,—
Augustine first delivering his message, which the drago-
man, as they would say in the East, explained to the King.[5]

---

[1] See Lewis (Isle of Thanet, p. 83,) "Under an oak that grew in the middle of the island, which all the German pagans had in the highest veneration." He gives no authority. The oak was held sacred by the Germans as well as by the Britons. (Grimm, i. 62.)
Probably the recollection of this meeting determined the forms of that which Augustine afterwards held with the British Christians at Bristol. Then, as now, it was in the open air, under an oak—then, as now, Augustine was seated. (Bede, ii. 2, § 9.) In the same chapel of St. Gregory's convent at Rome, which contains the picture of the departure of Augustine, is one—it need hardly be said, with no attempt at historical accuracy — of his reception by Ethelbert.

[2] As indicated by the names of places. (Hasted, iv. 292.)

[3] "Formose atque aurate." (Acta Sanct., 326.)

[4] Acta Sanct., 399.

[5] Exchange English travellers for Roman missionaries, Arab sheikhs for Saxon chiefs, and the well-known interviews, on the way to Petra, give us some notion of this celebrated dialogue.

The King heard it all attentively, and then gave this most characteristic answer, bearing upon it a stamp of truth which it is impossible to doubt : " *Your words are fair, and your promises—but because they are new and doubtful, I cannot give my assent to them, and leave the customs which I have so long observed, with the whole Anglo-Saxon race. But because you have come hither as strangers from a long distance, and as I seem to myself to have seen clearly, that what you yourselves believed to be true and good, you wish to impart to us, we do not wish to molest you ; nay rather we are anxious to receive you hospitably, and to give you all that is needed for your support, nor do we hinder you from joining all whom you can to the faith of your religion.*"

Such an answer, simple as it was, really seems to contain the seeds of all that is excellent in the English character—exactly what a king should have said on such an occasion—exactly what, under the influence of Christianity, has grown up into all our best institutions. There is the natural dislike to change, which Englishmen still retain ; there is the willingness at the same time to listen favourably to anything, which comes recommended by the energy and self-devotion of those who urge it ; there is, lastly, the spirit of moderation and toleration, and the desire to see fair play, which is one of our best gifts, and which, I hope, we shall never lose. We may, indeed, well be thankful, not only that we had an Augustine to convert us, but that we had an Ethelbert for our King.

From the Isle of Thanet, the missionaries crossed the broad ferry to Richborough, the "Burgh" or castle of "Rete" or "Retep," as it was then called, from the old Roman fortress of Rutupiæ, of which the vast ruins still remain. Underneath the overhanging cliff of the castle, so the tradition ran, the King received the missionaries.[1] They

---

[1] Sandwich MS. in Boys' Sandwich (p. 838). An old hermit lived amongst the ruins in the time of Henry VIII., and pointed out to Leland what seems to have been a memorial of this in a Chapel of St. Augustine, of which some slight remains are still to be traced in the northern bank of the fortress.

There was also a head or bust, said to be of Queen Bertha, embedded in the walls — remaining till the time of Elizabeth. The curious crossing in the centre was then called by the common people, " St. Augustine's Cross " (Camden, p. 342). For this question see the Note at the end of this Lecture.

c

then advanced to Canterbury along the vale of the Stour.
As they came within sight of the city—the rude wooden
city on the banks of the river, they formed themselves into
a long procession ; they lifted up again the tall silver cross,
and the rude painted board; there were with them the
choristers, whom Augustine had brought from Gregory's
school on the Cælian hill, trained in the chants which were
called after his name, and they sang one of those Litanies [1]
which Gregory had introduced for the plague at Rome.
"We beseech thee, O Lord, in all thy mercy, that thy wrath
and thine anger may be removed from this city, and from
thy holy house. Allelujah." [2] Doubtless, as they uttered
that last word, they must have remembered that they were
thus fulfilling to the letter the very wish that Gregory had
expressed, when he first saw the Saxon children in the
market-place at Rome.

Every one of the events which follow is connected with
some well-known locality. The place that Ethelbert gave
them first, was "Stable-gate," by an old heathen temple,
where his servants worshipped, near the present church
of St. Alfege, as a "resting-place," where they "stabled"
till he had made up his mind ; and by their good and
holy lives, it is said, as well as by the miracles they were
supposed to work, he was at last decided to encourage
them more openly, and allow them to worship with the
Queen at St. Martin's. [3]

In St. Martin's they worshipped, and no doubt the
mere splendour and strangeness of the Roman ritual
produced an instant effect on the rude barbarian mind.
And now came the turning point of their whole mission,
the baptism of Ethelbert. It was, unless we except the

[1] Fleury, H.E., book xxxv. 1.
[2] Bede (II. i. § 87) supposes that it was to this that Gregory alludes in his Commentary on Job, when he says, "Lo the language of Britain, which once only knew a barbarous jargon, now has begun in divine praises to sound Allelujah." It is objected to this that the Commentary on Job was written during Gregory's mission to Constantinople, some years before this event, and that therefore the passage must relate to the victory gained by Germanus over the Britons in the Welsh mountains, by the shout of "Hallélujah." But, considering the doubt whether Gregory could have heard of the proceedings of Germanus, it may well be a question, whether the allusion in the Commentary on Job was not added after he had heard of this fulfilment of his wishes. At any rate, it illustrates the hold which the word "Hallelujah" had on his mind in connexion with the conversion of Britain.   [3] Thorn, 1758.

conversion of Clovis, the most important baptism that the world had seen since that of Constantine. We know the day—it was the Feast of Whit-Sunday—on the 2nd of June, in the year of our Lord 597. Unfortunately we do not with certainty know the place. The only authorities of that early age tell us merely that he was baptised, without specifying any particular spot. Still, as St. Martin's Church is described as the scene of Augustine's ministrations, and amongst other points, of his administration of baptism, it is in the highest degree probable that the local tradition is correct. And although the venerable font, which is there shown as that in which he was baptised, is proved by its appearance to be of a later date, yet it is so like that which appears in the representation of the event in the seal of St. Augustine's Abbey, and is in itself so remarkable, that we may perhaps fairly regard it as a monument of the event ;—in the same manner as the large porphyry basin in the Lateran Church at Rome commemorates the baptism of Constantine, though still less corresponding to the reality of that event than the stone font of St. Martin's to the place of the immersion of Ethelbert.[1]

The conversion of a king was then of more importance than it has ever been before or since. The baptism of any one of these barbarian chiefs almost inevitably involved the baptism of the whole tribe, and therefore we are not to be surprised at finding that when this step was once achieved, all else was easy. Accordingly, by the end of that year, Gregory wrote to his brother Patriarch of the distant Church of Alexandria (so much interest did the event excite to the remotest ends of Christendom), that ten thousand Saxons had been baptised on Christmas Day[2]— baptised, as we learn from another source, in the broad waters of the Swale,[3] at the mouth of the Medway.

[1] Neither Bede (79), nor Thorn (1759), says a word of the scene of the baptism. But Gocelin (*Acta Sanc.* 383), speaks distinctly of a "baptistery" or "urn" as used. The first mention of the font at St. Martin's that I find, is in Stukeley, p. 117 (in the 17th century).

[2] Greg. Epp. vii. 30.

[3] See Fuller's Church Hist., ii. § 7, 9, where he justly argues, after his quaint

fashion, that the Swale, mentioned by Gocelin (*Acta Sanct.*, p. 390), Gervase (Act. Pont. 1551), and Camden (p. 136), cannot be that of Yorkshire. Indeed, Gregory's letter is decisive. The legend represents the crowd as miraculously delivered from drowning, and the baptism as performed by two and two upon each other at the command, though not by the act, of Augustine.

The next stage of the mission carries us to another spot. Midway between St. Martin's and the town was another ancient building—also, it would appear, although this is less positively stated—once a British Church, but now used by Ethelbert as a temple in which to worship the gods of Saxon Paganism. Like all the Saxon temples we must imagine it embosomed in a thick grove of oak or ash. This temple, according to a principle which, as we shall afterwards find, was laid down by Gregory himself, Ethelbert did not destroy, but made over to Augustine for a regular place of Christian worship. Augustine dedicated the place to St. Pancras, and it became the Church of St. Pancras, of which the spot is still indicated by a ruined arch of ancient brick, and by the fragment of a wall, still showing the mark,[1] where, according to the legend, the old demon who, according to the belief at that time, had hitherto reigned supreme in the heathen temple, laid his claws to shake down the building in which he first heard the celebration of Christian services and felt that his rule was over. But there is a more authentic and instructive interest attaching to that ancient ruin, if you ask why it was that it received from Augustine the name of St. Pancras ? Two reasons are given. First, St. Pancras or Pancrasius was a Roman boy of noble family, who was martyred[2] under Diocletian at the age of fourteen, and being thus regarded as the patron saint of children, would naturally be chosen as the patron saint of the first-fruits of the nation which was converted out of regard to the three English children in the market-place : and, secondly, the monastery of St. Andrew on the Cælian Hill, which Gregory had founded, and from which Augustine came, was built on the very property which had belonged to the family of St. Pancras, and therefore the name of St. Pancras was often in

[1] The place now pointed out, can hardly be the same as that indicated by Thorn (1760) as "the south wall of the church." But every student of local tradition knows how easily they are transplanted to suit the convenience of their perpetuation. The present mark is apparently that mentioned by Stukeley (p. 117), who gives a view of the church as then standing.

[2] The Roman Church of St. Pancrazio behind the Vatican (so famous in the siege of Rome by the French in 1849), is on the scene of Pancrasius' martyrdom.

Gregory's mouth (one of his sermons was preached on St. Pancras' day) and would thus naturally occur to Augustine also. That rising ground on which the chapel of St. Pancras stands, with St. Martin's hill behind, was to him a Cælian Mount in England, and this, of itself, would suggest to him the wish, as we shall presently see, to found his first monastery as nearly as possible with the same associations as that which he had left behind.

But Ethelbert was not satisfied with establishing those places of worship outside the city. Augustine was now formally consecrated as the first Archbishop of Canterbury, and Ethelbert determined to give him a dwelling-place and a house of prayer within the city also. Buildings of this kind were rare in Canterbury, and so the King retired to Reculver—built there a new palace out of the ruins of the old Roman fortress, and gave up his own palace and an old British or Roman church in its neighbourhood, to be the seat of the new archbishop and the foundation of the new cathedral. If the baptism of Ethelbert may in some measure be compared to the baptism of Constantine, so this may be compared to that hardly less celebrated act of the same Emperor (made up of some truth and more fable)—his donation of the "States of the Church" to Pope Sylvester; his own retirement to Constantinople in consequence of this resignation to the Pope of Rome. It is possible that Ethelbert may have been in some measure influenced in his step by what he may have heard of this story. His wooden palace was to him what the Lateran was to Constantine—Augustine was his Sylvester—Reculver was his Byzantium. At any rate, this grant of house and land to Augustine was a step of immense importance not only in English but European history, because it was the first instance in England, or in any of the countries occupied by the barbarian tribes, of an endowment by the State. As St. Martin's and St. Pancras' witnessed the first beginning of English Christianity, so Canterbury Cathedral is the earliest monument of an English Church Establishment—of the English constitution

of the union of Church and State.[1] Of the actual building
of this first Cathedral, nothing now remains ; yet there is
much, even now, to remind us of it.   First there is the
venerable chair, in which for so many generations, the
primates of England have been enthroned, and which,
though probably of a later date, may yet rightly be called
" St. Augustine's Chair ;"[2] for, though not the very one in
which he sate, it no doubt represents the ancient episcopal
throne, in which after the fashion of the bishops of that
time, he sate behind the altar (for that was its proper place,
and there, as is well known, it once stood) with all his clergy
round him, as may still be seen in several ancient churches
abroad. Next, there is the name of the cathedral. It was
then, as it is still, properly, called "Christ Church," or "the
Church of our Saviour."   We can hardly doubt that this
is a direct memorial of the first landing of Augustine,
when he first announced to the pagan Saxons, the faith
and name of Christ, and spread out before their eyes, on
the shore of Ebbe's Fleet, the rude painting on the large
board, which, we are emphatically told, represented to
them " Christ our Saviour."   And, thirdly, there is the
curious fact, that the old church, whether as found, or as
restored by Augustine, was in many of its features an
exact likeness of the old St. Peter's at Rome—doubtless
from his recollection of that ancient edifice in what may
be called his own cathedral city in Italy.   There, as at
St. Peter's,[3] the altar was originally at the west end ;—
there, as at St. Peter's, there was a crypt made in
imitation of the ancient catacombs, in which the bones of
the Apostles were originally found ; and this was the first
beginning of the crypt which still exists, and which is so
remarkable a part of the present cathedral.   Lastly, then,
as now, the chief entrance into the cathedral was through
the south door,[4] which is a practice derived, not from the

---

[1] That the parallel of Constantine
was present to the minds of those
concerned is evident, not merely from
the express comparison by Gocelin
(*Acta Sanct.* p. 383), of Ethelbert to
Constantine, and Augustine to Sylvester, but from the appellation of
" Helena" given by Gregory to Bertha,
or (as he calls her) Edilburga.—Epp.
ix. 60.

[2] The arguments against the antiquity
of the chair are: 1. The use of Purbeck
marble. 2. The old throne was of one
piece of stone, the present is of three.

[3] Willis's Canterbury Cathedral, ii.
pp. 20—32.   [4] *Ibid.*, p. 11.

Roman, but from the British times, and therefore from the ruined British church which Augustine first received from Ethelbert. It is so still in the remains of the old British churches which are preserved in Cornwall and Scotland, and I mention it here because it is perhaps the only point in the whole cathedral which reminds us of that earlier British Christianity, which had almost died away before Augustine came.

Finally, in the neighbourhood of the Church of St. Pancras, where he had first begun to perform Christian service, Ethelbert granted to Augustine the ground, on which was to be built the monastery, that afterwards grew up into the great abbey called by his name. It was, in the first instance, called the Abbey of St.Peter and St. Paul, after the two apostles of the city of Rome, from which Augustine and his companions had come, and though in after times it was chiefly known by the name of its founder Augustine, yet its earlier appellation was evidently intended to carry back the thoughts of those who first settled within its walls far over the sea, to the great churches which stood by the banks of the Tiber, over the graves of the two Apostles. This monastery was designed chiefly for two purposes. One object was, that the new clergy of the Christian mission might be devoted to study and learning. And it may be interesting to remember here, that of this original intention of the monastery, two relics possibly exist, although not at Canterbury. In the library at Corpus Christi College at Cambridge, and in the Bodleian library at Oxford, two ancient MS. Gospels still exist, which have at least a fair claim to be considered the very books which Gregory sent to Augustine as marks of his good wishes to the rising monastery, when Lawrence and Peter returned from Britain to Rome, to tell him the success of their mission, and from him brought back these presents. They are, if so, the most ancient books that ever were read in England ; as the Church of St. Martin is the mother church, and the Cathedral of Canterbury the mother cathedral of England, so these books, are, if I may so call them, the mother books of England—the first beginning of English literature, of English learning, of English

education. And St. Augustine's Abbey was thus the
mother school, the mother university of England, the seat
of letters and study, at a time when Cambridge was a
desolate fen, and Oxford a tangled forest in a wide
waste of waters.[1] They remind us that English power
and English religion have, as from the very first, so ever
since, gone along with knowledge, with learning, and
especially with that knowledge and that learning, which
those two old manuscripts give—the knowledge and
learning of the Gospel.

This was one intention of St. Augustine's monastery—
the other is remarkable, as explaining the situation of the
Abbey. It might be asked why so important an Abbey,
constructed for study and security, should have been built
outside the city walls ? One reason, as I have said, may
have been to fix it as near as possible to the old church of
St. Pancras. But another and that the chief reason, is
instructive as showing us how much there is in all these
events, occasioned by the customs of the distant country
from which Augustine came. He desired to have in this
land of strangers a spot of consecrated ground where his
bones should repose after death. But such a place according
to the usages which he brought with him from Rome, he
could not have within the walls of Canterbury. No interment was allowed in Rome within the walls of the city. The
great cemeteries were always outside the town, along the
sides of the great high-ways by which it was approached.
It was in fact the same in all ancient cities—we see it in
Jewish history as well as in the Roman ; only persons of
the very highest importance were allowed what we now
call intra-mural interment. So it was here. Augustine the
Roman fixed his burial-place by the side of the great
Roman road, which then ran from Deal to Canterbury over
St. Martin's hill, and entering the town by the gateway

---

[1] A MS. history of the foundation of
St. Augustine's Abbey (in the library
of Trinity Hall, Cambridge, to which it
was given by one into whose hands it
fell at the time of the Dissolution),
contains an account of eight MSS., said
to be those sent over by Gregory. Of
these, all have long since disappeared,
with three exceptions,—a Bible which,
however, has never been heard of since
1604, and the two MSS. Gospels still
shown at Corpus, Cambridge, and in the
Bodleian at Oxford. The arguments
for their genuineness are stated by
Wanley, in Hickes' Thesaurus (ii. pp.
172, 173).

which still marks the course of the old road.[1]   The
cemetery of St. Augustine was an English Appian way, as
the church of St. Pancras was an English Cælian hill ; and
this is the reason why St. Augustine's Abbey instead of
the Cathedral, has enjoyed the honour of burying the last
remains of the first Primate of the English Church, and of
the first King of Christian England.

For now we have arrived at the end of their career.
Nothing of importance is known of Augustine in
connexion with Canterbury, beyond what has been
said above. We know that he penetrated as far west
as the banks of the Severn, on his important mission
to the Welsh Christians, and it would also seem that he
must[2] have gone into Dorsetshire ; but these would lead us
into regions and topics remote from our present subject.

His last act at Canterbury, of which we can speak with
certainty, was his consecration of two monks who had been
sent out after him by Gregory to two new sees—two new
steps further into the country, still under the shelter of
Ethelbert.   Justus became Bishop of Rochester, and
Mellitus Bishop of London.   And still the same association
of names which we have seen at Canterbury was continued.   The memory of " *St. Andrew's* Convent" on the
Cælian Hill was perpetuated in the Cathedral Church of
St. Andrew on the banks of the Medway.   The names of
St. Peter and *St. Paul*, which had been combined in the
Abbey at Canterbury, were preserved apart in St. Peter's
at Westminster and St. Paul's in London, which thus
represent the great Roman Basilicas, on the banks of the
Thames.   How like the instinct with which the colonists
of the New World reproduced the nomenclature of
Christian and civilised Europe, was this practice of
recalling in remote and barbarous Britain the familiar
scenes of Christian and civilised Italy !

It was believed that Augustine expired on the 26th of

---

[1] Bede, i. 33, § 79.

[2] See the account of his conference
with the Welsh, in Bede ; the stories of
his adventures in Dorsetshire, in the
Acta Sanctorum, p. 391. The story of
his journey into Yorkshire, has probably
arisen from the mistake, before noticed,
respecting the Swale. The whole question of his miracles and of the legendary
portions of his life, is too long to be
discussed in this place.

May, 605,[1] his patron and benefactor, Gregory the Great, having died on the 12th of March of the previous year, and he was interred,[2] according to the custom of which I have spoken, by the road-side in the ground now occupied by the Kent and Canterbury Hospital. The Abbey which he had founded was not yet finished, but he had just lived to see its foundation.[3] Ethelbert came from Reculver to Canterbury, a few months before Augustine's death, to witness the ceremony, and the monks were settled there under Peter, the first companion of Augustine, as their head. Peter did not long survive his master. He was lost, it is said, in a storm off the coast of France, two years afterwards, and his remains were interred in the Church of St. Mary at Boulogne.[4] Bertha and her chaplain also died about the same time, and were buried beside Augustine. There now remained of those who had first met in the Isle of Thanet ten years before, only Ethelbert himself, and Lawrence, who had been consecrated Archbishop by Augustine himself before his death, an unusual and almost unprecedented step,[5] but one which it was thought the unsettled state of the newly converted country demanded. Once more Ethelbert and Lawrence met, in the year 613, eight years after Augustine's death, for the consecration of the Abbey Church, on the site of which there rose in after times the noble structure whose ruins still remain, preserving in the fragments of its huge western tower, even to our own time, the name of Ethelbert. Then the bones[6] of Augustine were removed from their resting-place by the Roman road, to be deposited in the north transept of the church; where they remained, till in the 12th century they were moved once again, and placed under the high altar at the east end. Then also the remains of Bertha and of Luidhard were brought within the same church, and laid in the transept or apse dedicated to St. Martin;[7] thus

[1] Thorn (1765) gives the year, Bede, (ii. 3, § 96), the day.
[2] Thorn, 1767.
[3] Thorn, 1761. Christmas, A.D. 605, was, according to our reckoning, on Christmas, 604.
[4] Thorn, 1766.
[5] Thorn, 1765 ; Bede, ii. 4, § 97.

[6] Thorn, 1767. The statement in Butler's "Lives of the Saints" (May 26), is a series of mistakes.
[7] The mention of this apse, or "porticus" of St. Martin, has led to the mistake, which from Fuller's time (ii. 7, § 32) has fixed the grave of Bertha in the Church of St. Martin's on

still keeping up the recollection of their original connexion with the old French saint, and the little chapel where they had so often worshipped on the hill above—Luidhard[1] on the north, and Bertha on the south side of the altar.

Three years longer Ethelbert reigned. He lived, as has been already said, no longer at Canterbury, but in the new palace which he had built for himself within the strong Roman fortress of Reculver, at the north-western end of the estuary of the Isle of Thanet, though in a different manner. The whole aspect of the place is even more altered than that of its corresponding fortress of Richborough, at the other extremity. The sea, which was then a mile or more from Reculver, has now advanced up to the very edge of the cliff on which it stands, and swept the northern wall of the massive fortress into the waves; but the three other sides, overgrown with ivy and elder-bushes, still remain, with the strong masonry which Ethelbert must have seen and handled, and within the enclosure stand the venerable ruins of the church with its two towers, which afterwards rose on the site of Ethelbert's palace.

This wild spot is the scene which most closely connects itself with the remembrance of that good Saxon king, and it long disputed with St. Augustine's Abbey, the honour of his burial-place. Even down to the time of King James I., a monument was to be seen in the south transept of the church of Reculver, professing to cover his remains,[2] and down to our own time, I am told, a board was affixed to the wall, with the inscription "Here lies Ethelbert, Kentish king whilom." This, however, may have been Ethelbert II., and all authority leans to the story that, after a long reign of forty-eight years (dying on the 24th of February, 616), he

the hill. But the elegant Latin inscription, which the excellent Rector of St. Martin's has caused to be placed over the rude stone tomb, which popularly bears her name, in his beautiful church, is so cautiously worded that, even if she were buried much further off than she is, the claim which is there set up, would hardly be contradicted.

[1] Luidhard is so mere a shadow, that it is hardly worth while collecting what is known or said of him. His name is variously spelt Lethard, Ledvard, and Luidhard. His French Bishopric is variously represented to be Soissons or Senlis. This tomb in the abbey was long known, and his relics were carried round Canterbury in a gold chest on the Rogation Days.—(*Acta Sanct.*, Feb. 24, pp. 468, 470.)

[2] Weever. Funeral Monuments, 260.

was laid side by side with his first wife Bertha,[1] on the south
side of St. Martin's altar in the Church of St. Augustine,[2]
and there somewhere in the field around the ruins of the
Abbey, his bones, with those of Bertha and Augustine,[3]
probably still repose and may possibly be discovered.

These are all the direct traces which Augustine and
Ethelbert have left amongst us.   Viewed in this light they
will become so many finger-posts, pointing your thoughts,
along various roads, to times and countries far away—
always useful and pleasant in this busy world in which
we live.   But in that busy world itself they have left
traces also, which we shall do well briefly to consider
before we bid farewell to that ancient Roman Prelate and
that ancient Saxon Chief.   I do not now speak of the one
great change of our conversion to Christianity, which is
too extensive and too serious a subject to be treated of on
the present occasion.   But the particular manner in which
Christianity was thus planted, is in so many ways best
understood by going back to that time, that I shall not
scruple to call your attention to it.

First, the arrival of Augustine explains to us at once
why the Primate of this great Church—the first subject
of this great empire, should be Archbishop, not of
London, but of Canterbury.   It had been Gregory's intention to have fixed the primacy in London, but the local

---

[1] That he had a second wife appears
from the allusion to her in the story of
his son Eadbald (Bede, ii. § 102), but
her name is never mentioned.

[2] Thorn, 1767; Bede, ii. §§ 100, 101.

[3] In the *Acta Sanctorum* for Feb. 24
(p. 478), a strange ghost-story is told of
Ethelbert's tomb, not without interest
from its connexion with the previous
history. The priest who had the charge
of the tomb had neglected it. One
night as he was in the chapel, there
suddenly issued from the tomb in a
blaze of light which filled the whole
apse, the figure of a boy, with a torch
in his hand ; long golden hair flowed
round his shoulders; his face was as
white as snow ; his eyes shone like stars.
He rebuked the priest, and retired into
his tomb. Is it possible that the story

of this apparition was connected with
the traditional description of the three
children at Rome ?

There was a statue of Ethelbert in
the south chapel or apse of St. Pancras
(Thorn, 1677), long since destroyed.
But in the screen of the Cathedral
choir, of the 15th century, he may still
be seen as the founder of the Cathedral,
with the model of the church in his
hand. He was canonised; but probably as a saint he was less popularly
known than St. Ethelbert of Hereford,
with whom he is sometimes confused.

His epitaph was a curious instance
of rhyming Latinity :—

Rex Ethelbertus hic clauditur in polyandro,
Fana pians, Christo meat absque meandro.—

(Speed, 215.)

feelings which grew out of Augustine's landing in Kent were too strong for him, and they have prevailed to this day.[1] Humble as Canterbury may now be, yet so long as an Archbishop of Canterbury exists,—so long as the Church of England exists, we can never forget that we have had the glory of being the cradle of English Christianity. And that glory we had in consequence of a few simple causes—far back in the mist of ages—the shore between the cliffs of Ramsgate and of the South Foreland, which made the shores of Kent the most convenient landing-place for the Italian missionaries; —the marriage of the wild Saxon king of Kent with a Christian princess;—and the good English common sense of Ethelbert when the happy occasion arrived.

Secondly, we may see in the present constitution of Church and State in England, what are far more truly the footmarks of Gregory and Augustine, than that fictitious footmark which he was said to have left at Ebbe's Fleet.

There are letters from Gregory to Augustine, which give him excellent advice for his missionary course— advice which all missionaries would do well to consider, and of which the effects are to this day visible amongst us. Let me mention two or three of these points. The first, perhaps, is more curious than generally interesting. Any of you who have ever read or seen the state of foreign churches and countries, may have been struck by one great difference, which I believe distinguishes England from all other Churches in the world; and that is, the great size of its dioceses. In foreign countries, you will generally find a bishop's see in every large town, so that he is, in fact, more like a clergyman of a large parish than what we call the bishop of a diocese. It is a very important characteristic of the English Church, that the opposite should be the case with us. In some respects it has been a great disadvantage; in other respects, I believe, a great advantage.

---

[1] Greg. Epp., xii. 15. Gervase (*Act. Pont.*, pp. 1131, 1132), thinking that by this letter the Pope established three primacies, one at London, one at Canterbury, and one at York, needlessly perplexes himself to reconcile such a distribution with the geography of Britain, and arrives at the conclusion that the Pope, "licet Sancti Spiritus sacrarium esset," yet had fallen into the error of supposing each of the cities to be equidistant from the other.

But whether for good or evil, it has proceeded, in the first instance, from Gregory's instructions to Augustine. He gave him orders to divide the country into twenty-four bishoprics, and so it was gradually done, and so it has remained ever since. Britain, as I have said several times, was to him almost an unknown island. Probably he thought it might be about the size of Sicily or Sardinia, the only large islands he had ever seen, and that twenty-four bishoprics would be sufficient. At any rate, so he divided, and so, with the variation of giving only four, instead of twelve, to the province of York, it was followed out by Augustine and his successors. The kings of the various kingdoms seem to have encouraged the practice, each making his kingdom co-extensive with a bishopric;[1] so that the bishop of the diocese was also chief pastor of the tribe, succeeding in all probability to the post which the chaplain or high priest of the king had held in the days of Paganism.

But further, Gregory gave directions as to the two points, which probably most perplex missionaries, and which at once beset Augustine. The first concerned his dealings with other Christian communities. Augustine had passed through France, and saw there customs very different from what he had seen in Rome ; and he was now come to Britain, where there were still remnants of the old British churches, with customs very different from what he had seen either in France or Rome. What was he to do ? The answer of Gregory was, that whatever custom he found really good and pleasing to God, whether in the Church of Italy, or of France, or any other, he was to adopt it, and use it in his new Church of England. *"Things,"* he says, *" are not to be loved for the sake of places, but places for the sake of things."* [2]

It was indeed a truly wise and liberal maxim ;—one which would have healed many feuds, one which perhaps Augustine himself might have followed more than he did. It would be too much to say, that the effect of this advice has reached to our own time ; but it often happens that the first turn given to the spirit of an institution lasts long after its first founder has passed away, and in

[1] See Kemble's "Saxons," book ii. c. 8.   [2] Bede, i. 27, § 60.

channels quite different from those which he contemplated; and when we think what the Church of England is now, I confess there is a satisfaction in thinking, that at least in this respect it has in some measure fulfilled the wishes of Gregory the Great. There is no Church in the world which has combined such opposite and various advantages from other Churches more exclusive than itself,—none in which various characters and customs from the opposite parts of the Christian world, could have been able to find such shelter and refuge.

Another point was, how to deal with the Pagan customs and ceremonies which already existed in the Anglo-Saxon kingdom. Were they to be entirely destroyed?—or were they to be tolerated so far as was not absolutely incompatible with the Christian religion? And here again Gregory gave to Augustine the advice which, certainly as far as we could judge, St. Paul would have given, and which in spirit at least is an example always. "He had thought much on the subject," he says, and he came to the conclusion that heathen temples were not to be destroyed, but turned whenever possible into Christian churches,[1]— that the droves of oxen which used to be killed in sacrifice were still to be killed for feasts for the poor; and that the huts which they used to make of boughs of trees round the temples, were still to be used for amusements on Christian festivals. And he gives as the reason for this, that "*for hard and rough minds it is impossible to cut away abruptly all their old customs, because he who wishes to reach the highest place, must ascend by steps and not by jumps.*"[2]

How this was followed out in England is evident. In Canterbury, we have already seen how the old heathen temple of Ethelbert was turned into the Church of St. Pancras. In the same manner, the sites granted by Ethelbert for St. Paul's in London, and St. Peter's in

[1] To Ethelbert he had expressed himself, apparently in an earlier letter, more strongly against the temples.— (Bede, i. 32, § 76.) "Was it settled policy," asks Dean Milman, "or mature reflection which led the Pope to devolve the more odious duty of the total abolition of idolatry on the temporal power—the barbarian king; while it permitted the milder or more winning course to the clergy, the protection of the hallowed places and images of the heathen from insult by consecrating them to holier uses?"—(Hist. of Latin Christianity, ii. 59.)

[2] Bede, i. 30, 74.

Westminster, were both originally places of heathen worship. This appropriation of heathen buildings is the more remarkable, inasmuch as it had hitherto been very unusual in Western Christendom. In Egypt, indeed, the temples were usually converted into Christian churches, and the intermixture of Coptic saints with Egyptian gods is one of the strangest sights that the traveller sees in the monuments of that strange land. In Greece also, the Parthenon and the Temple of Theseus are well-known instances. But in Rome it was very rare. The Pantheon, now dedicated to All Saints, is almost the only example ; and this dedication itself took place four years after Gregory's death, and probably in consequence of his known views. The fragment of the Church of St. Pancras—the nucleus, as we have seen, of St. Augustine's Abbey—thus becomes a witness to an important principle ; and the legend of the Devil's claw reads us a true lesson— that the evil spirit can be cast out of institutions without destroying them. Gregory's advice is, indeed, but the counterpart of John Wesley's celebrated saying about church music : that "it was a great pity the Devil should have all the best tunes to himself:" and the principle which it involved, coming from one in his commanding position, probably struck root far and wide, not only in England, but throughout Christendom. One familiar instance is to be found in the toleration of the heathen names of the days of the week. Every one of these is called, as we all know, after the name of some Saxon god or goddess, whom Ethelbert worshipped in the days of his Paganism. Through all the changes of Saxon and Norman, Roman Catholic and Protestant, these names have survived, but, most striking of all, through the great change from heathenism to Christianity.[1] They have

[1] See a full and most interesting discussion of the whole subject of the heathen names of the week days, in Grimm's "Deutsche Mythologie," vol. i. 111-128. It may be worth while, in connexion with this subject of the preservation of heathen names, to notice the curious fact, that about three miles south of Canterbury, on the ancient Roman road now called Stone-street, there is a farm-house and pond, still called. Hermansole, with which tradition has connected the belief of some Saxon antiquity. (See Hasted's "Kent," i. 25 ; iii. 731.) The name immediately suggests the well-known sacred pillars which existed in ancient Germany under the name of *Hermansaule*, "the pillars of Herman." (Grimm, "Deutsche Myth.," i. 9.)

survived, and rightly, because there is no harm in their intention ; and if there is no harm, it is a clear gain to keep up old names and customs, when their evil intention is passed away. They, like the ruin of St. Pancras, are standing witnesses of Gregory's wisdom and moderation —standing examples to us that Christianity does not require us to trample on the customs, even of a heathen world, if we can divest them of their mischief.

Lastly, the mission of Augustine is one of the most striking instances in all history of the vast results which may flow from a very small beginning,—of the immense effects produced by a single thought in the heart of a single man, carried out consistently, deliberately, and fearlessly. Nothing in itself could seem more trivial than the meeting of Gregory with the three Yorkshire slaves in the market-place at Rome, yet this roused a feeling in his mind which he never lost ; and through all the obstacles which were thrown first in his own way, and then in the way of Augustine, his highest desire concerning it was more than realised. And this was even the more remarkable when we remember who and what his instruments were. You may have observed that I have said little of Augustine himself, and that for two reasons : first, because so little is known of him ; secondly, because I must confess, that what little is told of him leaves an unfavourable impression behind. We cannot doubt that he was an active, self-denying man—his coming here through so many dangers of sea and land proves it,—and it would be ungrateful and ungenerous not to acknowledge how much we owe to him. But still almost every personal trait which is recorded of him shows us that he was not a man of any great elevation of character,—that he was often thinking of himself, or of his order, when we should have wished him to be thinking of the great cause he had in hand. We see this in his drawing back from his journey in France,—we see it in the additional power which he claimed from Gregory over his own companions,—we see it in the warnings sent to him by Gregory, that he was not to be puffed up by the wonders he had wrought in

D

Britain,—we see it in the haughty severity with which he
treated the remnant of British Christians in Wales, not
rising when they approached, and uttering that male-
diction against them, which ·sanctioned, if it did not
instigate, their massacre by the Saxons,—we see it in the
legends which grew up after his death, telling us how,
because the people of Stroud insulted him by fastening a
fish tail to his back,[1] he cursed them, and brought down
on the whole population the curse of being born with tails.

I mention all this; not to disparage our great benefactor and first archbishop ; but partly, because we ought
to have our eyes open to the truth even about our best
friends,—partly to show what I have said before, from
what small beginnings and through what weak instruments
Gregory accomplished his mighty work. It would have
been a mighty work—even if it had been no more than
Gregory and Augustine themselves imagined. They
thought, no doubt, of the Anglo-Saxon conversion, as we
might think of the conversion of barbarous tribes in India
or Africa,—numerous and powerful themselves, but with
no great future results. How far beyond their widest
vision that conversion has reached, may best be seen at
Canterbury.

Let any one sit on the hill of the little church of
St. Martin, and look on the view which is there spread
before his eyes. Immediately below are the towers of the
great Abbey of St. Augustine, where Christian learning and
civilisation first struck root in the Anglo-Saxon race;[2] and
within which now, after a lapse of many centuries, a new
institution has arisen, intended to carry far and wide to
countries of which Gregory and Augustine never heard,

[1] Gocelin notices the offence, without
expressly stating the punishment (c. 41),
and places it in Dorsetshire. The
story is given in Harris's "Kent," 303;
in Fuller's ".Church Hist.," ii. 7. § 22;
and in Ray's "Proverbs," (p. 233) who
mentions it especially as a Kentish
story, and as one that was very generally
believed in his time on the continent.
There is a long and amusing discussion
on the subject in Lambard's "Kent,"
p. 400.
[2] I have forborne to dwell on any

traces of Augustine's mission, besides
those which were left at the time.
Otherwise the list would be much
enlarged by the revival of the ancient
associations, visible in St. Augustine's
College, in St. Gregory's Church and
burial ground, and in the restored
Church of St. Martin ; where the
windows, although of modern date, are
interesting memorials of the past—
especially that which represents the
well-known scene of St. Martin dividing
the cloak.

the blessings which they gave to us. Carry your view on,—and there rises high above all the magnificent pile of our cathedral, equal in splendour and state to any, the noblest temple or church, that Augustine could have seen in ancient Rome, rising on the very ground which derives its consecration from him. And still more than the grandeur of the outward buildings that rose from the little church of Augustine and the little palace of Ethelbert, have been the institutions of all kinds, of which these were the earliest cradle. From Canterbury, the first English Christian city —from Kent, the first English Christian kingdom—has, by degrees, arisen the whole constitution of Church and State in England which now binds together the whole British empire. And from the Christianity here established in England has flowed, by direct consequence, first, the Christianity of Germany,—then, after a long interval, of North America,—and lastly, we may trust, in time, of all India, and all Australasia. The view from St. Martin's Church is indeed one of the most inspiriting that can be found in the world ; there is none to which I would more willingly take any one, who doubted whether a small beginning could lead to a great and lasting good,—none which carries us more vividly back into the past, or more hopefully forward to the future.

NOTE.—The statements respecting the spot of Augustine's landing are so various, that it may be worth while to give briefly the different claimants, in order to simplify the statement in pp. 12—17.

1. Ebbe's Fleet.—For this the main reasons are : 1. The fact that it was the *usual* landing-place in ancient Thanet, as is shown by the tradition that Hengist, S. Mildred, and the Danes, came there. (Lewis, p. 83. Hasted, iv., 289.) 2. The fact that Bede's whole narrative emphatically lands Augustine in Thanet, and not on the main land. 3. The present situation with the local tradition, as described in p. 12.

2. The spot called the Boarded Groin, Lewis, p. 83, also marked in the Ordnance Survey as the landing-place of the Saxons. But this must then have been covered by the sea.

3. Stonar, near Sandwich. Sandwich MS., in Boys' Sandwich, p. 836. But this, even if not covered by the sea, must have been a mere island. (Hasted, iv., 585.)

4. Richborough. Ibid. p. 838. But this was not in the Isle of Thanet,—and the story is probably founded, partly on Thorn's narrative, (1758) which, by speaking of "Retesburgh, *in insula Thaneti*," shows that he means the whole port, and partly on its having been actually the scene of the final debarkation on the mainland, as described in p. 17.

MAP OF THE ISLE OF THANET AT THE TIME OF THE LANDING OF
ST. AUGUSTINE.

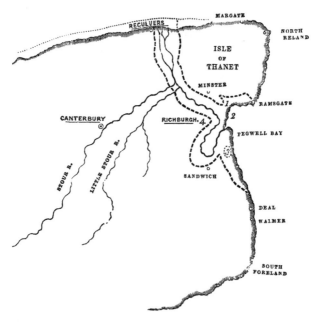

Present line of coast ———
Present towns, as *Deal*.
Ancient line of coast . . . . . .

Ancient towns. *Reculver*.
1, 2, 3, 4, the alleged landing-places.

THE

MURDER OF BECKET.

REPRINTED, WITH ADDITIONS, FROM THE "QUARTERLY REVIEW,"
SEPTEMBER, 1853.

MURDER OF BECKET.

EVERY one is familiar with the reversal of popular judgments respecting individuals or events of our own time. It would be an easy, though perhaps an invidious task, to point out the changes from obloquy to applause, and from applause to obloquy, which the present generation has witnessed ; and it would be instructive to examine in each case, how far these changes have been justified by the facts. What thoughtful observers may thus notice in the passing opinions of the day, it is the privilege of history to track through the course of centuries. Of such vicissitudes in the judgment of successive ages, one of the most striking is to be found in the conflicting feelings with which different epochs have regarded the contest of Becket with Henry II. During its continuance, the public opinion of England and of Europe was, if not unfavourable to the Archbishop, at least strongly divided. After its tragical close, the change from indifference or hostility to unbounded veneration was instantaneous and universal. This veneration, after a duration of more than three centuries, was superseded, at least in England, by a contempt as general and profound as had been the previous admiration. And now, after three centuries more, the revolution of the wheel of fortune has again brought up, both at home and abroad, worshippers of the memory of St. Thomas of Canterbury, who rival the most undoubting devotee that ever knelt at his shrine in the reign of the Plantagenet kings. Indications [1] are not wanting, that the pendulum which has been so violently swung to and fro, is at last about to settle into its proper place ; and we may trust that on this, as on many other controverted historical points, a judgment will be pronounced in our own times, which, if not irreversible, is less likely to be reversed than those which have gone before. But it may contribute to the decision upon the merits of the general question if a complete picture is presented of the passage of his career which has left by far the most indelible impression,—its terrible close. And even though the famous catastrophe had not turned the course of events for generations to come, and exercised an influence which is not yet fully exhausted, it would still deserve to be minutely described, from its intimate connexion with the stateliest of English cathedrals, and with the first great poem of the English language.

The labour of Dr. Giles has collected no less than nineteen biographies, or fragments of biographies, all of which appear to have been written within fifty years of the murder, and some of which are confined to that single subject. [2] To these we must add the French biography in verse [3] by Guernes, or Garnier, of Pont S. Maxence, which was composed only five years after the event—the more interesting from being the sole record which gives the words of the actors in the language in which they spoke ; and, although somewhat later, that by Robert of Gloucester

---

[1] The Rev. J. C. Robertson, of Bekesbourne, was perhaps the first author who, in two articles in the "English Review" of 1846, took a detailed and impartial survey of the whole struggle. To these articles I have to acknowledge a special obligation, as having first introduced me to the copious materials from which this account is derived. To this general estimate of the controversy, I have now to add the narrative given by the Dean of St. Paul's, in the third volume of "The History of Latin Christianity," and the "History of England," by Dr. Pauli, to whose kindness I have been also much indebted for some of the sources of the 'martyr-

dom.' An interesting account of Becket's death is affixed to the collection of his letters published in the "Remains of the late Mr. Froude." But besides the one-sided view by which that account is pervaded, it is almost exclusively drawn from a single source, the narrative of Fitzstephen.

[2] Vitæ et Epistolæ S. Thomæ Cantuariensis, ed. Giles. 6 volumes.

[3] The concluding fragment of the poem has been published by the great scholar Immanuel Bekker, in the Berlin Transactions, 1838, pt. 2, pp. 25—168. From fragment in the Wolfenbüttel MSS. (The whole MS. is in the British Museum.)

in the 13th,[1] and by Grandison Bishop of Exeter in the 14th century.[2] We must also include the contemporary or nearly contemporary chroniclers — Gervase, Diceto, Hoveden, and Giraldus Cambrensis ; and, in the next century, Matthew Paris and Brompton.

Of these twenty-nine narrators, four—Edward Grim, William Fitzstephen, John of Salisbury (who unfortunately supplies but little), and the anonymous author of the Lambeth MS.—claim to have been eye-witnesses. Three others—William of Canterbury, Benedict, afterwards abbot of Peterborough, and Gervase of Canterbury—were monks of the convent, and, though not present at the massacre, were probably somewhere in the precincts. Herbert of Bosham, Roger of Pontigny, and Garnier, though not in England at the time, had been on terms of intercourse more or less intimate with Becket, and the two latter, especially, seem to have taken the utmost pains to ascertain the truth of the facts they relate. From these several accounts we can recover the particulars of the death of Archbishop Becket to the minutest details. It is true that, being written by monastic or clerical historians after the national feeling had been roused to enthusiasm in his behalf, allowance must be made for exaggeration, suppression, and every kind of false colouring which could set off their hero to advantage. It is true, also, that on some few points the various authorities are hopelessly irreconcilable. But still a careful comparison of the narrators with each other, and with the localities, leads to a conviction that on the whole the facts have been substantially preserved, and that, as often happens, the truth can be ascertained in spite, and even in consequence, of attempts to distort and suppress it. If this be so, few occurrences in the middle ages have been so graphically and copiously described, and few give such an insight into the manners and customs, the thoughts and feelings, not only of the man himself, but of the entire age, as the eventful tragedy, known successively as the "martyrdom," the

---

[1] This metrical Life and Martyrdom of S. Thomas (composed in the reign of Henry III.) has been printed for the Percy Society, and edited by Mr. Black.

[2] Grandison's Life exists only in MS. The copy which I have used is in the Bodleian Library. (MS. 493.)

" accidental death," the " righteous execution," and the
" murder " of Thomas à Becket.

The year 1170 witnessed the termination of the
struggle of ten years between the King and the Archbishop ; in July, the final reconciliation had been effected
with Henry, in France ; in the beginning of December
Becket had landed at Sandwich[1]—the port of the
monks of Canterbury—and thence entered the metropolitical city, after an absence of six years, amidst the
acclamations of the people. The cathedral was hung with
silken drapery ; magnificent banquets were prepared ; the
churches resounded with organs and hymns ; the palace-
hall with trumpets ; and the Archbishop preached in the
chapter-house on the text, " Here we have no abiding
city, but we seek one to come." [2] Great difficulties, however, still remained. In addition to the general question
of the immunities of the clergy from secular jurisdiction,
which was the original point in dispute between the King
and Archbishop, another had arisen within this very year,
of much less importance in itself, but which now threw
the earlier controversy into the shade,[3] and eventually
brought about the final catastrophe. In the preceding
June, Henry, with the view of consolidating his power in
England, had caused his eldest son to be crowned King,
not merely as his successor, but as his colleague ; insomuch that by contemporary chroniclers he is always called
" the young King," sometimes even " Henry III." [4] In the
absence of the Archbishop of Canterbury, the ceremony of
coronation was performed by Roger of Bishop's Bridge,
Archbishop of York, assisted by Gilbert Foliot and
Jocelyn the Lombard, Bishops of London and of Salisbury,
under (what was at least believed to be) the sanction of a
Papal brief.[5] The moment the intelligence was communicated to Becket, who was then in France, a new blow
seemed to be struck at his rights ; but this time it was

---

[1] Garnier, 59, 9.
[2] Fitzstephen, Ed. Giles, i. 283.
[3] Giles, Epp. i. 65.
[4] Hence, perhaps, the precision with which the number "III." is added (for the first time) on the coins of Henry III.
[5] See Milman's "Hist. of Latin Chris- tianity," iii. 510, 511.

not the privileges of his order, but of his office, that were attacked. The inalienable right[1] of crowning the sovereigns of England, from the time of Augustine downwards inherent in the see of Canterbury, had been infringed, and with his usual ardour he procured from the Pope letters of excommunication against the three prelates who had taken part in the daring act, probably with the authority of the Pope himself. These letters he had with him, unknown to the King, at the time of the reconciliation, and his earliest thought on landing in England was to get them conveyed to the offending bishops, who were then at Dover. They started for France from that port as he landed at Sandwich, leaving however a powerful auxiliary, in the person of Randulf de Broc, a knight to whom the King had granted possession of the archiepiscopal castle of Saltwood, and who was for this, if for no other reason, a sworn enemy to Becket and his return. The first object of the Archbishop was to conciliate the young King, who was then at Woodstock, and his mode of courting him

---

[1] This contest with Becket for the privileges of the see of York, though the most important, was not the only one which Archbishop Roger sustained. At the court of Northampton their crosses had already confronted each other, like hostile spears.—Fitzstephen, 226. It was a standing question between the two Archbishops, and Roger maintained the pre-eminence of his see against Becket's successor in a somewhat singular manner. "In 1176," says Fuller, "a synod was called at Westminster, the Pope's legate being present thereat; on whose right hand sat Richard Archbishop of Canterbury, as in his proper place; when in springs Roger of York, and, finding Canterbury so seated, fairly sits him down on Canterbury's lap." . . . . "It matters as little to the reader as to the writer," the historian continues, "whether Roger beat Richard—or Richard beat Roger; yet, once for all, we will reckon up the arguments which each see alleged for its proceedings :" which accordingly follow with his usual racy humour.—Fuller's "Church Hist.," iii. § 3. Nor was York the only see which contested the Primacy of Canterbury at this momentous crisis. Gilbert Foliot endeavoured in his own person to revive the claims of London, which had been extinct from the fabulous age of Lucius son of Cole. "He aims," says John of Salisbury, in an epistle burning with indignation, "he aims at transferring the metropolitical see to London, where he boasts that the Archflamen once sate, whilst Jupiter was worshipped there. And who knows but that this religious and discreet bishop is planning the restoration of the worship of Jupiter ; so that if he cannot get the Archbishopric in any other way, he may have at least the name and title of Archflamen. He relies," continues the angry partisan, "on an oracle of Merlin, who, inspired by I know not what spirit, is said before Augustine's coming to have prophesied the transference of the dignity of London to Canterbury."—Ussher, "Brit. Eccl. Ant." 711. The importance attached to this question of coronation may be further illustrated by the long series of effigies of the Primates of Germany, in Mayence Cathedral, where the Archbishops of that see—the Canterbury of the German Empire—are represented in the act of crowning the German Emperors, evidently as the most characteristic trait in their archiepiscopal careers.

was characteristic. Three magnificent [1] chargers, of which his previous experience of horses enabled him to know the merits, were the gift by which he hoped to win over the mind of his former pupil ; and he himself, after a week's stay at Canterbury, followed the messenger who was to announce his present to the Prince. He passed through Rochester in state, entered London in a vast procession that advanced three miles out of the city to meet him, and took up his quarters at Southwark, in the palace of the aged Bishop of Winchester, Henry of Blois, brother of King Stephen.[2] Here he received orders from the young King to proceed no further, but return instantly to Canterbury. In obedience to the command, but professedly (and this is a characteristic illustration of much that follows) from a desire to be at his post at Christmas-day, he relinquished his design, and turned for the last time from the city of his birth to the city of his death.

One more opening of reconciliation occurred. Before he finally left the vicinity of London, he halted for a few days at his manor-house at Harrow, probably to make inquiries about a contumacious priest who then occupied the vicarage of that town. He sent thence to the neighbouring abbey of St. Albans to request an interview with the Abbot Simon. The Abbot came over with magnificent presents from the good cheer of his abbey ; and the Archbishop was deeply affected on seeing him, embraced and kissed him tenderly, and urged him, pressing the Abbot's hand to his heart, and quivering with emotion, to make a last attempt on the mind of the Prince. The Abbot went to Woodstock, but returned without success. Becket, heaving a deep sigh, and shaking his head significantly, said, "Let be—let be. Is it not so, is it not so, that the days of the end hasten to their completion ? " He then endeavoured to console his friend :—" My Lord Abbot, many thanks for your fruitless labour. The sick man is sometimes beyond the reach of physicians, but he will soon bear his own

[1] Fitzstephen, 284, 285.
[2] This interview is given at length in Matthew Paris, who, as a monk of

St. Albans, probably derived it from the traditions of the Abbey. Hist. Angl. 124. Vit. Abbat. 91.

judgment." He then turned to the clergy around him, and said, with the deep feeling of an injured Primate, " Look you, my friends, the Abbot, who is bound by no obligations to me, has done more for me than all my brother-bishops and suffragans;" alluding especially to the charge which the Abbot had left with the cellarer of St. Albans, to supply the Archbishop with everything during his own absence at Woodstock. At last the day of parting came. The Abbot, with clasped hands, intreated Becket to spend the approaching festival of Christmas and St. Stephen's day at his own abbey of the great British martyr. Becket, moved to tears, replied :—" O, how gladly would I come, but it has been otherwise ordered. Go in peace, dear brother, go in peace to your church, which may God preserve ; but I go to a sufficient excuse for my not going with you. But come with me, and be my guest and comforter in my many troubles." They parted on the high ridge of the hill of Harrow to meet no more.

It was not without reason that the Archbishop's mind was filled with gloomy forebodings. The first open manifestations of hostility proceeded from the family of the Brocs of Saltwood. Already, tidings had reached him that Randulf de Broc had seized a vessel laden with wine from the King, and had killed the crew, or imprisoned them in Pevensey Castle. This injury was promptly repaired at the bidding of the young King, to whom the Archbishop had sent a complaint through the Prior of Dover,[1] and to the friendly Abbot of St. Albans. But the enmity of the Brocs was not so easily allayed. No sooner had the Primate reached Canterbury than he was met by a series of fresh insults. Randulf, he was told, was hunting down his archiepiscopal deer with his own dogs in his own woods ; and Robert, another of the same family, who had been a monk in the novitiate, but had since taken to a secular life, sent out his nephew John to waylay and cut off the tails of a sumpter mule and a horse of the Archbishop. This jest, or outrage (according as we regard it), which occurred on Christmas-eve, took deep possession of Becket's

---

[1] Fitzstephen, 286

mind.[1] On Christmas-day, after the solemn celebration of the usual midnight mass, he entered the cathedral for the services of that great festival. Before the performance of high mass he mounted the pulpit (probably in the nave), and preached on the text, " On earth, peace to men of good will." It was the reading (perhaps the true reading) of the Vulgate version ; and had once before afforded him the opportunity of rejecting, on his return, the argument that he ought to come in peace. " There is no peace," he said, " but to men of good will."[2] On this limitation of the universal message of Christian love, he now proceeded to discourse. He began by speaking of the sainted fathers of the church of Canterbury, the presence of whose bones made doubly hallowed the consecrated ground. " One martyr," he said, " they had already"—Alfege, murdered by the Danes, whose tomb stood on the north side of the high altar ; " it was possible," he added, " that they would soon have another."[3] The people who thronged the nave were in a state of wild excitement ; they wept and groaned, and an audible murmur ran through the church, " Father, why do you desert us so soon ? to whom will you leave us ?" But, as he went on with his discourse, the plaintive strain gradually rose into a tone of fiery indignation. "You would have thought," says Herbert of Bosham, who was present, " that you were looking at the prophetic beast, which had at once the face of a man and the face of a lion." He spoke—the fact is recorded by all the biographers, without any sense of its extreme incongruity —he spoke of the insult of the docked tail[4] of the sumpter mule, and in a voice of thunder[5] excommunicated Randulf and Robert de Broc ; and in the same sentence included the Vicar of Thirlwood, and Nigel of Sackville, the Vicar

---

[1] Fitzstephen, 287.
[2] Fitzstephen, 283.
[3] Fitzstephen, 292.
[4] According to the popular belief, the excommunication of the Broc family was not the only time that Becket avenged a similar offence. Lambard, in his "Perambulations of Kent," says that the people of Stroud, near Rochester, insulted Becket as he rode through the

town, and like the Brocs, cut off the tails of his horses. Their descendants, as a judgment for the crime, were ever after born with horses' tails. (See, however, the previous Lecture, p. 34.) A curse lighted also on the blacksmiths of a town, where one of that trade had "dogged his horse." (Fuller's Worthies.)
[5] Herbert, i. 323 ; Garnier, 63, 4.

of Harrow, for occupying those incumbencies without his authority, and refusing access to his officials.[1]   He also publicly denounced and forbade communication with the three bishops who, by crowning the young King, had not feared to incroach upon the prescriptive rights of the church of Canterbury.   " May they be cursed," he said in conclusion, " by Jesus Christ, and may their memory be blotted out of the assembly of the saints, whoever shall sow hatred and discord between me and my Lord the King."[2]   With these words he dashed the candle on the pavement,[3] in token of the extinction of his enemies ; and as he descended from the pulpit, to pass to the altar to celebrate mass, he repeated to his Welsh crossbearer, Alexander, the prophetic words, " One martyr, St. Alfege, you have already—another, if God will, you will have soon."[4]   The service in the cathedral was followed by the banquet in his hall, at which, although Christmas-day fell this year on a Friday, it was observed that he ate as usual, in honour of the joyous festival of the Nativity.[5] On the next day, Saturday, the Feast of St. Stephen, and on Sunday, the Feast of St. John, he again celebrated mass ;[6] and towards the close of the day, under cover of the dark, he sent away, with messages to the King of France and the Archbishop of Sens, his faithful servant Herbert of Bosham, telling him that he would see him no more, but that he was anxious not to expose him to the further suspicions of Henry.   Herbert departed with a heavy heart,[7] and with him went Alexander, the Welsh crossbearer.   The Archbishop sent off another servant to the Pope, and two others to the Bishop of Norwich, with a letter relating to Hugh Earl of Norfolk.   He also drew up a deed appointing his priest William to the chapelry of Penshurst, with an excommunication against any one who should take it from him.[8]   These are his last recorded public acts.   On the night of the same Sunday he received a warning letter from France, announcing that

[1] Garnier, 71, 15.
[2] Fitzstephen, 292.
[3] Grim, ed. Giles, i. 68.
[4] Fitzstephen, 292.
[5] Herbert, 324, 325.
[6] Herbert, 324.
[7] Fitzstephen, 292, 293.
[8] Anon. Passio Tertia, Ed. Giles, ii. 156.

he was in peril from some new attack. What this was is
now to be told.

The three prelates of York, London, and Salisbury,
having left England as soon as they heard that the
excommunication had been issued against them, arrived
in France a few days before Christmas,[1] and immediately
proceeded to the King, who was then at the castle of Bur,
near Bayeux.[2] It was a place already famous in history
as the scene of the interview between William and Harold,
when the oath was perfidiously exacted and sworn which
led to the conquest of England. All manner of rumours
about Becket's proceedings had reached the ears of Henry,
and he besought the advice of the three prelates. The
Archbishop of York answered cautiously, " Ask counsel
from your barons and knights ; it is not for us to say what
must be done." A pause ensued ; and then it was added
—whether by Roger or by some one else does not clearly
appear—" As long as Thomas lives, you will have neither
good days, nor peaceful kingdom, nor quiet life."[3] These
words goaded the king into one of those paroxysms of
fury to which all the earlier Plantagenet princes were
subject, and which was believed by themselves to arise
from a mixture of demoniacal blood in their race. It is
described in Henry's son John as " something beyond
anger : he was so changed in his whole body that a man
would hardly have known him. His forehead was drawn
up into deep furrows ; his flaming eyes glistened ; a livid
hue took the place of colour."[4] Henry himself is said at
these moments to have become like a wild beast ; his eyes,
naturally dove-like and quiet, seemed to flash lightning ;
his hands struck and tore whatever came in their way : on
one occasion he flew at a messenger who brought him bad
tidings, to tear out his eyes ; in his previous controversy
with Becket, he is represented as having flung down his
cap, torn off his clothes, thrown the silk coverlet from his
bed, and rolled upon it, gnawing the straw and rushes.
Of such a kind was the frenzy which struck terror through

[1] Herbert, 319.
[2] Garnier, 65, who gives the interview
in great detail.
[3] Fitzstephen, 390.
[4] Richard of Devizes, § 40.

all hearts at the Council of Clarendon, and again at
Northampton, when with tremendous menaces, sworn upon
his usual oath "the eyes of God," he insisted on Becket's
appearance.[1] Of such a kind was the frenzy which he
showed on the present occasion.   " A fellow," he exclaimed, " that has eaten my bread has lifted up his heel
against me—a fellow that I loaded with benefits dares
insult the King and the whole royal family, and tramples
on the whole kingdom—a fellow that came to court on a
lame sumpter mule sits without hindrance on the throne
itself."   " What sluggard wretches," he burst forth again
and again, " what cowards have I brought up in my court,
who care nothing for their allegiance to their master ! not
one will deliver me from this low-born priest !"[2] and with
these fatal words he rushed out of the room.

There were present among the courtiers four knights,
whose names long lived in the memory of men, and on
which every ingenuity was exercised to extract from them
an evil augury of the deed which has made them famous
—Reginald Fitzurse, " son of the Bear," and of truly
"bearlike" character (so the Canterbury monks represented
it) ; Hugh de Moreville, " of the city of death "—of whom
a dreadful story was told of his having ordered a young
Saxon to be boiled alive on the false accusation of his
wife ; William de Tracy—a brave soldier, it was said, but
" of parricidal wickedness ;" Richard le Brez or le Bret,
commonly known as Brito, from the Latinised version of
his name in the Chronicles—more fit, they say, to have
been called the " Brute."[3]   They are all described as on
familiar terms with the King himself, and sometimes, in
official language, as gentlemen of the bed-chamber.[4] They
also appear to have been brought together by old associations.   Fitzurse, Moreville, and Tracy had all sworn
homage to Becket while Chancellor.   Fitzurse, Tracy,
and Bret had all connexions with Somersetshire.   Their

[1] Roger, 124, 104.
[2] Will. Cant., Ed. Giles, ii. p. 30; Grim,
68; Gervase, 1414.
[3] Will. Cant., 31. This play on the
word will appear less strange, when we
remember the legendary superstructure

built on the identity of the Trojan
Brutus with the primitive *Briton*. See
Lambard's " Kent," p. 306. Fitzurse is
called simply " Reginald Bure."
[4] Cubicularii.

rank and lineage can even now be accurately traced through the medium of our county historians and legal records. Fitzurse was the descendant of Urso, or Ours, who had, under the Conqueror, held Grittleston in Wiltshire, of the Abbey of Glastonbury. His father, Richard Fitzurse, became possessed in the reign of Stephen of the manor of Willeton in Somersetshire, which had descended to Reginald a few years before the time of which we are speaking.[1] He was also a tenant in chief in Northamptonshire, in tail in Leicestershire.[2] Moreville was a man of high rank and office. He was this very year Justice itinerant of the counties of Northumberland and Cumberland, where he inherited the barony of Burgh-on-the-Sands and other possessions from his father Roger and his grandfather Simon. He was likewise forester of Cumberland, owner of the castle of Knaresborough, and added to his paternal property that of his wife, Helwise de Stute-ville.[3] Richard the Breton was, it would appear from an incident in the murder, intimate with Prince William, the King's brother.[4] He and his brother Edmund had succeeded to their father Simon le Bret, who had probably come over with the Conqueror from Brittany, and settled in Somersetshire, where the property of the family long continued.[5] Tracy was the younger of two brothers, sons of John de Sudely and Grace de Traci. He took the name of his mother, who was daughter of William de Traci, a natural son of Henry I. On his father's side he was descended from the Saxon Ethelred. He was born at Toddington, in Gloucestershire,[6] where, as well as in Devonshire,[7] he held large estates.

It is not clear on what day the fatal exclamation of the King was made; Fitzstephen [8] reports it as taking place on Sunday, the 27th of December. Others,[9] who ascribe a more elaborate character to the whole plot, date it a few days before, on Tuesday the 24th,—the whole

[1] Collinson's Somersetshire, iii. 487.
[2] Liber Nigri Scaccarii, 216—88.
[3] Foss's Judges of England, i. 279.
[4] Fitzstephen, 303.
[5] Collinson's Somersetshire, iii. 514.
[6] Rudder's Gloucestershire, 770;

Pedigree of the Tracys in Britton's Toddington.
[7] Liber Nigri Scaccarii, 115—221.
[8] Fitstephen, 290.
[9] Garnier, 65, 17; so also Gervase, Chron., 1414.

Court taking part in it, and Roger Archbishop of York
giving full instructions to the knights as to their future
course.   However this may be, it was generally believed
that they left Bur on the night of the King's fury.   They
then, it was thought, proceeded by different roads to the
French coast, and crossed the Channel on the following
day.   Three courtiers, who, on their disappearance, were
sent to stop their progress,[1] arrived on the coast too late.
Two of them landed, as was afterwards noticed with mali-
cious satisfaction, at the port of *"Dogs"* near Dover,[2] two
of them at Winchilsea,[3] and all four arrived at the same
hour [4] at the fortress of Saltwood Castle, the property of
the see of Canterbury, but now occupied, as we have seen,
by Becket's chief enemy—Dan Randolph of Broc—who
came out to welcome them.[5]   Here they would doubtless
be told of the excommunication launched against their
host on Christmas-day.   In the darkness of the night—
the long winter night of the 28th of December [6]—it was
believed that, with candles extinguished, and not even
seeing each other's faces, the scheme was concerted.
Early in the morning of the next day they issued orders
in the King's name [7] for a troop of soldiers to be levied
from the neighbourhood to march with them to Canterbury.   They themselves mounted their chargers, and
galloped along the old Roman road from Lymne to Canterbury, which, under the name of Stone Street, runs in a
straight line of nearly fifteen miles from Saltwood to the
hills immediately above the city.   They proceeded
instantly to St. Augustine's Abbey, outside the walls, and
took up their quarters with Clarembald, the Abbot.[8]

The Abbey was in a state of considerable confusion at
the time of their arrival.   A destructive fire had ravaged
the buildings two years before,[9] and the reparations
could hardly have been yet completed.   Its domestic state
was still more disturbed.   It was now nearly ten years
since a feud had been raging between the inmates and

[1] Fitzstephen, 291.
[2] Grim. 69; Gervase, Chron., 1414.
[3] Garnier, 66, 67.
[4] Fitzstephen, 290.
[5] Garnier, 66, 29

[6] Garnier, 66, 22.
[7] Grim, 69; Roger, i. 160; Fitzstephen, 293; Garnier, 66, 6.
[8] Gervase, Chron., 1414.
[9] Thorn's Chronicles, 1817.

their Abbot, who had been intruded on them in 1161, as Becket had been on the ecclesiastics of the Cathedral,— but with the ultimate difference, that, whilst Becket had become the champion of the clergy, Clarembald had stood fast by the King, his patron, which perpetuated the quarrel between the monks and their superior. He would, therefore, naturally be eager to receive the new comers, and with him they concerted measures for their future movements.[1] Having sent orders to the mayor or provost of Canterbury to issue a proclamation in the King's name, forbidding any one to offer assistance to the Archbishop,[2] the knights once more mounted their chargers, and, accompanied by Robert of Broc, who had probably attended them from Saltwood, rode under the long line of wall which still separates the city and the precincts of the cathedral from St. Augustine's monastery, till they reached the great gateway which opened into the court of the Archbishop's palace.[3] They were followed by a band of about a dozen armed men, whom they placed in the house of one Gilbert,[4] which stood hard by the gate.

It was Tuesday the 29th of December. Tuesday, his friends remarked, had always been a significant day in Becket's life. On a Tuesday he was born and baptised— on a Tuesday he had fled from Northampton—on a Tuesday he had left the King's court in Normandy—on a Tuesday he had left England on his exile—on a Tuesday he had received warning of his martyrdom in a vision at Pontigny—on a Tuesday he had returned from that exile—it was now on a Tuesday that the fatal hour came[5] —and (as the next generation observed) it was on a Tuesday that his enemy King Henry was buried—on a Tuesday that the martyr's relics were translated[6]— and Tuesday was long afterwards regarded as the

---

[1] Gervase Chron., 1414.

[2] Garnier, 66, b. 10.

[3] The Archbishop's palace is now almost entirely destroyed, and its place occupied by modern houses. But an ancient gateway on the site of the one here mentioned, though of later date, still leads from *Palace* Street into these houses.

[4] Fitzstephen, 297.

[5] Robert of Gloucester, Life of Becket, 285.

[6] Alan, i. 377; Matthew Paris, 97. It was the fact of the 29th of December falling on a Tuesday that fixes the date of his death to 1170, not 1171; Gervase, 1418.

week-day especially consecrated to the saint, with whose
fortunes it had thus been so strangely interwoven.[1]
Other omens were remarked. A soldier who was in the
plot whispered to one of the cellarmen of the Priory that
the Archbishop would not see the evening of Tuesday.
Becket only smiled. A citizen of Canterbury, Reginald
by name, had told him that there were several in England
who were bent on his death ; to which he answered,
with tears, that he knew he should not be killed out of
church.[2] He himself had told several persons in France
that he was convinced he should not outlive the year,[3]
and in two days the year would be ended.

Whether these evil auguries weighed upon his mind, or
whether his attendants afterwards ascribed to his words a
more serious meaning than they really bore, the day
opened with gloomy forebodings. Before the break of
dawn, the Archbishop startled the clergy of his bed-
chamber by asking whether it would be possible for any
one to escape to Sandwich before daylight, and, on being
answered in the affirmative, added, " Let any one escape
who wishes." That morning he attended mass in the
cathedral ; then passed a long time in the chapter-house,
confessing to two of the monks, and receiving, as seems
to have been his custom, three scourgings.[4] Then came
the usual banquet in the great hall of the Palace, at three
in the afternoon. He was observed to drink more than
usual, and his cup-bearer, in a whisper, reminded him of
it.[5] " He who has much blood to shed," answered Becket,
" must drink much." [6]

The dinner [7] was now over ; the concluding hymn or
" grace " was finished ; [8] and Becket had retired to his
private room,[9] where he sat on his bed,[10] talking with his
friends ; whilst the servants, according to the practice
which is still preserved in our old collegiate establishments, remained in the hall making their meal of

---

[1] See the deed quoted in Journal of
British Archæol. Assoc., April, 1854.
[2] Grandison, c. 5. See p. 71.
[3] Benedict, 71. [4] Garnier, 70, b. 25.
[5] Anon. Lambeth, ed. Giles, ii. 121 ;
Roger, 169 ; Garnier, 77 b. 2.

[6] Grandison, c. 5. See p. 53.
[7] Grandison, c. 5.
[8] For the account of his dinners, see
Herbert, 63, 64, 70, 71.
[9] Grim, 70 ; Benedict, ii. 55.
[10] Roger, 163.

the broken meat which was left.[1] The floor of the hall
was strewn with fresh hay and straw,[2] to accommodate
with clean places those who could not find room on the
benches ;[3] and the crowd of beggars and poor,[4] who daily
received their food from the Archbishop, had gone [5] into
the outer yard, and were lingering before their final dis-
persion. It was at this moment that the four knights
dismounted in the court before the hall,[6] the doors were
all open, and they passed through the crowd without
opposition. Either to avert suspicion or from deference
to the feeling of the time, which forbade the entrance of
armed men into the peaceful precincts of the cathedral,[7]
they left their weapons behind, and their coats of mails
were concealed by the usual cloak and gown,[8] the dress of
ordinary life. One attendant, Radulf, an archer, followed
them. They were generally known as courtiers ; and the
servants invited them to partake of the remains of the
feast. They declined, and were pressing on, when, at the
foot of the staircase leading from the hall to the Archbishop's room, they were met by William Fitz-Nigel, the
seneschal who had just parted from the Primate with a
permission to leave his service, and join the King in
France. When he saw the knights, whom he immediately
recognised, he ran forward and gave them the usual kiss
of salutation, and at their request ushered them to the
room where Becket sate. " My lord," he said, " here are
four knights from King Henry, wishing to speak to you." [9]
" Let them come in," said Becket. It must have been a
solemn moment, even for those rough men, when they first
found themselves in the presence of the Archbishop.
Three of them, Hugh de Moreville, Reginald Fitzurse, and
William de Tracy, had known him long before in the
days of his splendour as Chancellor and favourite of the
King. He was still in the vigour of strength, though in

[1] Garnier, 20, b. 10.
[2] Fitzstephen, 189. This was in
winter. In summer it would have been
fresh rushes and green leaves.
[3] Grim, 70 ; Fitzstephen, 294.
[4] Garnier, 66, b. 17.
[5] Fitzstephen, 310.
[6] Gervase, 1415.
[7] Grim, 70 ; Roger, 161.
[8] Garnier, 66, b. 25, 67, b. 10 :
Roger, 161 ; Grim, 70 ; See the Archbishop's permission in p. 54.
[9] Garnier, 67, 15.

his fifty-third year ; his countenance, if we may judge of
it from the accounts at the close of the day, still retained
its majestic and striking aspect ; his eyes were large and
piercing, and always glancing to and fro ;[1] and his tall[2]
figure, though really spare and thin, had a portly look
from the number of wrappings which he wore beneath his
ordinary clothes. Round about him sate or lay on the
floor, the clergy of his household—amongst them, his
faithful counsellor, John, Archdeacon of Salisbury,
William Fitzstephen his chaplain, and Edward Grim, a
Saxon monk, of Cambridge,[3] who had arrived but a few
days before on a visit.

When the four knights appeared, Becket, without looking at them, pointedly continued his conversation with the
monk who sate next him, and on whose shoulder he was
leaning.[4] They, on their part, entered without a word,
beyond a greeting exchanged in a whisper to the attendants who stood near the door,[5] and then marched straight
to where the Archbishop sate, and placed themselves on
the floor at his feet, among the clergy who were reclining
around. Radulf the archer sate behind them,[6] on the
boards. Becket now turned round for the first time, and
gazed steadfastly on each in silence,[7] which he at last
broke by saluting Tracy by name. The conspirators continued to look mutely at each other, till Fitzurse,[8] who
throughout took the lead, replied, with a scornful expression, "God help you !"   Becket's face grew crimson,[9]
and he glanced round at their countenances,[1] which seemed
to gather fire from Fitzurse's speech. Fitzurse again broke
forth,—"We have a message from the King over the
water—tell us whether you will hear it in private, or in the
hearing of all."[2] "As you wish," said the Archbishop.
"Nay, as *you* wish," said Fitzurse.[3] "Nay, as *you* wish,"
said Becket. The monks at the Archbishop's intimation

[1] Herbert, 63.
[2] Fitzstephen, 185.
[3] Herbert, 337.
[4] Garnier, 67, 20, 26.
[5] Benedict, 55.
[6] Roger, 161; Garnier, 67.
[7] Roger, 161.

[8] Roger, 161.
[9] Grim, 70 ; Garnier, 67, 18.
[1] Roger, 161.
[2] Grim, 70; Roger, 161 ; Garnier, 67, b. 10—15.
[3] Roger, 161 ; Garnier, 67, b. 19.

withdrew into an adjoining room ; but the doorkeeper ran
up and kept the door ajar, that they might see from the
outside what was going on.[1] Fitzurse had hardly begun
his message, when Becket, suddenly struck with a
consciousness of his danger, exclaimed, "This must not
be told in secret," and ordered the doorkeeper to recall
the monks.[2] For a few seconds the knights were left
alone with Becket; and the thought occurred to them, as
they afterwards confessed, of killing him with the cross-
staff which lay at his feet —the only weapon within their
reach.[3] The monks hurried back, and Fitzurse, apparently
calmed by their presence, resumed his statement of the
complaints of the King. These complaints,[4] which are
given by the various chroniclers in very different words,
were three in number. "The King over the water commands you to perform your duty to the King on this side
the water, instead of taking away his crown." "Rather
than take away his crown," replied Becket, "I would give
him three or four crowns."[5] "You have excited disturb-
ances in the kingdom, and the King requires you to
answer for them at his court." "Never," said the Archbishop, "shall the sea again come between me and my
church, unless I am dragged thence by the feet." "You
have excommunicated the bishops, and you must absolve
them." "It was not I," replied Becket, "but the Pope,
and you must go to him for absolution." He then
appealed, in language which is variously reported, to the
promises of the King at their interview in the preceding
July. Fitzurse burst forth, "What is it you say ? You
charge the King with treachery." "Reginald, Reginald,"
said Becket, "I do no such thing ; but I appeal to the
archbishops, bishops, and great people, five hundred and
more, who heard it, and you were present yourself, Sir

[1] Roger, 161 ; Benedict, 55.
[2] Roger, 162 ; Benedict, 56 ; Garnier,
67. b. 20.
[3] Grim, 71 ; Roger, 162 ; Garnier,
67 , b. 25. It was probably Tracy's
thought, as his was the confession
generally known.
[4] In this dialogue I have not
attempted to give more than the words
of the leading questions and answers, in
which most of the chroniclers are agreed.
Where the speeches are recorded with
great varieties of expression, it is impossible to distinguish accurately between what was really spoken, and what
was afterwards written as likely to have
been spoken.
[5] Benedict, 56 ; Garnier, 68.

Reginald." "I was not," said Reginald, "I never saw
nor heard anything of the kind." "You were," said
Becket, "I saw you."[1] The knights, irritated by contradiction, swore again and again, "by God's wounds," that
they had borne with him long enough.[2] John of Salisbury, the prudent counsellor of the Archbishop, who
perceived that matters were advancing to extremities,
whispered, "My lord, speak privately to them about this."
"No," said Becket; "they make proposals and demands
which I cannot and ought not to admit."[3]

He, in his turn, complained of the insults he had
received. First came the grand grievances of the preceding week. "They have attacked my servants, they
have cut off my sumpter-mule's tail, they have carried off
the casks of wine that were the King's own gift."[4] It
was now that Hugh de Moreville, the gentlest of the four,[5]
put in a milder answer: "Why did you not complain to
the King of these outrages? Why did you take upon
yourself to punish them by your own authority?" The
Archbishop turned round sharply upon him: "Hugh!
how proudly you lift up your head! When the rights of
the Church are violated, I shall wait for no man's permission to avenge them. I will give to the King the
things that are the King's, but to God the things that are
God's. It is my business, and I alone will see to it."[6]
For the first time in the interview the Archbishop had
assumed an attitude of defiance; the fury of the knights
broke at once through the bonds which had partially
restrained it, and displayed itself openly in those
impassioned gestures which are now confined to the half-
civilised nations of the south and east, but which seem to
have been natural to all classes of mediæval Europe.
Their eyes flashed fire;[7] they sprang upon their feet, and
rushing close up to him, gnashed their teeth, twisted their
long gloves, and wildly threw their arms above their
heads. Fitzurse exclaimed, "You threaten us, you

---

[1] He was remarkable for the tenacity
of his memory, never forgetting what
he had heard or learned (Gervase,
Chron.).
[2] Benedict, 59; Garnier, 68, 16.

[3] Fitzstephen, 295.
[4] Roger, 163; Benedict, 61; Gervase,
1415; Garnier, 68, b. 26.
[5] Benedict, 62.
[6] Roger, 163, 164.

threaten us ;[1] are you going to excommunicate us all ? "
One of the others added, "As I hope for God's mercy, he
shall not do that; he has excommunicated too many
already." The Archbishop also sprang from his couch,
in a state of strong excitement. "You threaten me," he
said, "in vain ; were all the swords in England hanging
over my head, you could not terrify me from my obedience
to God, and my lord the Pope.[2] Foot to foot shall you
find me in the battle of the Lord.[3] Once I gave way.
I returned to my obedience to the Pope, and will never
more desert it. And besides, you know what there is
between you and me ; I wonder the more that you should
thus threaten the Archbishop in his own house." He
alluded to the fealty sworn to him while Chancellor by
Moreville, Fitzurse, and Tracy, which touched the tenderest
nerve of the feudal character. "There is nothing," they
rejoined, with an anger which they doubtless felt to be
just and loyal, "there is nothing between you and us
which can be against the King."[4]

Roused by the sudden burst of passion on both sides,
many of the servants and clergy, with a few soldiers of
the household, hastened into the room, and ranged themselves round the Archbishop. Fitzurse turned to them
and said, "You who are on the King's side, and bound to
him by your allegiance, stand off." They remained
motionless, and Fitzurse called to them a second time,
"Guard him ; prevent him from escaping." The Archbishop said, "I shall not escape." On this the knights
caught hold of their old acquaintance, William Fitz-Nigel,
who had entered with the rest, and hurried him with them,
saying, "Come with us." He called out to Becket, "You
see what they are doing with me." "I see," replied
Becket ; "this is their hour, and the power of darkness."[5]
As they stood at the door, they exclaimed,[6] "It is you who
threaten ;" and in a deep under-tone they added some

[1] Fitzstephen, 296. "Minæ, minæ,"
a common expression as it would seem.
Compare Benedict, 71.

[2] Roger, 163; Benedict, 61; Gervase,
1415.

[3] Benedict, 61.

[4] Fitzstephen, 296 ; Grim, 72 ; Anon.
Passio Quinta, 174.

[5] Fitzstephen, 296.

[6] Garnier, 68, b. 15. For the general
fact of the acuteness of his senses,
both hearing and smell, see Roger, 95.

menace, and enjoined on the servants obedience to their orders. With the quickness of hearing for which he was remarkable, he caught the words of their defiance, and darted after them to the door, entreating them to release Fitz-Nigel; [1] then he implored Moreville, as more courteous than the others, to return [2] and repeat their message ; and lastly, in despair and indignation, he struck his neck repeatedly with his hand, and said, " Here, here you will find me." [3]

The knights, deaf to his solicitations, kept their course, seizing another soldier as they went, Radulf Morin, and passed through the hall and court, crying, " To arms ! to arms ! " A few of their companions had already taken post within the great gateway, to prevent the gate being shut ; the rest, at the shout, poured in from the house where they were stationed hard by, with the watchword, " King's men ! King's men ! " (Réaux ! Réaux !) The gate was instantly closed, to cut off communication with the town ; the Archbishop's porter was removed, and in front of the wicket, which was left open, William Fitz-Nigel, and a soldier attached to the household of Clarembald, Simon of Croil, kept guard on horseback. [4] The knights threw off their cloaks and gowns under a large sycamore in the garden, [5] appeared in their armour, and girt on their swords. [6] Fitzurse armed himself in the porch, [7] with the assistance of Robert Tibia, trencherman of the Archbishop. Osbert and Algar, two of the servants, seeing their approach, shut and barred the door of the hall, and the knights in vain endeavoured to force it open. [8] But Robert de Broc, who had known the palace during the time of its occupation by his uncle Randolf, [9]

"Vix aliquid in ejus presentiâ licet longiusculè et submisse dici posset, quod non audiret si aurem apponere voluisset."   [1] Fitzstephen, 296.

[2] Benedict, 62 ; Garnier, 69.

[3] Grim. 73; Roger, 163; Garnier, 69, b. 5 (though he places this speech earlier).

[4] Fitzstephen, 298.

[5] Gervase, Act. Pont., 1672.

[6] Garnier, 70, 11.

[7] Fitzstephen, 298. The porch of the hall, built, doubtless on the plan of the one here mentioned, by Archbishop Langton about fifty years later, still in part remains, incorporated in one of the modern houses now occupying the site of the Palace. There is a similar porch, in a more complete state, the only fragment of a similar hall, adjoining the palace at Norwich.

[8] Fitzstephen, 297, 298.

[9] Fitzstephen, 298; Roger, 165; Garnier 70.

called out, "Follow me, good sirs, I will show you another way!" and got into the orchard behind the kitchen. There was a staircase leading thence to the ante-chamber between the hall and the Archbishop's bedroom. The wooden steps were under repair, and the carpenters had gone to their dinner, leaving their tools on the stairs.[1] Fitzurse seized an axe, and the others hatchets, and thus armed they mounted the staircase to the ante-chamber,[2] broke through an oriel-window which looked out on the garden,[3] entered the hall from the inside, attacked and wounded the servants who were guarding it, and opened the door to the assailants.[4] The Archbishop's room was still barred and inaccessible.

Meanwhile Becket, who resumed his calmness as soon as the knights had retired, reseated himself on his couch, and John of Salisbury again urged moderate counsels,[5] in words which show that the estimate of the Archbishop in his lifetime justifies the impression of his vehement and unreasonable temper which has prevailed in later times, though entirely lost during the centuries which elapsed between his death and the Reformation. "It is wonderful, my Lord, that you never take any one's advice; it always has been, and always is your custom, to do and say what seems good to yourself alone." "What would you have me do, Dan John?"[6] said Becket. "You ought to have taken counsel with your friends, knowing as you do that these men only seek occasion to kill you." "I am prepared to die," said Becket. "We are sinners," said John, "and not yet prepared for death; and I see no one who wishes to die without cause except you."[7] The Archbishop answered, "Let God's will be done."[8] "Would to God it might end well," sighed John, in despair.[9] The dialogue was interrupted by one of the monks rushing in to announce that the knights were arming. "Let them arm," said Becket. But in a few

[1] Roger, 165; Benedict, 63.
[2] Grim. 73; Fitzstephen, 298; Garnier, 70, b. 1.
[3] Garnier, 70, b. 2.
[4] Benedict, 63.
[5] Fitzstephen, 298; Benedict, 62.
[6] Roger, 164; Garnier, 69, b. 25.
[7] Garnier, 70, b. 10.
[8] Roger, 164; Benedict, 62; Garnier, 70, 10.
[9] Benedict, 62.

minutes the violent assault on the door of the hall, and
the crash of a wooden partition in the passage from the
orchard, announced that the danger was close at hand.
The monks, with that extraordinary timidity which they
always seem to have displayed, instantly fled, leaving only
a small body of his intimate friends or faithful attendants.[1]
They united in entreating him to take refuge in the
cathedral. " No," he said ; " fear not ; all monks are
cowards." [2]   On this some sprang upon him, and
endeavoured to drag him there by main force ; others
urged that it was now five o'clock, that vespers were
beginning, and that his duty called him to attend the
service.   Partly forced, partly persuaded by the argument,[3] partly feeling that his doom called him thither,
he rose and moved, but seeing that his cross-staff was
not, as usual, borne before him, he stopped and called for
it.[4]   He remembered, perhaps, the memorable day at the
Council of Northampton, when he had himself borne the
cross [5] through the royal Hall, to the dismay and fury of
his opponents.   His ordinary cross-bearer, Alexander the
Welshman, had, as we have seen, left him for France [6] two
days before, and the cross-staff was, therefore, borne
by one of his clerks, Henry of Auxerre.[7]   They first
attempted to pass along the usual passage to the cathedral,
through the orchard, to the western front of the church.
But both court and orchard being by this time thronged
with armed men,[8] they turned through a room which
conducted to a private door,[9] that was rarely used, and
which led from the palace to the cloisters of the monastery.
One of the monks ran before to force it, for the key was
lost.   Suddenly the door flew open as if of itself,[10] and in
the confusion of the moment, when none had leisure or
inclination to ask how so opportune a deliverance

---

[1] Garnier, 70, b. 16.
[2] Roger, 165 ; Fitzstephen, 298.
[3] Fitzstephen, 299. He had dreamed,
or anticipated, that he should be killed
in church, and had communicated his
apprehensions to the abbots of Pontigny
and Clairvaux (Benedict, 65), and, as we
have seen, to a citizen of Canterbury on
the eve of this day.

[4] Fitzstephen, 299 ; Benedict, 64.
[5] Herbert, 143.
[6] Herbert, 330.
[7] Fitzstephen, 299.
[8] Roger, 165.
[9] Garnier, 71.
[10] Grim, 73 ; Roger. 166 ; Garnier,
71, b. 9.

occurred, it was natural for the story to arise which is
related, with one exception,[1] in all the narratives of the
period—that the bolt came off as though it had merely
been fastened on by glue, and left their passage free.
This one exception is the account by Benedict, then a
monk of the monastery, and afterwards abbot of Peterborough, and his version, compared with that of all the
other historians, is an instructive commentary on a
thousand fables of a similar kind. Two cellarmen, he
says, of the monastery, Richard and William, whose
lodgings were in that part of the building, hearing the
tumult and clash of arms, flew to the cloister, drew back
the bolt from the other side, and opened the door to
the party from the palace. Benedict knew nothing of the
seeming miracle, as his brethren were ignorant of the
timely interference of the cellarmen. But both miracle
and explanation would at the moment be alike disre-
garded. Every monk in that terrified band had but a
single thought—to reach the church with their master in
safety. The whole march was a struggle between the
obstinate attempt of the Primate to preserve his dignity,
and the frantic eagerness of his attendants to gain the
sanctuary. As they urged him forward, he coloured and
paused, and repeatedly asked them what they feared.
The instant they had passed through the door which led
to the cloisters, the subordinates flew to bar it behind
them, which he as peremptorily forbade.[2] For a few steps
he walked firmly on, with the cross-bearer and the monks
before him ; halting once, and looking over his right
shoulder, either to see whether the gate was locked, or
else if his enemies were pursuing. Then the same
ecclesiastic who had hastened forward to break open the
door, called out, "Seize him, and carry him."[3] Vehemently

[1] Benedict, 64. It is curious that a
similar miracle was thought to have
occurred on his leaving the royal castle
at Northampton. He found the gate
locked and barred. One of his servants
caught sight of a bundle of keys hanging
aloft, seized it, and with wonderful
quickness (*quod quasi miraculum quibus-
dam visum est*), picked out the right
key from the tangled mass, and opened
the door (Roger, 142). The cellarman,
Richard, was the one who had received
intimation of the danger (as mentioned
in p. 52), and who would therefore be
on the watch.

[2] Fitzstephen, 292.
[3] Roger, 166.

he resisted, but in vain. Some pulled him from before, others pushed him from behind;[1] half carried, half drawn, he was borne along the northern and eastern cloister, crying out, "Let me go, do not drag me." Thrice they were delayed, even in that short passage, for thrice he broke loose from them—twice in the cloister itself, and once in the chapter-house, which opened out of its eastern side.[2] At last they reached the door at the lower north transept of the cathedral, and here was presented a new scene.

The vespers had already begun, and the monks were singing the service in the choir, when two boys rushed up the nave, announcing, more by their terrified gestures than by their words, that the soldiers were bursting into the palace and monastery.[3] Instantly the service was thrown into the utmost confusion ; part remained at prayer—part fled into the numerous hiding-places the vast fabric affords ; and part went down the steps of the choir into the transept to meet the little band at the door.[4] " Come in, come in !" exclaimed one of them, " come in, and let us die together." The Archbishop continued to stand outside, and said, " Go and finish the service. So long as you keep in the entrance, I shall not come in." They fell back a few paces, and he stepped within the door, but, finding the whole place thronged with people, he paused on the threshold and asked, " What is it that these people fear ?" One general answer broke forth, " The armed men in the cloister." As he turned and said, " I shall go out to them," he heard the clash of arms behind.[5] The knights had just forced their way into the cloister, and were now (as would appear from their being thus seen through the open door) advancing along its southern side. They were in mail, which covered their faces up to their eyes, and carried their swords drawn.[6] With them was Hugh of Horsea, surnamed Mauclerc, a sub-deacon, chaplain of Robert de Broc.[7] Three had hatchets.[8]

[1] Garnier, 71, 27.
[2] Roger, 166. It is from this mention of the Chapter-house, which occupied the same relative position as the present one, that we ascertain the sides of the cloister by which Becket came.
[3] Will. Cant. 32.
[4] Fitzstephen, 249.
[5] Benedict, 64 ; Herbert, 330.
[6] Garnier, 71, b. 10.
[7] Gervase, Act. Pont., 1672.
[8] Garnier. 71. b. 12.

Fitzurse, with the axe he had taken from the carpenters, was foremost, shouting as he came, "Here, here, king's men!" Immediately behind him followed Robert Fitzranulph[1] with three other knights, whose names are not preserved; and a motley group—some their own followers, some from the town—with weapons, though not in armour, brought up the rear.[2] At this sight, so unwonted in the peaceful cloisters of Canterbury, not probably beheld since the time when the monastery had been sacked by the Danes, the monks within, regardless of all remonstrances, shut the door of the cathedral, and proceeded to barricade it with iron bars.[3] A loud knocking was heard from the terrified band without, who, having vainly endeavoured to prevent the entrance of the knights into the cloister, now rushed before them to take refuge in the church.[4] Becket, who had stepped some paces into the cathedral, but was resisting the solicitations of those immediately about him to move up into the choir for safety, darted back, calling aloud as he went, "Away you cowards! By virtue of your obedience I command you not to shut the door—the church must not be turned into a castle."[5] With his own hands he thrust them away from the door, opened it himself, and catching hold of the excluded monks, dragged them into the building, exclaiming, "Come in, come in—faster, faster!"[6]

At this moment the ecclesiastics who had hitherto clung round him fled in every direction; some to the altars in the numerous side chapels, some to the secret chambers with which the walls and roof of the cathedral are filled. Even John of Salisbury, his tried and faithful counsellor, escaped with the rest. Three only remained—Robert, Canon of Merton, his old instructor; William Fitzstephen (if we may believe his own account), his lively and worldly-minded chaplain; and Edward Grim, the Saxon monk,[7] Two hiding-places had been specially pointed out to the

---

[1] Foss's Judges, i. 243.
[2] Fitzstephen, 300.
[3] Herbert, 331; Benedict, 65.
[4] Anon. Lambeth, 121. Herbert (331) describes the knocking, but mistakingly supposes it to be the knights.

[5] Garnier, 71, b. 24. This speech occurs in all.
[6] Benedict, 65.
[7] Fitzstephen, 301.

Archbishop.   One was the venerable crypt of the church,
with its many dark recesses and chapels, to which a door
then as now opened immediately from the spot where
he stood ; the other was the chapel of St. Blaise in
the roof, itself communicating by a gallery with the
triforium of the cathedral, to which there was a ready
access through a staircase cut in the thickness of the
wall at the corner of the transept.[1]   But he positively
refused.   One last resource remained to the staunch companions who stood by him.   They urged him to ascend to
the choir, and hurried him, still resisting, up one of the
two flights of steps which led thither.[2]   They no doubt
considered that the greater sacredness of that portion of
the church would form their best protection.   Becket
seems to have given way, as in leaving the palace, from the
thought flashing across his mind that he would die at his
post. He would go (such at least was the impression left on
their minds) to the high altar, and perish in the Patriarchal
Chair, in which he and all his predecessors from time
immemorial had been enthroned.[3]   But this was not to be.

   What has taken long to describe must have been compressed in action within a few minutes.   The knights, who
had been checked for a moment by the sight of the closed
door, on seeing it unexpectedly thrown open, rushed into
the church.   It was, we must remember, about five o'clock
in a winter evening ;[4] the shades of night were gathering,
and were deepened into a still darker gloom within the
high and massive walls of the vast cathedral, which was
only illuminated here and there by the solitary lamps
burning before the altars.   The twilight,[5] lengthening from
the shortest day a fortnight before, was but just sufficient
to reveal the outline of objects.   The transept [6] in which

[1] Fitzstephen, 301.   [2] Roger, 166.
[3] Anon. Lambeth, 121; Gervase,
Chron. 1443.
   [4] " Nox longissima instabat."   Fitzstephen, 301.
   [5] The 29th of December of that year
corresponded (by the change of style)
to our 4th of January.
   [6] Garnier, 74, b. 11 :

" Pur l'iglise del *nort* e en l'ele del *nort*,
   Envers le *nort* suffri li bons sainz Thomas
      mort."

For the ancient arrangements of " the
martyrdom," see Willis's Account of
Canterbury Cathedral, 18, 40, 71, 96.
The chief changes since that time
are :—

   1. The removal of the Lady Chapel
in the Nave.
   2. The removal of the central pillar.
   3. The enlargement of the Chapel of
St. Benedict.

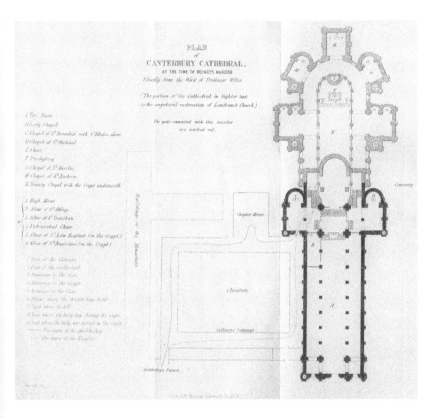

The material originally positioned here is too large for reproduction in this reissue. A PDF can be downloaded from the web address given on page iv of this book, by clicking on 'Resources Available'.

the knights found themselves is the same as that which
—though with considerable changes in its arrangements—
is still known by its ancient name of " The Martyrdom."
Two staircases led from it, one from the east to the
northern aisle, one on the west, to the entrance of the
choir. At its south-west corner, where it joined the nave,
was the little chapel and altar of the Virgin, the especial
patroness of the Archbishop. Its eastern apse was formed
by two chapels, raised one above the other ; the upper in
the roof, containing the relics of St. Blaise, the first martyr
whose bones had been brought into the church, and which
gave to the chapel a peculiar sanctity ; the lower containing [1] the altar of St. Benedict, under whose rule from
the time of Dunstan the monastery had been placed.
Before and around this altar were the tombs of four
Saxon and two Norman archbishops. In the centre of
the transept was a pillar, supporting a gallery leading to
the chapel of St. Blaise,[2] and hung at great festivals with
curtains and draperies. Such was the outward aspect,
and such the associations, of the scene which now, perhaps,
opened for the first time on the four soldiers. But the
darkness, coupled with the eagerness to find their victim,
would have prevented them from noticing anything more
than its prominent features. At the moment of their
entrance the central pillar exactly intercepted their view
of the Archbishop ascending (as would appear from this
circumstance) the eastern staircase.[3] Fitzurse, with his
drawn sword in one hand, and the carpenter's axe in the
other, sprang in first, and turned at once to the right of
the pillar. The other three went round it to the left. In
the dim twilight they could just discern a group of figures
mounting the steps.[4] One of the knights called out to
them "Stay." Another, "Where is Thomas Becket, traitor

4. The removal of the Chapel of St. Blaise.
5. The removal of the eastern stair-case.

In the two last points, a parallel to the old arrangement may still be found in the southern transept.
[1] It may de mentioned, as an instance of Hume's well-known inaccuracy, that he represents Becket as taking refuge "in the church of St. Benedict," evidently thinking, if he thought at all, that it was a parish church dedicated to that saint.
[2] Garnier, 72-9, b. 6. Willis's Canterbury Cathedral, p. 47.
[3] Garnier, 72, 10.
[4] Garnier, 72, 11.

to the King ?"   No answer was returned.   None could
have been expected by any who remembered the indignant
silence with which Becket had swept by when the same
word had been applied by Randulf of Broc at Northampton.[1]   Fitzurse rushed forward, and, stumbling
against one of the monks, on the lower step,[2] not still
able to distinguish clearly in the darkness, exclaimed,
" Where is the Archbishop ? "   Instantly the answer came
—" Reginald, here I am, no traitor, but the Archbishop
and Priest of God ; what do you wish ?"[3]—and from
the fourth step,[4] which he had reached in his ascent,
with a slight motion of his head—noticed apparently
as his peculiar manner in moments of excitement[5]—
Becket descended to the transept.   Attired, we are told,
in his white rochet,[6] with a cloak and hood thrown over
his shoulders, he thus suddenly confronted his assailants.
Fitzurse sprang back two or three paces, and Becket
passing[7] by him took up his station between the central
pillar[8] and the massive wall which still forms the
south-west corner of what was then the chapel of St.
Benedict.[9]   Here they gathered round him, with the
cry, "Absolve the bishops whom you have excommunicated."   " I cannot do other than I have done," he
replied, and turning[1] to Fitzurse, he added—" Reginald,
you have received many favours at my hands ; why do
you come into my church armed ? "   Fitzurse planted
the axe against his breast, and returned for answer,
" You shall die,—I will tear out your heart."[2]   Another,
perhaps in kindness, struck him between the shoulders
with the flat of his sword, exclaiming, " Fly ; you are
a dead man."[3]   " I am ready to die," replied the Primate,
"for God and the Church, but I warn you in the name of
God Almighty to let my men escape."[4]

[1] Roger, 142.   [2] Garnier, 72, 14.
[3] Gervase, Act. Pont., 1672; Garnier,
72, 15.
[4] Gervase, Act. Pont., 1673.
[5] As in his interview with the
Abbot of St. Alban's, at Harrow.
See p. 43.
[6] Grandison, c. 9.
[7] Grim, 75; Roger, 166.

[8] Roger, 166.
[9] Willis's Canterbury, 41.   It was
afterwards preserved purposely.
[1] Garnier, 72, 20.
[2] Grim, 79; Anon. Passio Quinta,
176.
[3] Grim, 75, 76 ; Roger, 166.
[4] Garnier, 72, b. 25; Fitzstephen,
302; Grim, 76 ; Roger. 166.

The well-known horror which in that age was felt at an act of sacrilege, together with the sight of the crowds who were [1] rushing in from the town through the nave, turned their efforts for the next few moments to carrying him out of the church.[2] Fitzurse threw down the axe,[3] and tried to drag him out by the collar of his long cloak,[4] calling "Come with us—you are our prisoner." "I will not fly, you detestable fellow,"[5] was Becket's reply, roused to his usual vehemence, and wrenching the cloak out of Fitzurse's grasp.[6] The four knights, to whom was now added Hugh Mauclerc, chaplain of Robert de Broc,[7] struggled violently to put him on Tracy's shoulders ;[8] but Becket set his back against the pillar,[9] and resisted with all his might, whilst Grim [1] threw his arms around him to aid his efforts. In the scuffle Becket fastened upon Tracy, shook him by his coat of mail, and, exerting his great strength, flung him down on the pavement.[2] It was hopeless to carry on the attempt to remove him. And in the final struggle, which now began, Fitzurse, as before, took the lead. But, as he approached with his drawn sword, the sight of him kindled afresh the Archbishop's anger, now heated by the fray ; the spirit of the Chancellor rose within him, and with a coarse [3] epithet, not calculated to turn away his adversary's wrath, exclaimed "You profligate wretch, you are my man—you have done me fealty—you ought not to touch me."[4] Fitzurse, roused to frenzy, retorted—"I owe you no fealty or

---

[1] Anon. Lamb.,122; Fitzstephen, 302.
[2] Grim, 76 ; Roger, 166.
[3] Fitzstephen, 302 ; Benedict, 88.
[4] Garnier, 72, 20, 30.
[5] "Vir abominabilis." Gervase, Act. Pont., 1673.
[6] Garnier, 73, 21.
[7] Roger, 166; Garnier, 71.
[8] Roger, 166.
[9] Garnier, 72, 73, b. 5 ; Grim, 75.
[1] Fitzstephen, 302 ; Garnier, 73, b. 6.
[2] Benedict, 66; Roger, 166; Gervase, Act. Pont. 1173 ; Herbert, 331; Garnier, 72, b. 30. All but Herbert and Garnier believe this to have been Fitzurse, but the reference of Herbert to Tracy's confession is decisive.

[3] "Lenonem appellans'," Roger, 167 ; Grim, 66. It is this part of the narrative that was so ingeniously, and, it must be confessed, not altogether without justice, selected as the ground of the official account of Becket's death, published by King Henry VIII., and representing him as having fallen in a scuffle with the knights, in which he and they were equally aggressors. The violence of Becket's language was well known. His usual name for Geoffry Riddel, Archdeacon of Canterbury, was Archdevil. Anselm, the king's brother, he called a "catamite and bastard."
[4] Grim, 66.

homage, contrary to my fealty to the King,"[1] and waving
the sword over his head, cried "Strike, strike!" (Ferez,
ferez), but merely dashed off his cap.   The Archbishop
covered his eyes with his joined hands, bent his neck,
and said,[2] "I commend my cause and the cause of the
Church to God, to St. Denys of France, to St. Alfege, and
to the saints of the Church." Meanwhile Tracy, who,
since his fall, had thrown off his hauberk[3] to move more
easily, sprang forward, and struck a more decided blow.
Grim, who up to this moment had his arm round Becket,
threw it up to intercept the blade, Becket exclaiming,
"Spare this defence."   The sword lighted on the arm of
the monk, which fell wounded or broken;[4] and he fled
disabled to the[5] nearest altar, probably that of St. Benedict
within the chapel.   It is a proof of the confusion of the
scene, that Grim, the receiver of the blow, as well as most
of the narrators, believed it to have been dealt by Fitzurse,
while Tracy, who is known to have been[6] the man from
his subsequent boast, believed that the monk whom he had
wounded was John of Salisbury.   The spent force of the
stroke descended on Becket's head, grazed the crown, and
finally rested on his left shoulder,[7] cutting through the
clothes and skin.   The next blow, whether struck by Tracy
or Fitzurse, was only with the flat of the sword, and again
on the bleeding head,[8] which Becket drew back as if
stunned, and then raised his clasped hands above it.   The

---

[1] Grim, 66; Roger, 167; Garnier, 73, b. 11.

[2] Garnier, 73, 25. These are in several of the accounts made his last words (Roger, 167; Alan, 336, and Addit. to John of Salisbury, 376); but this is doubtless the moment when they were spoken.

[3] Garnier, 73, b. 1.

[4] Garnier, 73, b. 18. The words in which this act is described in almost all the chronicles have given rise to a curious mistake:—"Brachium Edwardi *Grim ferè* abscidit." By running together these two words, later writers have produced the name of "Grimfere." Many similar confusions will occur to classical scholars. In most of the mediæval pictures of the murder, Grim

is represented as the cross-bearer, which is an error.   Grandison alone speaks of Grim, "*cum cruce*." The acting cross-bearer, Henry of Auxerre, had doubtless fled. Another error respecting Grim has been propagated in much later times by Thierry, who, for the sake of supporting his theory that Becket's cause was that of the Saxons against the Normans, represents him as remonstrating against the Primate's acquiescence in the Constitutions of Clarendon. For this statement there seems to be no authority.

[5] Will. Cant. 32.

[6] Will. Cant. 33; Fitzstephen, 302; Garnier, 73, b. 17.

[7] Garnier, 73, b. 8.

[8] Will. Cant. 32. Grim, 66.

blood from the first blow was trickling down his face in a thin streak ; he wiped it with his arm, and when he saw the stain, he said—" Into thy hands, O Lord, I commend my spirit." At the third blow, which was also from Tracy, he sank on his knees—his arms falling—but his hands still joined as if in prayer. With his face turned towards the altar of St. Benedict, he murmured in a low voice, which might just have been caught by the wounded Grim,[1] who was crouching close by, and who alone reports the words— " For the name of Jesus, and the defence of the Church, I am willing to die." Without moving hand or foot,[2] he fell flat on his face as he spoke, in front of the corner wall of the chapel, and with such dignity that his mantle, which extended from head to foot, was not disarranged. In this posture he received from Richard the Breton a tremendous blow, accompanied with the exclamation (in allusion to a quarrel of Becket with Prince William) " Take this for love of my lord William, brother of the King."[3] The stroke was aimed with such violence that the scalp or crown of the head [4]—which, it was remarked, was of unusual size— was severed from the skull, and the sword snapped in two on the marble pavement.[5] Hugh of Horsea, the subdeacon

---

[1] Grim, 66.

[2] Gervase, Chron., 2466.

[3] Fitzstephen, 303.

[4] Grim, 77; Roger, 167; Passio Quinta, 177. Great stress was laid on this, as having been the part of his head which had received the sacred oil (John of Salisbury, 376). There was a dream, by which he was said to have been troubled, at Pontigny— curious, as in some respects so singularly unlike, in others so singularly like, his actual fate. He was at Rome, pleading his cause before the Pope and cardinals, the adverse cardinals rushed at him with a shout that drowned the remonstrances of the Pope, and tried to pluck out his eyes with their fingers, then vanished, and were succeeded by a band of savage men, who struck off his scalp, so that it fell over his forehead (Grim, 58).

[5] Benedict, 66. For the pavement being marble, see Benedict, 66, and Garnier, 79, b. 19. Baronius (vol. xix. p. 379) calls it "lapideum pavimentum."

A spot is still shown in Canterbury Cathedral, with a square piece of stone said to have been inserted in the stone pavement in the place of a portion taken out and sent to Rome. That the spot so marked is precisely the place where Becket fell, is proved by its exact accordance with the localities so minutely described in the several narratives ; and that a piece was taken to Rome by the legates in 1173, and deposited in Sta. Maria Maggiore, is also well authenticated (see Baronius, vol. xix. 396). But whether the flagstones now remaining are really the same, must, perhaps, remain in doubt. The piece sent to Rome, I ascertained, after diligent inquiry, to be no longer in existence. Another story states that Benedict, when appointed Abbot of Peterborough in 1177, being vexed at finding that his predecessor had pawned or sold the relics of the abbey, returned to Canterbury, and carried off, amongst other memorials of St. Thomas, the stones of the pavement which had been sprinkled

who had joined them as they entered the church,[1] taunted by the others with having taken no share in the deed, planted his foot on the neck of the corpse, thrust his sword into the ghastly wound, and scattered the brains over the pavement—" Let us go—let us go," he said in conclusion ; " the traitor is dead ; he will rise no more."[2]

This was the final act. One only of the four knights had struck no blow. Hugh de Moreville throughout retained the gentler disposition for which he was distinguished, and contented himself with holding back at the entrance of the transept the crowds who were pouring in through the nave.[3]

The murderers rushed out of the church, through the cloisters, into the palace. Tracy, in a confession made long afterwards to Bartholomew Bishop of Exeter, said that their spirits, which had before been raised to the highest pitch of excitement, gave way when the deed was perpetrated, and that they retired with trembling steps, expecting the earth to open and swallow them up.[4] Such, however, was not their outward demeanour, as it was recollected by the monks of the place. With a savage burst of triumph they ran, shouting as if in battle, the royal watchword [5]—" The King's men, the King's men !" wounding, as they went, a servant of the Archdeacon of Sens for lamenting the murdered prelate.[6] Robert de Broc, as knowing the palace, had gone before to take possession of the private apartments. There they broke open the bags and coffers, and seized many papal bulls, charters,[7] and other documents, which Randulph de Broc sent to the King. They then traversed the whole of the palace, plundering gold and silver vases ; [8] the magnificent vestments and utensils employed in the services of the

---

with his blood, and had two altars made from them for Peterborough Cathedral. Still, as the whole floor must have been flooded, he may have removed only those adjacent to the flagstone from which the piece was taken—a supposition with which the present appearance of the flagstone remarkably corresponds.

[1] Benedict (66) ascribes this to Brito ; the anonymous Passio Quinta (177) to Fitzurse ; Herbert (345) and Grandison (iv. 1) to Robert de Broc. The rest to Mauclerc.

[2] Fitzstephen, 303 ; Roger, 268 ; Benedict, 67 ; Garnier, 74, 25.

[3] Roger, 108 ; Grim, 77 ; Garnier, 74, 11.

[4] Herbert, 351 ; Grandison, c. 9.

[5] Garnier, 74, b. 1 ; Grim, 79 ; Roger, 168 ; Fitzstephen, 305.

[6] Fitzstephen, 305.

[7] Garnier, 74, 5.

[8] Fitzstephen, 305.

church ; the furniture and books of the chaplains' rooms, and, lastly, the horses from the stables, on which Becket had prided himself to the last.[1] The amount of plunder was estimated by Fitzstephen at 2000 marks. To their great surprise they found two haircloths among the effects of the Archbishop, and threw them away. As the murderers left the cathedral, a tremendous storm of thunder and rain burst over Canterbury, and the night fell in thick darkness [2] upon the scene of the dreadful deed.

The crowd was every instant increased by the multitudes flocking in from the town on the tidings of the event. There was still at that moment, as in his lifetime, a strong division of feeling—and Grim overheard even one of the monks declare that the Primate had paid a just penalty for his obstinacy,[3] and was not to be lamented as a martyr. Others said, "He wished to be king, and more than king—let him be king; let him be king." [4] Whatever horror was expressed, was felt (as in the life-long remorse of Robert Bruce for the slaughter of the Red Comyn in church) not at the murder, but at the sacrilege.

At last, however, the cathedral was cleared, and the gates shut ;[5] and for a time the body lay entirely deserted. It was not till the night had quite closed in, that Osbert, the chamberlain[6] of the Archbishop, entering with a light, found the corpse lying on its face,[7] the scalp hanging by a piece of skin : he cut off a piece of his shirt to bind up the frightful gash. The doors of the cathedral were again opened, and the monks returned to the spot. Then, for the first time, they ventured to give way to their grief, and a loud lamentation resounded through the stillness of the night. When they turned the body with its face upwards, all were struck by the calmness and beauty of the countenance : a smile still seemed to play on the features—the colour on the cheeks was fresh—and the eyes were closed as if in sleep.[8] The top of the head, wound round with Osbert's

[1] Herbert, 352.
[2] Fitzstephen, 304.
[3] Grim, 79, 80.
[4] Benedict , 67.
[5] Roger, 169.
[6] Fitstephen, 305.
[7] Grandison, iv. 1.
[8] Will. Cant. 33. The same appearances are described on the subsequent morning, in Herbert, 358; Grandison, c. 9.

shirt, was bathed in blood, but the face was marked only
by one faint streak that crossed the nose from the right
temple to the left cheek.[1]   Underneath the body they
found the axe which Fitzurse had thrown down, and a
small iron hammer, brought, apparently, to force open the
door ; close by were lying the two fragments of Le Bret's
broken sword, and the Archbishop's cap, which had been
struck off in the beginning of the fray.   All these they
carefully preserved.   The blood, which, with the brains,
were scattered over the pavement, they collected and
placed in vessels ; and as the enthusiasm of the hour
increased, the bystanders, who already began to esteem
him a martyr, cut off pieces of their clothes to dip in
the blood, and anointed their eyes with it.   The cloak
and outer pelisse, which were rich with sanguinary stains,
were given to the poor—a proof of the imperfect apprehension as yet entertained of the value of these relics,
which a few years afterwards would have been literally
worth their weight in gold, and which were now sold for
some trifling sum.[2]

After tying up the head with clean linen, and fastening
the cap over it, they placed the body on a bier, and carried
it up the successive flight of steps which led from the
transept through the choir—" the glorious choir," as it was
called, " of Conrad "—to the high altar, in front of which
they laid it down.   The night was now far advanced, but
the choir was usually lighted—and probably, therefore, on
this great occasion—by a chandelier with twenty-four wax
tapers.   Vessels were placed underneath the body to catch
any drops of blood that might[3] fall, and the monks sat
weeping around.[4]   The aged Robert, canon of Merton, the
earliest friend and instructor of Becket, and one of the
three who had remained with him to the last, consoled
them by a narration of the austere life of the martyred
prelate which hitherto had been only known to himself,
as the confessor of the Primate, and to Brun the
valet.[5]   In proof of it he thrust his hand under the

---

[1] Benedict, 68 ; or (as Robert of Gloucester states it), " from the left half of
his forehead to the left half of his chin."
[2] Benedict, 68.

[3] Benedict, 69.
[4] Roger, 168.
[5] Fitzstephen, 308.

garments, and showed the monk's habit and haircloth
shirt which he wore next to his skin. This was the one
thing wanted to raise the enthusiasm of the bystanders to
the highest pitch. Up to that moment there had been a
jealousy of the elevation of the gay Chancellor to the
Archbishopric of Canterbury. The Primacy involved the
abbacy of the cathedral monastery, and the Primates
therefore had been, with two exceptions, always chosen
from the monks. The fate of these two had, we are told,
weighed heavily on Becket's mind. One was Stigand, the
last Saxon archbishop, who ended his life in a dungeon,
after the Conquest ; the other was Elsey, who had been
appointed in opposition to Dunstan, and who, after having
triumphed over his predecessor Odo by dancing on his
grave, was overtaken by a violent snow-storm in passing
the Alps, and, in spite of the attempts to resuscitate him
by plunging his feet in the bowels of his horse, was
miserably frozen to death. Becket himself, it was believed,
had immediately after his consecration received, from a
mysterious [1] apparition, an awful warning against appearing in the choir of the cathedral in his secular dress as
Chancellor. It now for the first time appeared that,
though not formally a monk, he had virtually become one
by his secret austerities. The transport of the fraternity
on finding that he had been one of themselves, was beyond
all bounds. They burst at once into thanksgivings, which
resounded through the choir ; fell on their knees ; kissed
the hands and feet of the corpse, and called him by the
name of "SAINT THOMAS," [2] by which, from that time
forward, he was so long known to the European
world. At the sound of the shout of joy there
was a general rush to the choir, to see the saint in
sackcloth who had hitherto been known as the chancellor in purple and fine linen.[3] A new enthusiasm
was kindled by the spectacle ; Arnold, a monk, who
was goldsmith to the monastery, was sent back, with
others, to the transept to collect in a basin any vestiges of
the blood and brains, now become so precious ; and

[1] Grim, 16.
[2] Fitzstephen, 308.
[3] Fitzstephen, 308 ; Gervase, Chron.
1416.

benches were placed across the spot, to prevent its being
desecrated by the footsteps of the crowd.[1] This perhaps
was the moment that the great ardour of the citizens
first began for washing their hands and eyes with the
blood. One instance of its application gave rise to a
practice which became the distinguishing characteristic of
all the subsequent pilgrimages to the shrine. A citizen
of Canterbury dipped a corner of his shirt in the blood,
went home, and gave it, mixed in water, to his wife, who
was paralytic, and who was said to have been cured.
This suggested the notion of mixing the blood with water,
which, endlessly diluted, was kept in innumerable vials,
to be distributed to the pilgrims ; [2] and thus, as the
palm [3] was a sign of a pilgrimage to Jerusalem, and a
scallop-shell of the pilgrimage to Compostella, so a leaden
vial or bottle suspended from the neck became the mark
of a pilgrimage to Canterbury.

Thus passed the night ; and it is not surprising that
in [4] the red glare of an Aurora Borealis, which, after the
stormy evening, lighted up the midnight sky, the excited
populace, like that at Rome after the murder of Rossi,
should fancy that they saw the blood of the martyr go up
to heaven ; or that, as the wax lights sank down in the
cathedral, and the first streaks of the grey winter morning
broke through the stained windows of Conrad's choir, the
monks who sate round the corpse should imagine that the
right arm of the dead man was slowly raised in the sign
of the cross, as if to bless his faithful followers.[5]

Early in the next day a rumour or message came to
the monks that Robert de Broc forbade them to bury the
body among the tombs of the archbishops, and that he
threatened to drag it out, hang it on a gibbet, tear it
with horses, cut it to pieces,[6] or throw it in some pond or
sink to be devoured by swine or birds of prey, as a fit
portion for the corpse of his master's enemy. " Had
St. Peter so dealt with the King," he said, " by the body

[1] Fitzstephen, 308.
[2] Fitzstephen, 309.
[3] Garnier, 78, b. 16 ; Anon. Lambeth,
p. 134.
[4] Fitzstephen, 304.

[5] Anon. Passio Quinta, 156; Hoveden,
299.
[6] Fitzstephen, 309 ; Anon. Lambeth,
134 ; Benedict, 69 ; Roger, 168 ; Herbert, 327 ; Grim, 81 ; Garnier, 76, b. 1.

of St. Denys, if I had been there I would have driven my sword into his skull." [1] They accordingly closed [2] the doors, which apparently had remained open through the night to admit the populace, and determined to bury the corpse in the crypt. Thither they carried it, and in that venerable vault proceeded to their mournful task, assisted by the Abbot of Boxley and the Prior [3] of Dover, who had come to advise with the Archbishop about the vacancy of the Priory at Canterbury. [4] A discussion seems to have taken place whether the body should be washed, according to the usual custom, which ended in their removing the clothes for the purpose. The mass of garments in which he was wrapt is almost incredible, and appears to have been worn chiefly for the sake of warmth, and in consequence of his naturally chilly temperament. [5] First, there was the large brown mantle, with white fringes of wool ; below this there was a white surplice, and again below this a white fur garment of lambs' wool. Next these were two short woollen pelisses, which were cut off with knives and given away, and under these the black cowled garment of the Benedictine [6] order, and the shirt [7] without sleeves or fringe, that it might not be visible on the outside. The lowermost covering was the hair-cloth, which had been made of unusual roughness, and within the hair-cloth was a warning [8] letter he had received on the night of the 27th. The existence of the austere garb had been pointed out on the previous night by Robert of Merton ; but, as they proceeded in their task, their admiration increased. The haircloth encased the whole body, down to the knees ; the hair drawers, [9] as well as the rest of the dress, being covered on the outside with white linen so as to escape observation ; and the whole so fastened together as to admit of being readily taken off for his daily scourgings, of which yesterday's portion was still apparent in the stripes on his body. [1] Such austerity had

[1] Garnier, 76, b. 7.
[2] Gervase, Chron. 1417.
[3] The Prior of Dover was no less a person than Richard, the Archbishop's chaplain, and his successor in the primacy. Matt. Paris, Hist., 127 ; Vit. Abb. St. A., 16, 91.   [4] Fitzstephen, 109.

[5] Garnier, 77, 1.
[6] Matt. Paris, 104.
[7] Garnier, 77 ; Herbert, 330.
[8] Fitzstephen, 203 ; Roger, 169 ; Benedict, 20.
[9] Garnier, 77, 40.
[1] Anon. Passio Tertia, 156.

hitherto been unknown to English saints, and the marvel
was increased by the sight [1]—to our notions so revolting—
of the innumerable vermin with which the haircloth
abounded—boiling over with them, as one account describes
it, like water [2] in a simmering caldron. At the dreadful
sight all the enthusiasm of the previous night revived with
double ardour. They looked at each other in silent
wonder ; then exclaimed, " See, see what a true monk
he was, and we knew it not ; " and burst into alternate
fits of weeping and laughter, between the sorrow of
having lost such a head, and the joy of having found
such a saint.[3] The discovery of so much mortifica-
tion, combined with the more prudential reasons for has-
tening the funeral, induced them to abandon the thought
of washing a corpse already, as it was thought, sufficiently
sanctified, and they at once proceeded to lay it out for
burial.

Over the haircloth, linen shirt, monk's cowl, and linen
hose,[4] they put first the dress in which he was consecrated, and which he had himself desired to be preserved [5]
—namely, the alb, super-humeral, chrismatic, mitre, stole,
and maniple ; and, over these, according to the usual
custom in Archiepiscopal funerals, the Archbishop's in-
signia, namely, the tunic, dalmatic, chasuble, the pall with
its pins, the chalice, the gloves, the rings, the sandals, and
the pastoral staff [6] —all of which, being probably kept in
the treasury of the cathedral, were accessible at the
moment. Thus arrayed, he was laid by the monks in
a new marble sarcophagus [7] which stood in the ancient
crypt,[8] at the back of the shrine of the Virgin, between
the altars of St. Augustine and St. John the Baptist,[9]
the first Archbishop as it was observed, and the bold
opponent of a wicked king. The remains of the blood
and brains were placed outside the tomb, and the doors

[1] Roger, 169 ; Fitzstephen, 309.
[2] Passio Quinta, 161.
[3] Roger, 169 ; Garnier, 77, b. 30.
[4] Fitzstephen ; Benedict, 70 ; Matt.
Paris, 124.
[5] Fitzstephen, 309.
[6] Fitzstephen, 309.

[7] Grim, 82 ; Benedict, 70 ; Gervase,
Chron. 1417.
[8] Benedict, 70 ; Addit. ad Alan., 377 ;
Matt. Paris, 124.
[9] Fitzstephen, 309 ; Grandison, c. 9 ;
Gervase, Act. Pont., 1673. (Gervase
was present.) Alan. 339 ; M. Paris, 125 ;

of the crypt closed against all entrance.[1] No mass was said over the Archbishop's grave ;[2] for from the moment that armed men had entered, the church was supposed to have been desecrated ; the pavement of the cathedral[3] was taken up ; the bells ceased to ring ; the walls were divested of their hangings ; the crucifixes were veiled ; the altars stripped, as in Passion week ; and the services were conducted without chanting[4] in the chapter-house. This desolation continued till the next year, when Odo the Prior, with the monks, took advantage of the arrival of the Papal legates, who came to make full inquiry into the murder, and to request their influence with the bishops to procure a re-consecration. The task was intrusted[5] to the Bishops of Exeter and Chester; and on the 21st of December, the Feast of St. Thomas the Apostle, 1171 (the day of St. Thomas of Canterbury was not yet authorised), Bartholomew, Bishop of Exeter, again celebrated mass, and preached a sermon on the text, "For the multitude of the sorrows that I had in my heart, thy comforts have refreshed my soul."[6]

Within three years the popular enthusiasm was confirmed by the highest authority of the Church. The Archbishop of York, had, some time after the murder, ventured to declare that Becket had perished, like Pharaoh, in his pride, and the government had endeavoured to suppress the miracles. But the Papal court, vacillating, and often unfriendly in his lifetime, now lent itself to confer the highest honours on his martyrdom.[7] In 1172 legates were sent by Alexander III. to investigate the alleged miracles, and they carried back to Rome the tunic stained with blood, and a piece of the pavement on which the brains were scattered—relics which were religiously deposited in the Basilica of Sta. Maria Maggiore.[8] In 1173

Garnier, 75. The arrangements of this part of the crypt were altered within the next fifty years; but the spot is still ascertainable, behind the Chapel of "Our Lady Undercroft," and underneath what is now the Trinity Chapel.

[1] Gervase, Chron. 1417.

[2] Fitzstephen, 310 ; Matt. Paris, 125 ; Diceto, 338.

[3] Diceto (338) speaks of the dirt of the pavement from the crowd who trod

it with dusty and muddy feet. M. Paris, 126. [4] Gervase, Chron. 1417.

[5] Gervase, 1421. [6] M. Paris, 125.

[7] Milman's Lat. Christianity, iii. 532.

[8] Baronius, xiv. 396. A fragment of the tunic and small blue bags said to contain portions of the brain are still shown in the reliquary of this church. The stone, as I have said, has disappeared.

a Council was called at Westminster to hear letters read
from the Pope, authorising the invocation of the martyr
as a saint.   All the bishops who had opposed him
were present, and, after begging pardon for their offence,
expressed their acquiescence in the decision of the Pope.
In the course of the same year he was regularly canonised,
and the 29th of December was set apart as the Feast
of St. Thomas of Canterbury.   His sister Mary was
appointed Abbess of Barking.[1]

A wooden altar, which remained unchanged through
the subsequent alterations and increased magnificence of
the Cathedral, was erected on the site of the murder, in
front of the ancient stone wall of St. Benedict's Chapel.
It was this which gave rise to the mistaken tradition,
repeated in books, in pictures, and in sculptures, that the
Primate was slain whilst praying at the altar.[2]   The crypt
in which the body had been laid so hastily and secretly
became the most sacred spot in the church, and, even after
the "translation" of the relics, in 1220, continued to be
known down to the time of the Reformation as "Becket's
Tomb,"[3]   The subsequent history of those sacred spots
must be reserved for a separate consideration.

It remains for us now to follow the fate of the murderers.   On the night of the deed the four knights rode to
Saltwood, leaving Robert de Broc in possession of the
palace, whence, as we have seen, he brought or sent the
threatening message to the monks on the morning of the
30th.   They vaunted their deeds to each other, and it was
then that Tracy claimed the glory of having wounded
John of Salisbury.   The next day they rode forty miles by
the sea-coast to South-Malling, an archiepiscopal manor

---

[1] Matt. Paris, 126. At this Council a
scene took place between Roger of York
and Richard of Canterbury, similar to
one already mentioned.   Roger nearly
lost his life under the sticks and fists of
the opposite party, who shouted out, as
he rose from the ground with crushed
mitre and torn cope, "Away, away, traitor
of St. Thomas — thy hands still reek
with his blood!"   Anglia Sacra, i. 72.

[2] The gradual growth of the story is
curious :—1. The posthumous altar of

the martyrdom is represented as standing there at the time of his death. 2.
This altar is next confounded with the
altar within the chapel of St. Benedict.
3. This altar is again transformed into
the High Altar. And, 4. In these successive changes the furious altercation
is converted into an assault on a meek
unprepared worshipper, kneeling before the altar.

[3] See Gough's Sepulchral Monuments,
i. 26.

near Lewes. On entering the house, they threw off their arms and trappings on the large dining-table which stood in the hall, and after supper gathered round the blazing hearth ; suddenly the table started back, and threw its burden on the ground. The attendants, roused by the crash, rushed in with lights and replaced the arms. But soon a second still louder crash was heard, and the various articles were thrown still further off. Soldiers and servants with torches searched in vain under the solid table to find the cause of its convulsions, till one of the conscience-stricken knights suggested that it was indignantly refusing to bear the sacrilegious burden of their arms. So ran the popular story ; and, as late as the fourteenth century, it was still shown in the same place—the earliest and most memorable instance of a "rapping," "leaping," and "turning table." [1] From South-Malling they proceeded to Knaresborough Castle, a royal fortress then in the possession of Hugh de Moreville, where they remained for a year. [2]

From this moment they disappear for a time in the black cloud of legend with which the monastic historians have enveloped their memory. Dogs, it was said, refused to eat the crumbs that fell from their table. [3] Struck with remorse, they went to Rome to receive the sentence of Pope Alexander III., and by him were sent to expiate their sins in the Holy Land. Moreville, Fitzurse, and Brito—so the story continues—after three years' fighting, died, and were buried, according to some accounts, in front of the church of the Holy Sepulchre, according to others, in front of the church of " the Black Mountain," [4] with an inscription on their graves,—.

"Hic jacent miseri qui martyrisaverunt
Beatum Thomam Archiepiscopum Cantuariensem."

---

[1] Grandison, iv. 1. "Monstratur ibidem ipsa tabula in memoriam miraculi conservata." See, also, Giraldus, in Wharton's Anglia Sacra, 425.

[2] Brompton, 1064 ; Diceto, 557.

[3] Brompton, 1064 ; Hoveden, 299.

[4] Baronius, xix. 399. The legend hardly aims at probabilities. The "Church of the Black Mountain" may possibly be a mountain so called in Languedoc, near the abbey of St. Papoul. But the front of the Church of the Holy Sepulchre is, and always must have been, a square of public resort to all the pilgrims of the world, where no tombs either of murderer or saint could have ever been placed. In Bartlett's "Jerusalem Revisited," p. 107. the scene of this is transferred to the Mosque El Akka. But this is apparently a mere confusion of the author or of his editor.

Tracy alone, it was said, was never able to accomplish his vow.   The crime of having struck the first blow [1] was avenged by the winds of heaven, which always drove him back.   According to one story, he never left England.   According to another, and, as we shall see, more correct version, he reached the coast of Calabria, and was then seized at Cosenza, with a dreadful disorder, which caused him to tear his flesh from his bones with his own hands, calling, " Mercy, St. Thomas," and there he died miserably, after having made his confession to the bishop of the place.   His fate was long remembered among his descendants in Gloucestershire, and gave rise to the distich that—

> " The Tracys
> Have always the wind in their faces."

Such is the legend.   The real facts, so far as we can ascertain them, are in some respects curiously at variance with it,— in other respects, no less curiously confirm it.   On the one hand, the general fate of the murderers was far less terrible than the popular tradition delighted to believe.   It would seem that, by a singular reciprocity, the principle for which Becket had contended—that priests should not be subjected to secular courts—prevented the trial of a layman for the murder of a priest by any other than by a clerical tribunal.[2] The consequence was, that the perpetrators of what was thought the most heinous crime since the Crucifixion could be visited with no other penalty than excommunication.   That they should have performed a pilgrimage to Palestine is in itself not improbable, and one of them, as we shall see, certainly attempted it.   But they seem before long to have recovered their position.   Not only did the other enemies of Becket rise to high offices—John of Oxford being made within five years Bishop of Norwich, and Geoffry Riddel, Becket's " arch-devil," within four years Bishop of Ely—but even the murderers them-

---

[1] "Primus percussor," Baronius, xix. p. 399.   See Robert of Gloucester, 1301-2321; Fuller's Worthies, 357.

[2] Such at least seems the most probable explanation.   The fact of the law is stated, as in the text, by Speed (p. 511). The law was altered in 1176 (23 H. II.), that is, seven years from the date of the murder, at the time of the final settlement of the Constitutions of Clarendon, between Henry II. and the Papal Legate (Matt., Paris, 132), and from that time slayers of clergy were punished before the Grand Justiciary in the presence of the Bishop.

selves, within the first two years of the murder, were living at court on familiar terms with the King, and constantly joined him in the pleasures of the chase.[1] Moreville, who [2] had been justice itinerant in the counties of. Northumberland and Cumberland at the time of the murder, was discontinued from his office the ensuing year ; but in the first year of King John he is recorded as paying twenty-five marks and three good palfreys for holding his court so long as Helwise his wife should continue in a secular habit. He procured about the same period a charter for a fair and market at Kirk Oswald, and died shortly afterwards, leaving two daughters.[3] The sword he used at the murder is stated by Camden to have been preserved in the time of Queen Elizabeth ; and it is now said to be attached to his statue at Brayton Castle. Fitzurse is said to have gone over to Ireland, and there to have become the ancestor of the M'Mahon family in the north of Ireland —M'Mahon being the Celtic translation of Bear's son.[4] On his flight, the estate which he held in the Isle of Thanet, Barham or Berham Court, lapsed to his kinsman Robert of Berham—Berham being, as it would seem, the English, as M'Mahon was the Irish version, of the name Fitzurse.[5] His estate of Willeton, in Somersetshire, he made over, half to the knights of St. John the year after the murder, probably in expiation—the other half to his brother Robert, who built the chapel of Willeton. The descendants of the family lingered for a long time in the neighbourhood under the same name, successively corrupted into Fitzour, Fishour, and Fisher.[6] The family of Bret or Brito was carried on, as we shall shortly see, through at least two generations of female descendants. The village of Sanford, in Somersetshire, is still called from the family Sanford *Bret*.[7]

Robert Fitzranulph, who had followed the four knights into the church, retired at that time from the shrievalty of Nottingham and Derby, which he had held during the six previous years, and is said to have founded the priory of

---

[1] Gervase, 1422.
[2] Foss's Judges, i. 279, 280.
[3] Lysons' Cumberland, p. 127. Nichols' Pilgrimage of Erasmus, p. 220. He must not be confounded with his

namesake, the founder of Dryburgh Monastery. [4] Fuller's Worthies.
[5] Harris's Kent, 313.
[6] Collinson's Somersetshire, iii. 487.
[7] *Ibid*, iii. 514.

Beauchief in expiation of his crime.[1]   But his son William
succeeded to the office, and was in places of trust about
the court till the reign of John.[2]

The history of Tracy is the most remarkable of the
whole.   Within four years from the murder he appears as
Justiciary of Normandy ; he was present at Falaise in
1174, when William, king of Scotland, did homage to
Henry II., and in 1176 was succeeded in his office by
the Bishop of Winchester.[3]   This is the last authentic
notice of him.   But his name appears long subsequently
in the somewhat conflicting traditions of Gloucestershire
and Devonshire, the two counties where his chief estates
lay.   The local histories of the former endeavour to
identify him in the wars of John and of Henry III., as late
as 1216 and 1222.   But, even without cutting short his
career by any untimely end, such longevity as this would
ascribe to him—bringing him to a good old age of ninety
—makes it probable that he has been confounded with
his son or grandson.[4]   The Devonshire story is better
supported.   The bay of Woollacombe Sands, between Over
and Nether Woollacombe, was long pointed out as the
spot where "he lived a private life, when wind and weather
turned against him."[5]   This is confirmed by the statement
of William of Worcester, that he retired to the western
parts of England ; and also by the well-attested fact, that
he selected for his confessor Bartholomew Iscan, Bishop
of Exeter.[6]   According to this story, he was buried in
Morthoe Church.[7]   The tomb which is there shown as his,
is really that of the parish priest in the fourteenth century,
called, according to the custom of the time, *Sir* William
de Tracy, which has occasioned the mistake.

There can be little doubt, however, that his family
still continues in Gloucestershire.   His daughter married
Sir Gervase de Courtenay, and it is apparently from
their son, Oliver de Tracy, who took the name of
his mother, that the present Lord Wemyss and Lord
Sudely are both descended.   The pedigree, in fact,

[1] The tradition is disputed, but without reason, in Pegge's Beauchief Abbey,
p. 34.   [2] Foss's Judges, i. 202.
[3] Nichols's Pilgrimage of Erasmus.
p. 221.

[4] Rudder's Gloucestershire, 776.
[5] Risdon in Polewhill's Devonshire,
p. 480.   [6] Herbert, 351.
[7] Polewhill's Devonshire, p. 480.

contrary to all received opinions on the subject of judgments on sacrilege, "exhibits a very singular instance of an estate descending for upwards of seven hundred years in the male line of the same family." [1]

Two remarkable monuments still remain of his connexion with the murder. One is the Priory of Woodspring, of which the ruins still crown the banks of Bristol Channel, and which was founded in 1210 by William de Courtenay, probably his grandson, in honour of the Holy Trinity, the Blessed Virgin, and St. Thomas of Canterbury.[2] To this priory lands were bequeathed by Maud, the daughter, and Alice, the granddaughter, of the third murderer, Bret or Brito, in the hope, expressed by Alice, that the intercession of the glorious martyr might never be wanting to her and her children.[3] In the repairs of Woodspring Church, in 1852, a wooden cup, much decayed, was discovered in a hollow in the back of a statue fixed against the wall. The cup contained a substance, which was decided to be the dried residuum of blood. From the connexion of the priory with the murderers of Becket, and from the fact that the seal of the Prior contained a cup or chalice as part of its device, there can be little doubt that this ancient cup was thus preserved at the time of the Dissolution, as a valuable relic, and that the blood which it contained was that of the murdered Primate.[4]

The other memorial of Tracy is still more curious, as partially confirming, and certainly illustrating, the legendary account which has been given above of his adventure in Calabria. In the archives of Canterbury Cathedral a deed exists, by which "William de Tracy, for the love of God, and the salvation of his own soul and of his ancestors, and for the love of the blessed Thomas, Archbishop and Martyr," makes over to the Chapter of Canterbury the manor of Daccombe, for the clothing and support of a monk to celebrate masses for the souls of the living and dead. The deed is without date, and it might possibly, therefore, have been ascribed to a descendant of

---

[1] Rudder's Gloucestershire, 770. Britton's Toddington.
[2] Collinson's Somersetshire, iii. 487.
[3] Collinson's Somersetshire, iii. 543.
[4] Journal of Archæol. Institute, vol. vi. p. 400.

Tracy, and not to the murderer himself. But its date is fixed by the confirmation of Henry, attested as that confirmation is by " Richard, elect of Winchester," and " Robert, elect of Hereford," to the year 1173 (the only year when such a conjunction occurs in the two sees), that is, two years after the murder.[1] The manor of Daccombe or Dockham in Devonshire, is still held under the Chapter of Canterbury, and is thus a present witness of the remorse with which Tracy humbly begged that, on the scene of his deed of blood, masses might be offered—not for himself individually (this, perhaps, could hardly have been granted)—but as included in the general category of " the living and the dead." But, further, this deed is found in company with another document, by which it appears that one William Thaun, *before his departure to the Holy Land with his master*, made his wife swear to render up to the Blessed Thomas and the monks of Canterbury, all his lands, given to him by his lord, William de Tracy. He died on his journey, his widow married again, and her second husband prevented her fulfilment of her oath ; she, however, survived him, and the lands were duly rendered up. From this statement we learn that Tracy really did attempt, if not fulfil, a journey to the Holy Land. But the attestation of the bequest of Tracy himself enables us to identify the story still further. One of the witnesses is the Abbot of St. Euphemia, and there can be little doubt that this Abbey of St. Euphemia was the celebrated convent of that name in Calabria, not twenty miles from Cosenza, the very spot where the detention, though not the death, of Tracy, is thus, as it would appear, justly placed by the old story.

The figures of the murderers may be seen in the representations of the martyrdom, which on walls, or in painted windows, or in ancient frescoes have survived the attempted extermination of all the monuments of the traitor Becket by King Henry VIII. Sometimes three, sometimes four are given, but always so far faithful to history, that

---

[1] This deed (which is given in the Appendix to " Becket's Shrine,") is slightly mentioned by Lord Lyttelton in his History of Henry II., iv. 284, but he appears not to have seen it, and is ignorant of the circumstances which incontestably fix the date.

Moreville is stationed aloof from the massacre. Two vestiges of such representation still remain in Canterbury Cathedral. One is a painting on a board, now greatly defaced, at the head of the tomb of King Henry IV. It is engraved, though not quite correctly, in Carter's "Ancient Sculpture and Painting," and, through the help of the engraving, the principal figures can still be dimly discerned.[1] There is the common mistake of making the archbishop kneel at the altar, and of representing Grim, with his blood-stained arm, as the bearer of the cross. The knights are carefully distinguished from one another. Bret, with boars' heads embroidered on his surcoat, is in the act of striking. Tracy appears to have already dealt a blow, and the bloody stains are visible on his sword, to mark the "*primus percussor.*" Fitzurse, with bears on his coat, is "stirring the brains" of his victim, holding his sword with both hands perpendicularly, thus taking the part sometimes ascribed to him, though really belonging to Mauclerc. Moreville, distinguished by fleurs-de-lis, stands apart. All of them have beards of the style of Henry IV. On the ground lies the bloody scalp, or cap, it is difficult to determine which.[2] There is besides a sculpture over the south porch, where Erasmus states that he saw the figures of "the three murderers," with their names of "Tusci, Fusci, and Berri," underneath. These figures have disappeared; and it is as difficult to imagine where they could have stood, as it is to

[1] A correct copy has now been made by Mr. George Austin, of Canterbury.

[2] A much more faithful representation is given in an illuminated Psalter in the British Museum (Harl. 1502), undoubtedly of the period, and, as Becket is depicted without the nimbus, probably soon after, if not before, the canonisation. He is represented in white drapery, falling towards the altar. His grey cap is dropping to the ground, Fitzurse and Tracy are rightly given, with coats of mail up to their eyes. Moreville is without helmet or armour. Fitzurse is wounding Grim. A light hangs from the roof. The Palace (apparently), with the town wall, is seen in the distance. There is another illumination in the same Psalter, representing the burial. In the Journal of the Archæol. Assoc., April, 1854, there is a full account of a fresco in St. John's Church, Winchester; in the Archæologia (vol. ix.), of one at Brereton in Cheshire. The widest deviation from historical truth is to be found in the modern altar-piece of the Church of St. Thomas, which forms the chapel of the English College at Rome. The saint is represented in a monastic garb on his knees before the altar of a Roman Basilica; and behind him are the three knights, in complete classical costume, brandishing daggers like those of the assassins of Cæsar. The nearest likeness is in the choir of Sens Cathedral.

explain the origin of the names they bore; but in the portion which remains, there is a representation of an altar surmounted by a crucifix, placed between the figures of St. John and the Virgin, and marked as the altar of the martyrdom—"Altare ad punctum ensis,"— by sculptured fragments of a sword, which lie at its foot.

Thus far have we traced the history of the murderers, but the great expiation still remained. The King had gone from Bur to Argenton, a town situated on the high table-land of southern Normandy. There the news first reached him, and he instantly shut himself up for three days, refused all food,[1] except milk of almonds, rolled himself in sackcloth and ashes, vented his grief in frantic lamentations, and called God to witness that he was in no way responsible for the Archbishop's death, unless that he loved him too little.[2] He continued in this solitude for five weeks, neither riding, nor transacting public business, but exclaiming again and again, "Alas! alas! that it ever happened." [3]

The French King, the Archbishop of Sens, and others, had meanwhile written to the Pope, denouncing Henry in the strongest language as the murderer, and calling for vengeance upon his head;[4] and there was a fear that this vengeance would take the terrible form of a public excommunication of the King, and an interdict of the kingdom. Henry, as soon as he was roused from his retirement, sent off as envoys to Rome the Archbishop of Rouen, the Bishop of Worcester, and others of his courtiers, to avert the dreaded penalties by announcing his submission. The Archbishop of Rouen returned on account of illness, and Alexander III., who occupied the Papal See, and who after long struggles with his rival had at last got back to Rome, refused to receive the rest. He was, in fact, in the eyes of Christendom, not wholly guiltless himself, in consequence of the lukewarmness with which he had fought Becket's fights; and it was believed that he, like the King, had shut himself up on hearing the news as much

---

[1] Vita Quadrip., p. 143.
[2] Matt. Paris, 125.
[3] Vita Quadrip. 146.
[4] Brompton, 1064.

from remorse as from grief. At last, by a bribe of 500 marks,[1] an interview was effected on the heights of ancient Tusculum—not yet superseded by the modern Frascati. Two Cardinals, Theodore Bishop of Portus, and Albert, Chancellor of the Holy See, were sent to Normandy to receive the royal penitent's submission,[2] and an excommunication was pronounced against the murderers on Maundy Thursday,[3] which is still the usual day for the delivery of Papal maledictions. The worst of the threatened evils—excommunication and interdict—were thus avoided; but Henry still felt so insecure, that he crossed over to England, ordered all the ports to be strictly guarded to prevent the admission of the fatal document, and refused to see any one who was the bearer of letters.[4] It was during this short stay that he visited for the last time the old Bishop of Winchester,[5] Henry of Blois, brother of King Stephen, well known as the founder of the beautiful hospital of St. Cross, when the dying old man added his solemn warnings to those which were resounding from every quarter with regard to the deed of blood. From England Henry crossed St. George's Channel to his new conquests in Ireland, and it was on his return from the expedition that the first public expression of his penitence was made in Normandy.

He repaired to Argenton, where he had received the first intelligence of the fatal deed, and there remained for " forty days in penitence and sorrow." Thence he proceeded to his castle of Gorram,[6] now Goron, on the banks of the

[1] Gervase, 1418.
[2] Brompton, 1068.
[3] Gervase, 1418.
[4] Diceto, 556.
[5] Gervase, 1419.
[6] Ep. St. Thomæ in MSS. Cott. Claud. b. ii., f. 350, epist. 94, also preserved in the Vita Quadripartita, edited by Lupus at Brussels, pp. 146, 147, 871, where, however, the epistle is numbered 88 from a Vatican MS.

The castle in question was procured by Henry I. from Geoffery, third duke of Mayenne, and was well-known for its deer preserves. To the ecclesiastical historian of the 19th century, the town near which it is situated will possess a curious interest as the original seat of the family of Gorram, or Gorham,—which, after giving birth to Geoffrey, the abbot of St. Albans, and Nicholas the theologian, each famous in his day,—has become known in our generation through the celebrated Gorham controversy, which in 1850 invested for a time with an almost European interest the name of the Rev. George Cornelius Gorham, now Vicar of Bramford Speke. To his courtesy and profound antiquarian knowledge, I am indebted for the above references and all the facts to which they relate.

Colmont, where he first met the Pope's Legates, and exchanged the kiss of charity with them. This was on the 16th of May, the Tuesday before the Rogation days; the next day he went on to Savigny, where they were joined by the Archbishop of Rouen and many bishops and noblemen; and finally proceeded to the Council, which was to be held under the auspices of the Legate at Avranches.

The great Norman cathedral of that beautiful city stood on what was perhaps the finest situation of any cathedral in Christendom,—on the brow of the high ridge which sustains the town of Avranches, and looking over the wide bay, in the centre of which stands the sanctuary of Norman chivalry and superstition, the majestic rock of St. Michael, crowned with its fortress and chapel. Of this vast cathedral one granite pillar alone has survived the storm of the French Revolution, and that pillar marks the spot where Henry performed his first penance for the murder of Becket. It bears an inscription with these words :—" Sur cette pierre, ici, à la porte de la cathédrale d'Avranches, après le meurtre de Thomas Becket, Archévêque de Cantorbéry, Henri II., Roi d'Angleterre et Duc de Normandie, reçut à genoux, des légats du Pape, l'absolution apostolique, le Dimanche, xxii Mai, MCLXXII." [1]

The council was held in the church, on the Friday of the same week. On the following Sunday, being Rogation Sunday, or that which precedes the Ascension, the King swore on the Gospels that he had not ordered or wished the Archbishop's murder; but that as he could not put the assassins to death, and feared that his fury had instigated them to the act, he was ready on his part to make all satisfaction,—adding, of himself,

[1] This was the transcript made on the spot. Mr. Gorham has pointed out to me that the 22nd of May did not that year fall on a Sunday :
"In A.D. 1171, Sunday fell on May 23rd
In A.D. 1172,   „   „   May 21st
In A.D. 1173,   „   „   May 20th
The only year in the reign of Henry II. in which May 22nd fell on a Sunday, was A.D. 1155, 1160, 1166, 1177, 1183, 1188." There seems no reason to doubt the correctness of the year 1172, which is positively indeed fixed by the Cotton MS. Life of S. Thomas, before referred to; nor the general fact, that it was in the month of May; not as Gervase (p. 422) erroneously states, on the 27th of September, misled perhaps, as Mr. Gorham suggests, by some legal document, subsequently signed by the King.

that he had not grieved so much for the death of his
father or his mother.[1] He next swore adhesion to the
Pope, restitution of the property of the see of Canterbury, and renunciation of the Constitutions of Clarendon ;
and further promised, if the Pope required, to go a three
years' crusade to Jerusalem, or Spain, and to support 200
soldiers for the Templars.[2] After this, he said aloud,
" Behold, my Lords Legates, my body is in your hands ;
be assured that whatever you order, whether to go to
Jerusalem or to Rome, or to St. James (of Compostella),
I am ready to obey." The spectators, whose sympathy
is usually with the sufferer of the hour, were almost
moved to tears.[3] He was thence led by the legates to
the porch, where he knelt, but was raised up, brought
into the church, and reconciled. The young Henry, at
his father's suggestion, was also present, and, placing
his hand in that of Cardinal Albert,[4] promised to make
good his father's oath. The Archbishop of Tours was
in attendance, that he might certify the penance to the
French king.

Two years passed again, and the fortunes of the King
grew darker and darker with the rebellion of his sons.
It was this which led to the final and greater penance at
Canterbury. He was conducting a campaign against
Prince Richard in Poitou when the Bishop of Winchester
arrived with the tidings that England was in a state of
general revolt. The Scots had crossed the border, under
their King ; Yorkshire was in rebellion, under the standard
of Mowbray ; Norfolk, under Bigod ; the midland counties,
under Ferrers and Huntingdon ; and the Earl of Flanders
with Prince Henry was meditating an invasion of England
from Flanders. All these hostile movements were further
fomented and sustained by the revival of the belief, not
sufficiently dissipated by the penance at Avranches, that
the King had himself been privy to the murder of the saint,
who had now been canonised, and whose fame and miracles
were increasing year by year. It was on Midsummer-day

---

[1] Diceto, 557.
[2] Alan., in Vita Quadrip., 147.

[3] Gervase, 1422.
[4] Alan., in Vita Quadrip., 147, 148.

that the Bishop found the King at Bonneville.[1] So many messages had been daily despatched, and so much importance was attached to the character of the Bishop of Winchester, that the Normans, on seeing his arrival, exclaimed, " The next thing that the English will send over to fetch the King will be the Tower of London itself." [2] Henry saw at once the emergency. That very day, with the Queens Eleanor and Margaret, his son and daughter John and Joan, and the princesses, wives of his other sons, he set out for England. He embarked, in spite of the threatening weather, and the ominous looks of the captain. A tremendous gale sprang up, and the King uttered a public prayer on board the ship, that, " if his arrival in England would be for good, it might be accomplished ; if for evil, never."

The wind abated, and he arrived at Southampton on Monday, the 8th of July. From that moment he began to live on the penitential diet of bread and water, and deferred all business till he had fulfilled his vow. He rode to Canterbury with speed, avoiding towns as much as possible, and on Friday, the 12th of July, approached the sacred city, probably by a road of which traces still remain, over the Surrey hills, and which falls into what was then as now the London road by the ancient village and hospital of Harbledown. This hospital, or leper-house, now venerable with the age of seven centuries, was then fresh from the hands of its founder Lanfranc. Whether it had yet obtained the relic of the saint,—the upper leather of his shoe, which Erasmus saw, and which it is said, remained in the alms-house almost down to our own day—does not appear ; but he halted there, as was the wont of all pilgrims, and made a gift of 40 marks to the little church. And now, as he climbed the steep road beyond the hospital, and descended on the other side of the hill, the first view of the cathedral burst upon him, rising, not indeed in its present proportions, but still with its three towers and

[1] The chroniclers have made a confusion between June and July ; but *July* is right.—*Hoveden*, 308.

[2] Diceto, 573.

vast front, and he leaped off his horse, and went on foot
to the outskirts of the town. Here, at St. Dunstan's [1]
church, he paused again, entered the edifice with the
prelates who were present, stripped off his ordinary dress,
and walked through the streets in the guise of a penitent
pilgrim—barefoot, and with no other covering than a
woollen shirt, and a cloak thrown over it to keep off
rain.[2]

So, amidst a wondering crowd—the rough stones of the
streets marked with the blood that started from his feet—
he reached the cathedral. There he knelt, as at Avranches,
in the porch, then entered the church, and went straight
to the scene of the murder in the north transept. Here
he knelt again, and kissed the sacred stone on which the
Archbishop had fallen, the prelates standing round to
receive his confession. Thence he was conducted to the
crypt, where he again knelt, and with groans and tears
kissed the tomb, and remained long in prayer. At this
stage of the solemnity, Gilbert Foliot, Bishop of London—
the ancient opponent and rival of Becket—addressed the
monks and bystanders, announcing to them the King's
penitence for having by his rash words unwittingly occasioned the perpetration of a crime of which he himself was
innocent, and his intention of restoring the rights and
property of the church, and bestowing 40 marks yearly
on the monastery to keep lamps burning constantly at the
martyr's tomb.[3] The King ratified all that the bishop
had said, requested absolution, and received a kiss of
reconciliation from the prior. He knelt again at the tomb,
removed the rough cloak which had been thrown over his
shoulders, but still retained the woollen shirt to hide the
haircloth,[4] which was visible to near observation, next his
skin, placed his head and shoulders in the tomb, and there
received five strokes from each bishop and abbot who was

[1] Grim, 86.
[2] Garnier, 78, vol. 29. He was present.
[3] Garnier, 80, b. 9.
[4] Newburgh alone (118, 1) represents
the penance as having taken place in
the chapter-house, doubtless as the

usual place for discipline. The part
surrounding the tomb was superseded
in the next generation by the circular
vault which now supports the Trinity
Chapel. But the architecture must
have been like what is now seen in the
western portion of the crypt.

present, beginning with Foliot, who stood by with the "balai," or monastic rod, in his hand,[1] and three from each of the eighty monks. Fully absolved, he resumed his clothes, but was still left in the crypt, resting against one of the rude Norman[2] pillars, on the bare ground, with bare[3] feet still unwashed from the muddy streets, and passed the whole night fasting. At early matins he rose and went round the altars and shrines of the upper church, then returned to the tomb, and finally, after hearing mass, set off, with one of the usual phials of Canterbury pilgrims, containing water mixed with the martyr's blood, and rode to London, which he reached in a week.

So deep a humiliation of so great a prince was unparalleled within the memory of that generation. The submission of Theodosius to Ambrose, of Louis the Debonnaire at Soissons, of Otho III. at Ravenna, of Edgar to Dunstan, of the Emperor Henry IV. to Gregory VII., were only known as matters of history. It is not surprising that the usual figure of speech by which the chroniclers express it should be "the mountains trembled at the presence of the Lord"—"the mountain of Canterbury smoked before Him who touches the hills and they smoke."[4] The auspicious consequences were supposed to be immediate. The King had arrived in London on Sunday, and was so completely exhausted by the effects of the long day and night at Canterbury, that he was seized with a dangerous fever. On the following Thursday,[5] at midnight, the guards were roused by a violent knocking at the gates. The messenger, who announced that he brought good tidings, was reluctantly admitted into the King's bedroom. The King,

---

[1] Grim, 86. A lively representation of Henry's penance is to be seen in Carter's Ancient Sculpture and Painting (p. 50). The king is represented as kneeling, crowned but almost naked, before the shrine. Two great officers, one bearing the sword of State, stand behind him. The monks in their black Benedictine robes are defiling round the shrine, each with a large rod in his hand approaching the bare shoulders of the King. A good notion of this ceremony of the scourging is conveyed by the elaborate formalities with which it was nominally, and probably for the last time, exercised by Pope Julius II. and the Cardinals on the Venetian Deputies in 1509.—*Sketches of Venetian History*, c. 16.

[2] Garnier, 80, b. 29.
[3] Diceto, 575.
[4] Grim, 86.
[5] Gervase, Chron. 1427.

THE CRYPT, CANTERBURY CATHEDRAL.

starting from his sleep, said, "Who art thou?" The lad answered, "I am the boy of your faithful Count Ralph of Glanville, and I come to bring you good tidings." "Is our good Ralph well?" asked the King. "He is well," answered the boy, "and he has taken your enemy the King of the Scots prisoner at Richmond." The King was thunderstruck; the boy repeated his message, and produced the letters confirming it.[1] The King leaped from his bed, and returned thanks to God and "St. Thomas." The victory over William the Lion had taken place on the very Saturday on which he had left Canterbury, after having[2] made his peace with the martyr. On that same Saturday, the fleet, with which his son had intended to invade England from Flanders,[3] was driven back. It was in the enthusiasm of this crisis that Tracy, as it would seem, presented to the King the bequest of his manor of Daccombe to the monks of Canterbury; which accordingly received[4] then and there, at Westminster, the Royal confirmation. Once more, as far as we know, the penitent king and the penitent knight met, in the December of that same year, when, in the fortress of Falaise, the captured king of Scotland did homage to his conqueror, Tracy standing, as of old, by his master's side, but now in the high position of Justiciary of Normandy. Nor did the association of his capture with the Martyr's power pass away from the mind of William the Lion. He, doubtless in recollection of these scenes, reared on his return to Scotland the stately abbey of Aberbrothock, to the memory of St. Thomas of Canterbury.

Thus ended this great tragedy. Its effects on the constitution of the country, and on the religious feeling not only of England but of Europe, would open too large a field. It is enough if, from the narrative we have given, a clearer notion can be formed of that remarkable event than is to be derived from the works either of his professed apologists or professed opponents—if the scene can be more fully realised, the localities more accurately

[1] Brompton, 1095. The effect of this story is heightened by Gaufridus Vosiensis (Script. Rer. Franc., 443), who speaks of the announcement as taking place in Canterbury cathedral, after mass was finished. [2] Brompton, 1096. [3] M. Paris, p. 130. [4] See Appendix to "Becket's Shrine."

identified, the man and his age more clearly understood.
If there be any who still regard Becket as an ambitious
and unprincipled traitor, plotting for his own aggrandise-
ment against the welfare of the monarchy, they will
perhaps be induced, by the accounts of his last moments,
to grant to him the honour, if not of a martyr, at least of
an honest and courageous man, and to believe that such
restraints as the religious awe of high character, or of sacred
place and office, laid on men like Henry and his courtiers,
are not to be despised in any age, and in that lawless and
cruel time were almost the only safeguards of life and
property.   If there be any who are glad to welcome or
stimulate attacks, however unmeasured in language or
unjust in fact, against bishops and clergy, whether Roman
Catholic or Protestant, in the hope of securing the interests of Christian liberty against priestly tyranny, they
may take warning by the reflection, that the greatest
impulse ever given in this country to the cause of sacer-
dotal independence was the reaction produced by the
horror consequent on the deed of Fitzurse and Tracy
Those, on the other hand, who, in the curious change of
feeling that has come over our age, are inclined to
the ancient reverence for St. Thomas of Canterbury, as
the meek and gentle saint of holier and happier times than
our own, may, perhaps, be led to modify their judgment
by the description, taken not from his enemies, but from
his admiring followers, of the violence, the obstinacy, the
furious words and acts, which deformed even the dignity
of his last hour, and well nigh turned the solemnity of his
" martyrdom " into an unseemly brawl.   They may learn
to see in the brutal conduct of the assassins—in the abject
cowardice of the monks—in the savage mortifications
and the fierce passions of Becket himself—how little
ground there is for that paradise of faith and love which
some modern writers find for us in the age of the Plantagenet kings.[1]   And for those who believe that an indis-

[1] One of the ablest of Becket's
recent apologists (Ozanam, *Les Deux
Chanceliers*), who combines with his
veneration for the Archbishop that
singular admiration which almost all
continental Catholics entertain for the
late "Liberator" of Ireland, declares
that on O'Connell, if on any character
of this age, the mantle of the saint and
martyr has descended.   Perhaps the

criminate maintenance of ecclesiastical claims is the best
service they can render to God and the Church, and that
opposition to the powers that be is enough to entitle a
bishop to the honours of a saint and a hero, it may not be
without instruction to remember that the Constitutions of
Clarendon, which Becket spent his life in opposing, and of
which his death procured the suspension, are now incorporated in the English law, and are regarded without a
dissentient voice as among the wisest and most necessary
of English institutions ; that the especial point for which
he surrendered his life was not the independence of the
clergy from the encroachments of the Crown, but the
personal and now forgotten question of the superiority of
the see of Canterbury to the see of York ; and, lastly,
that the wretched superstitions of which the shrine of
St. Thomas became the centre, ended by completely
alienating the affections of thinking men from his memory,
and rendering the name of Becket a by-word of reproach
as little proportioned to his real deserts as had been the
reckless veneration paid to it by his worshippers in the
middle ages.

readers of our narrative will think that, in some respects, the comparison of the Frenchman is true in another sense than that in which he intended it. So fixed an idea has the similarity become in the minds of foreign Roman Catho-lics, that in a popular life of St. Thomas, published as one of a series at Prague, under the authority of the Archbishop of Cologne, the concluding moral is an appeal to the example of "the most glorious of laymen," as Pope Gregory XVI. called Daniel O'Connell, who as a second Thomas strove and suffered for the liberties of his country and his church.

EDWARD THE BLACK PRINCE.

THIS lecture, it will be seen, dwells almost entirely upon those points which give an interest to the tomb at Canterbury. For any general view of the subject, the reader must go to Froissart or to the biographies of Barnes and James; for any further details, to the excellent essays in the 20th, 22nd, 28th, and 32nd volumes of the Archæologia, and to the contemporary metrical life by Chandos, to which reference is made in the course of the lecture. The Ordinance founding his Chantry, and the Will which regulated his funeral and the erection of his tomb, are printed at the end, with notes by Mr. Albert Way.

EDWARD THE BLACK PRINCE.

LECTURE DELIVERED AT CANTERBURY, JUNE, 1852.

EVERY one who has endeavoured to study history, must be struck by the advantage which those enjoy who live within the neighbourhood of great historical monuments. To have seen the place where a great event happened—to have seen the picture, the statue, the tomb of an illustrious man, is the next thing to being present at the event in person—to seeing the scene with our own eyes. In this respect few spots in England are more highly favoured than Canterbury. It is not too much to say, that if any one were to go through the various spots of interest in or around our great Cathedral, and ask what happened here?—who was the man whose tomb we see?—why was he buried here?—what effect did his life or his death have on the world?—a real knowledge of the history of England would be obtained, such as the mere reading of books or hearing of lectures would utterly fail to supply. And it is my hope that by lectures of this kind you will be led to acquire this knowledge for yourselves far more effectually than by hearing anything which the lectures themselves convey—and you will have thus gained not only knowledge, but interest and amusement in the sight of what now seem to be mere stones or bare walls, but what would then be so many chapters of English history, so many portraits and pictures of famous men and famous events in the successive ages of the world.

Let me, before I begin my immediate subject, show you very briefly how this may be done. First, if any one asks why Canterbury is what it is—why from this small town the first subject in this great kingdom takes his title—why we have any Cathedral at all?—the answer is to be found in that great event, the most important that has ever occurred in English history, the conversion of Ethelbert, King of Kent, by the first missionary, Augustine. And if you would understand this, it will lead you to make out for yourselves the history of the Saxon Kings—who they were—whence they came—and who Augustine was, why he came—and what was the city of Rome, from whence he was sent forth. And then if you enter the Cathedral, you will find, in the tombs which lie within its walls, remembrances of almost every reign in the history of England. Augustine and the seven first Archbishops are buried at St. Augustine's; but from that time to the Reformation they have, with a very few exceptions, been buried in the Cathedral, and even where no tombs are left, the places where they were buried are for the most part known. And, the Archbishops being at that time not only the chief ecclesiastics, but also the chief officers of state in the kingdom, their graves tell you not merely the history of the English clergy, but also of the whole Commonwealth and State of England besides. It is for this reason that there is no church, no place in the kingdom, with the exception of Westminster Abbey, that is so closely connected with the general history of our common country. The Kings before the Reformation are for the most part in the Abbey, but their Prime Ministers—so to speak—are for the most part in Canterbury Cathedral.[1]

Ask who it was who first laid out the monastery, and who it was that laid the foundations of the Cathedral as it now stands, and you will find that it was Lanfranc, the

[1] It is hardly necessary to refer to Archbishop Parker's valuable record, compendiously given in Professor Willis's excellent History of Canterbury Cathedral, pp. 13, 134. I cannot forbear to express a hope that this series of illustrious tombs will not be in our time needlessly cut short for all future generations.

great Archbishop whom William the Conqueror brought over with him from Normandy, and who thus re-established the old church with his Norman workmen. Then look at the venerable tower on the south side of the Cathedral, and ask who lies buried within, and from whom it takes its name? and you will find yourself with Anselm, the wise counsellor of William Rufus and Henry I.—Anselm, the man who, perhaps of all who ever filled the see of Canterbury, is the most known by his life and writings throughout the world. And then we come to that celebrated event, the most remarkable that has happened at Canterbury since the arrival of Augustine, and of which the effect may be traced not in one part only, but almost through every stone in the Cathedral, though it took place only on one small spot—the murder of Thomas à Becket. Then, in the south aisle, the broken effigy of Hubert Walter brings before us, the camp of the Crusaders at Acre, where he was appointed Archbishop by Richard I. Next look at that simple tomb in St. Michael's Chapel, half in and half out of the church, and you will be brought to the time of King John; for it is the grave of Stephen Langton, who, more than any one man, won for us the Magna Charta. Then look back at the north transept, at the wooden statue that lies in the corner. That is the grave of Archbishop Peckham, in the reign of King Edward I., and close beside that spot King Edward I. was married. And now we come to the time at which the subject of my lecture begins, the reign of King Edward III. And so we might pass on to Archbishop Sudbury, who lost his head in the reign of Richard II.; to Henry IV., who lies there himself; to Chichele, who takes us on to Henry V. and Henry VI.; to Morton, who reminds us of Henry VII. and Sir Thomas More; to Warham, the friend of Erasmus, predecessor of Archbishop Cranmer; and then to the subsequent troubles— of which the Cathedral still bears the marks—in the Reformation and the Civil Wars.

On some future occasion, perhaps, I may be permitted to speak of the more important of these, as opportunity may occur. But for the present let us leave the Primates of Canterbury, and turn to our especial subject. Let us place ourselves in imagination by the tomb of the most illustrious layman who rests amongst us, Edward Plantagenet, Prince of Wales, commonly called the Black Prince. Let us ask whose likeness is it that we there see stretched before us—why was he buried in this place, amongst the Archbishops and sacred shrines of former times—what can we learn from his life or his death ?

A few words must first be given to his birth and childhood. He was born on the 15th of June, 1330, at the old palace of Woodstock, near Oxford, from which he was sometimes called Prince Edward of Woodstock.[1] He was, you will remember, the eldest son of King Edward III. and Queen Philippa, a point always to be remembered in his history, because, like Alexander the Great, and a few other eminent instances, he is one of those men in whom the peculiar qualities both of his father and his mother were equally exemplified. Every one knows the story of the siege of Calais, of the sternness of King Edward, and the gentleness of Queen Philippa, and it is the union of these qualities in their son which gave him the exact place which he occupies in the succession of our English princes, and in the history of Europe.

We always like to know where a famous man was educated. And here we know the place, and also see the reason why it was chosen. Any of you who have been at Oxford will remember the long line of buildings which overlook the beautiful curve of High Street, the buildings of "Queen's College," the College of the Queen. At the time of which I speak, that college was the greatest—two others only in any regular collegiate form existed in Oxford. It had but just been founded by the chaplain of Queen Philippa, and took its name from her. There it was that, according to tradition, the Prince of Wales, her son, as in the next generation, Henry V., was brought up. If we look at the events which followed, he could hardly have been twelve years old when he went. But there were then no schools in England, and their place was almost

[1] Archæol. xxii. 227.

entirely supplied by the Universities. Queen's College is
much altered in every way since the little Prince went
there; but they still keep an engraving of the vaulted room,
which he is said to have occupied;[1] and though most of
the old customs which prevailed in the college, and which
made it a very peculiar place even then, have long since
disappeared, some which are mentioned by the founder,
and which therefore must have been in use when the
Prince was there, still continue. You may still hear the
students summoned to dinner, as he was, by the sound
of a trumpet, and, in the hall, you may still see, as he
saw, the Fellows sitting all on one side of the table,
with the Head of the college in the centre, in imitation of
the "Last Supper," as it is commonly represented in
pictures.[2] The very names of the Head and the twelve
Fellows, (the number first appointed by the founder, in
likeness of our Lord and the Apostles,) who were presiding
over the college when the Prince was there, are known to
us.[3] He must have seen what has long since vanished
away, the thirteen beggars, deaf, dumb, maimed, or blind,
daily brought into the hall, to receive their dole of bread,
beer, potage, and fish.[4] He must have seen the seventy
poor scholars, instituted, after the example of the
seventy disciples, and learning from their two chaplains to
chant the service.[5] He must have heard the mill within
or hard by the college walls grinding the Fellows' bread.[6]
He must have seen the porter of the college going round[7]
the rooms betimes in the morning to shave the beards, and
wash the heads, of the Fellows. In these and many other
curious particulars, we can tell exactly what the customs
and appearance of the College was when the Prince was
there. It is more difficult to answer another question,
which we always wish to know about famous men—Who
were his companions? One youth, however, there was at
that time in Oxford, and at Queen's College, whom we
shall all recognise as an old acquaintance—John Wycliffe,
the first English Reformer, and the first translator of the

[1] It now hangs in the gallery above
the hall of Queen's College.
[2] Statutes of Queen's College, p. 11.
[3] Ib. pp. 9, 33.
[4] Ib. p. 30.
[5] Ib. p. 27.
[6] Ib. p. 29.
[7] Ib. pp. 28, 29.

Bible into English.   He was a poor boy, in a threadbare
coat,[1] and devoted to study, and the Prince probably never
exchanged looks or words with him.   But it is almost
certain that he must have seen him, and it is interesting to
remember that once at least in their lives the great soldier
of the age had crossed the path of the great Reformer. Each
thought and cared little for the other ; their characters,
and pursuits, and sympathies, were as different as were
their stations in life ; let us be thankful if we have learned
to understand them both, and see what was good in each,
far better than they did themselves.

We now pass to the next events of his life ; those
which have really made him almost as famous in war, as
Wycliffe has been in peace—the two great battles of
Cressy and of Poitiers.   I will not now go into the origin
of the war, of which these two battles formed the turning-
points. It is enough for us to remember that it was under-
taken by Edward III. to gain the crown of France, through
a pretended claim—for it was no more than a pretended
claim—through his mother.   And now, first, for Cressy.
I shall not undertake to describe the whole fight, but will
call your attention briefly to the questions which every
one ought to ask himself, if he wishes to understand anything about any battle whatever.   First, where was it
fought ; secondly, why was it fought ; thirdly, how was it
won ; and fourthly, what was the result of it ?   And to
this I must add, in the present instance, what part was
taken in it by the Prince, whom we left as a little boy at
Oxford, but who was now following his father as a young
knight in his first great campaign ?   The first of these
questions involves the second also.   If we make out
where a battle was fought, this usually tells us why it
was fought ; and this is one of the many proofs of the
use of learning geography together with history.   Each
helps us to understand the other.   Cressy is a little
village between Abbeville and Calais, and not far from
the scene of what was, perhaps, a still greater victory—

---

[1] So we may gather from Chaucer's description of the Oxford Clerk, at this very
period.

that of Agincourt.[1] Edward had made an incursion into
Normandy, and was retreating towards Flanders—or
Belgium, as we now call it—when he was overtaken by the
French King, Philip, who, with an immense army, had
determined to cut him off entirely, and so put an end to
the war. It was Saturday, the 28th of August, 1346, and
it was at four in the afternoon that the battle commenced.
It always helps us better to imagine any remarkable
event, when we know at what time of the day or night it
took place ; and on this occasion it is of great importance,
because it helps us at once to answer the third question
we asked—how was the battle won ? It was four in the
afternoon, and the French army advanced from the south-
east, after a hard day's march to overtake the retiring
enemy. Every one, from the King down to the peasants
on the road, crying, "Kill! kill!" were in a state of the
greatest excitement, drawing their swords, and thinking
that they were sure of their prey. What the French
King chiefly relied upon (besides his great numbers) was
the troop of fifteen thousand cross-bowmen from Genoa, in
Italy. These were made to stand in front : when, just as
the engagement was about to take place, one of those extraordinary incidents occurred, which often turn the fate of
battles, as they do of human life in general. A tremendous
storm gathered from the west, and broke in thunder, and
rain, and hail, on the field of battle. The sun was darkened,
and the horror was increased by the hoarse cries of crows
and ravens, which fluttered before the storm, and struck
terror into the hearts of the Italian bowmen, who were
unaccustomed to these northern tempests. And when at
last the sky had cleared, and they prepared their crossbows
to shoot, the strings had been so wet by the rain that
they could not draw them. By this time the evening sun
streamed out in full splendour [2] over the black clouds of
the western sky—right in their faces ; and at the same
moment the English archers, who had kept their bows in
cases during the storm, and so had their strings dry, let

---

[1] See the interesting details of the
battle, in Arch. vol. xxviii., taken from
records in the Town Hall at Abbeville.

[2] A sun issuing from a cloud was the
badge of the Black Prince, probably from
this occurrence.—Arch. xx. 106.

fly their arrows so fast and thick, that those who were present could only compare it to snow or sleet. Through and through the heads, and necks, and hands of the Genoese bowmen, the arrows pierced. Unable to stand it, they turned and fled ; and from that moment the panic and confusion was so great, that the day was lost.

But though the storm, and the sun, and the archers had their part, we must not forget the Prince. He was, we must remember, only sixteen, and yet he commanded the whole English army. It is said that the reason of this was, that the King of France had been so bent on destroying the English forces, that he had hoisted the sacred banner of France [1]—the great scarlet flag, embroidered with golden lilies, called the Oriflamme —as a sign that no quarter would be given ; and that when King Edward saw this, and saw the hazard to which he should expose not only the army, but the whole kingdom, if he were to fall in battle, he determined to leave it to his son. Certain it is, that, for whatever reason, he remained on a little hill on the outskirts of the field, and the young Prince, who had been knighted [2] a month before, went forward with his companions in arms, into the very thick of the fray ; and when his father saw that the victory was virtually gained, he forbore to interfere. " Let him *win his spurs*," he said, in words which have since become a proverb, " and *let the day be his.*" The Prince was in very great danger at one moment ; he was wounded and thrown to the ground, and only saved by one of the knights near him, who carried the great banner of Wales, throwing the banner over the boy as he lay on the ground, and standing upon it till he had driven back the assailants. [3] The assailants were driven back, and far through the long summer evening, and deep into the summer night, the battle raged. It was not till all was dark, that the Prince and his companions halted from their pursuit ; and then

---

[1] The Oriflamme of France, like the green standard of the Prophet in the Turkish Empire, had the effect of declaring the war to be what was called a "Holy war;" that is, a war of extermination.

[2] Arch. xxxi. 3.

[3] Arch. xxxviii. 184.

huge fires and torches were lit up, that the King might see where they were. And then took place the touching interview between the father and the son ; the King embracing the boy in front of the whole army, by the red light of the blazing fires, and saying, "*Sweet son, God give you good perseverance; you are my true son—right loyally have you acquitted yourself this day, and worthy are you of a crown*,"—and the young Prince, after the reverential manner of those times, "bowed to the ground, and gave all the honour to the King his father." The next day the King walked over the field of carnage with the Prince, and said, " *What think you of a battle—is it an agreeable game ?* "[1]

The general result of the battle was the deliverance of the English army from a most imminent danger, and subsequently the conquest of Calais, which the King immediately besieged and won, and which remained in the possession of the English from that day till the reign of Queen Mary. From that time the Prince became the darling of the English, and the terror of the French ; and, whether from this terror, or from the black armour which he wore on that day, or from the black banners and the black devices which he used in tournaments,[2] and which contrasted with the fairness of his complexion, he was called by them "Le Prince Noir," the Black Prince, and from them the name has passed to us ; so that all his other sounding titles, by which the old poems call him— "Prince of Wales, Duke of Aquitaine,"—are lost in the one memorable name which he won for himself in his first fight at Cressy.

And now we pass over ten years, and find him on the field of Poitiers. Again we must ask what brought him there, and why the battle was fought ? He was this time alone ; his father, though the war had rolled on since the battle of Cressy, was in England. But, in other respects, the beginning of the fight was very like that of

[1] Arch. xxviii. 187.
[2] See his Will (App. p. 134), where he speaks of the black drapery of his "hall." We may compare, too, the black pony upon which he rode, on his famous entry into London (Froissart). In war, he was dressed in the blue and scarlet coat of the arms of England and France.

Cressy. Gascony belonged to him by right, and from this he made a descent into the neighbouring provinces, and was on his return home, when the King of France —John, the son of Philip—pursued him, as his father had pursued Edward III., and overtook him suddenly on the high upland fields, which extend for many miles south of the city of Poitiers. It is the third great battle which has been fought in that neighbourhood— the first was that in which Clovis defeated the Goths, and established the faith in the Creed of Athanasius throughout Europe—the second was that in which Charles Martel drove back the Saracens, and saved Europe from Mahometanism—the third was this, the most brilliant of English victories over the French.[1] The spot, which is about six miles south of Poitiers, is still known by the name of the Battle-field. Its features are very slightly marked—two ridges of rising ground, parted by a gentle hollow ; behind the highest of these two ridges is a large tract of copse and underwood, and leading up to it from the hollow is a somewhat steep lane, there shut in by woods and vines on each side. It was on this ridge that the Prince had taken up his position, and it was solely by the good use which he made of this position that the

[1] The battle of Clovis is believed to have been at Voulon, on the road to Bordeaux,—that of Charles Martel is uncertain. The name of Moussain La Bataille, which it is thought may have a reference to the death of the Arab chief Musa (Moses), and the expression in the chronicles " in suburbio Pictaviensi," may lead to the belief that it was nearer Poitiers than Tours. Yet if it lasted, as is said, for a whole week, it may well have reached to the very banks of the Loire, according to the traditions of Tours. These three battles (with that of Moncontour, fought not far off, in 1569, after the siege of Poitiers by Admiral Coligny), are well described by M. S. Hippolyte, in a number of the "Spectateur Militaire." For my acquaintance with this work, as well as for any details which follow relating to the battle, I am indebted to the kindness and courtesy of M. Foucart of Poitiers, in whose company I visited the field of battle, in the summer of 1851. The site of the field has been much contested by antiquaries, but now appears to be fixed beyond dispute. The battle is said to have been fought " at Maupertuis, between Beauvoir and the Abbey of Nouillé." There is a place called Maupertuis near a village Beauvoir, on the north of Poitiers, which has led some to transfer the battle thither ; but, besides the general arguments, both from tradition and from the probabilities of the case in favour of the southern site, there is a deed in the municipal archives of Poitiers, in which the farm-house now called La Cardinière (from its owner Cardin, to whom it was granted by Louis XIV., like many estates in the neighbourhood, called from their owners), is said to be "*alias* Maupertuis." The fine Gothic ruin of the Abbey of Nouillé also remains, a quarter of an hour's walk from the field.

victory was won. The French army was arranged on the other side of the hollow in three great divisions, of which the King's was the hindmost ; the farm-house which marks the spot where this division was posted is visible from the walls of Poitiers. It was on Monday, Sept. 19, 1356, at 9 A.M., that the battle began. All the Sunday had been taken up by fruitless endeavours of Cardinal Talleyrand—a namesake of the famous minister of Napoleon—to save the bloodshed, by bringing the King and Prince to terms ; a fact to be noticed for two reasons, first because it shows the sincere and Christian desire which animated the clergy of those times, in the midst of all their faults, to promote peace and good-will amongst the savage men with whom they lived ; and secondly because it shows, on this occasion, the confidence of victory which had possessed the French King.

The Prince offered to give up all the castles and prisoners he had taken, and to swear not to fight in France again for seven years. But the King would hear of nothing but his absolute surrender of himself and his army on the spot. The Cardinal laboured till the very last moment, and then rode back to Poitiers, having equally offended both parties. The story of the battle, if we remember the position of the armies, is told in a moment. The Prince remained firm in his position—the French charged with their usual chivalrous ardour—charged up the lane—the English archers, whom the Prince had stationed behind the hedges on each side, let fly their showers of arrows, as at Cressy—in an instant the lane was choked with the dead—and the first check of such headstrong confidence was fatal. The Prince in his turn charged,—a general panic seized the whole French army,—the first and second division fled in the wildest confusion,—the third alone where King John stood made a gallant resistance, the King was taken prisoner, and by noon the whole was over. Up to the city gates of Poitiers the French army fled and fell, and you still see the convent in the city, and the ruined abbey near the field, where their dead bodies were buried. It was a wonderful day. It was 8000 to 60,000 ; the Prince who had gained the battle was still only twenty-six, that is a year younger than Napoleon at the beginning of his campaigns, and the characteristic result of the battle which distinguished it from among all others, was the number, not of the slain but of the prisoners—one Englishman often taking four or five Frenchmen. Perhaps, however, the best known part of the whole is the scene when the King first met the Prince in the evening, which cannot be better described than by old Froissart.

"The day of the battle at night, the Prince gave a supper in his lodgings to the French King and to most of the great lords that were prisoners. The Prince caused the King and his son to sit at one table, and other lords, knights, and squires at the others ; and the Prince always served the King very humbly, and would not sit at the King's table, although he requested him—he said he was not qualified to sit at the table with so great a prince as the King was. Then he said to the King, ' Sir, for God's sake make no bad cheer, though your will was not accomplished this day. For, Sir, the King, my father, will certainly bestow on you as much honour and friendship as he can, and will agree with you so reasonably that you shall ever after be friends ; and, Sir, I think you ought to rejoice, though the battle be not as you will, for you have this day gained the high honour of prowess, and have surpassed all others on your side in valour. Sir, I say not this in raillery, for all our party, who saw every man's deeds, agree in this and give you the palm and chaplet.' Therewith the Frenchmen whispered among themselves that the Prince had spoken nobly, and that most probable he would prove a great hero, if God preserved his life, to persevere in such good fortune."

It was after this great battle that we first hear of the Prince's connexion with Canterbury. On the 16th of April, 1357, the Prince with the French King, landed at Sandwich ; there they staid two days, and on the 19th entered Canterbury. Simon of Islip, who is buried in the nave of the Cathedral, chiefly known as the founder of Canterbury Hall, at Oxford, which is now part of Christ Church, but of which the Black Prince's fellow-student

Wycliffe became afterwards Master, was now Archbishop, and he no doubt would be there to greet them. The French King, if we may suppose that the same course was adopted here as when they reached London, rode on a magnificent cream-coloured charger, the Prince on a little black pony at his side. They came into the Cathedral and made their offerings at the shrine of S. Thomas, and no doubt the King was shown all the relics and memorials which the monks had to exhibit. Tradition[1] says, but without any probability of truth, that the old room above St. Anselm's Chapel, was used as King John's prison. He may possibly have seen it, but he is hardly likely to have lived there. At any rate they were only here for a day, and then again advanced on their road to London. One other tradition we may perhaps connect with this visit. Behind the hospital at Harbledown, is an old well, still called "the Black Prince's well." If this is the only time that he passed through Canterbury—and it is the only time that we hear of—then we may suppose that in the steep road underneath the hospital he halted, as we know that all pilgrims did, to see Becket's shoe, which was kept in the hospital, and that he may have gone down on the other side of the hill to wash as others did, in the water of the spring ; and we may well suppose that such an occasion would never be forgotten, and that his name would live long afterwards in the memory of the old alms-men.

The remembrance of his visit to Canterbury lingered in his mind, and in 1363, when he married his cousin Joan, he left a memorial of his marriage in the beautiful chapel still to be seen in the crypt of the Cathedral, where two priests were to pray for his soul, first in his lifetime, and also, according to the practice of those times, after his death. It is now by a strange turn of fortune which adds another link to the historical interest of the place, the entrance to the chapel of the French congregation—the descendants of the very nation whom he conquered at Poitiers ; but you can still trace the situation

[1] Gostling, "Walks about Canterbury," p. 263. For his later visit to Canterbury, see " Becket's Shrine."

of the two altars where his priests stood, and on the groined vaultings you can see his arms, and the arms of his father, and, in connection with the joyful event in thankfulness for which he founded the chapel, what seems to be the face of his beautiful wife, commonly known as the Fair Maid of Kent ; and for the permission to found this chantry, he left to the Chapter of Canterbury an estate which still belongs to them, the manor of " Fawkes' Hall." This ancient namesake of the more celebrated Guy was, as we learn from legal records, a powerful baron in the reign of John; and received from that king a grant of land in South Lambeth, where he built a hall or mansion-house, called from him Fawkes' Hall, or " La Salle de Fawkes." He would have little thought of the strange and universal fame his house would acquire in the form in which we are now so familiar with it in the gardens, the factories, the bridge, and the railway station, of *Vauxhall*.[1]

And now we have to go again over ten years, and we find the Prince engaged in a war in Spain, helping Don Pedro, King of Spain, against his brother. But this would take us too far away—I will only say that here also he won a most brilliant victory, the battle of Nejara, in 1367, and it is interesting to remember that the first great commander of the English armies, had a Peninsular war to fight as well as the last, and that the flower of English chivalry led his troops through the pass of Roncesvalles,

" Where Charlemagne and all his peerage fell,"

in the days of the old romances.

Once again, then, we pass over ten· years—for, by a singular coincidence, which has been observed by others, the life of the Prince thus naturally divides itself—and we find ourselves at the end, at. that last scene which is; in fact, the main connexion of the Black Prince with Canterbury. The expedition to Spain, though accompanied by one splendid victory, had ended disastrously. From that moment the fortunes of the Prince were overcast. A

---

[1] See Appendix, p. 131. For the history of Fawkes, see Foss's Judges, vol. ii. p. 256. Archæological Journal, vol. iv. p. 275.

long and wasting illness, which he contracted in the
southern climate of Spain, broke down his constitution ; a
rebellion, occasioned by his own wastefulness, which was
one of the faults of his character, broke out in his French
provinces ; his father was now sinking in years, and
surrounded by unworthy favourites—such was the state
in which the Prince returned, for the last time, to England.
For four years he lived in almost entire seclusion at
Berkhampstead, in preparation for his approaching end :
often he fell into long fainting fits, which his attendants
mistook for death. One of the traditions which connects
his name with the well at Harbledown, speaks of his
having had the water brought thence to him as he lay
sick—or, according to a more common but groundless
story, dying—in the Archbishop's palace at Canterbury.[1]
Once more, however, his youthful spirit, though in a
different form, shot up an expiring flame. His father, I
have said, was sinking into dotage, and the favourites of
the court were taking advantage of him, to waste the
public money. Parliament met—Parliament, as you must
remember, unlike the two great Houses which now sway
the destiny of the Empire, but still feeling its way towards
its present powers—Parliament met, to check this
growing evil ; and then it was that when they looked
round in vain for a leader to guide their counsels, and
support their wavering resolutions, the dying Prince came
forth from his long retirement, and was carried up to
London, to assist his country in this time of its utmost
need. His own residence was a palace which stood on
what is now called Fish Street Hill, the street opposite
the London Monument. But he would not rest there :
he was brought to the Royal Palace of Westminster, that
he might be close at hand to be carried from his sick bed
to the Parliament, which met in the chambers of the
palace. This was on the 28th of April, 1376. The spirit
of the Parliament and the nation revived as they saw
him, and the purpose for which he came was accomplished.
But it was his last effort. Day by day his strength

---

[1] There is no doubt that the well has
always been supposed to possess medi-
cinal qualities, and this was probably
the cause of Lanfranc's selection of that
spot for his leper-house.

ebbed away, and he never again moved from the Palace at
Westminster.   On the 7th of June, he signed his will, by,
which, as we shall presently see, directions were given for
his funeral and tomb.   On the 8th he rapidly sank.   The
beginning of his end cannot be better told than in the
words of the herald Chandos, who had attended him in all
his wars, and who was probably present :—

> Then the Prince caused his chambers to be opened
> And all his followers to come in,
> Who in his time had served him,
> And served him with a free will ;
> "Sirs," said he, " pardon me
> For, by the faith I owe you,
> You have served me loyally,
> Though I cannot of my means
> Render to each his guerdon ;
> But God by his most holy name
> And saints, will render it you."
> Then each wept heartily
> And mourned right tenderly,
> All who were there present,
> Earl, baron, and batchelor ;
> Then he said in a clear voice,
> " I recommend to you my son,
> Who is yet but young and small,
> And pray, that as you served me
> So from your heart you would serve him."
> Then he called the King his father,
> And the Duke of Lancaster his brother,
> And commended to them his wife,
> And his son, whom he greatly loved,
> And straightway entreated them ;
> And each was willing to give his aid,
> Each swore upon the book,
> And they promised him freely
> That they would comfort his son
> And maintain him in his right ;
> All the princes and barons
> Swore all round to this,
> And the noble Prince of fame
> Gave them an hundred thousand thanks.
> But till then, so God aid me,
> Never was seen such bitter grief
> As was at his departure.
> The right noble excellent Prince
> Felt such pain at heart,
> That it almost burst
> With moaning and sighing,
> And crying out in his pain
> So great suffering did he endure,
> That there was no man living
> Who had seen his agony,
> But would heartily have pitied him.[1]

---

[1] Chandos's " Poem of the Black
Prince," edited and translated for the
Roxburghe Club, by the Rev. H. O.
Coxe, Sub-librarian of the Bodleian
Library, at Oxford. May I take this
opportunity of expressing my grateful

In this last agony he was, as he had been through life, specially attentive to the wants of his servants and dependents; and after having made them large gifts, he called his little son to his bedside, and charged him on pain of his curse never to take them away from them as long as he lived.

The doors still remained open, and his attendants were constantly passing and re-passing, down to the least page, to see their dying master. Such a deathbed had hardly been seen since the army of Alexander the Great defiled through his room, during his last illness. As the day wore away, a scene occurred which showed how, even at that moment, the stern spirit of his father still lived on in his shattered frame. A knight, Sir Richard Strong by name, who had offended him by the evil counsel he had given to the King, came in with the rest. Instantly the Prince broke out into a harsh rebuke, and told him to leave the room, and see his face no more. This burst of passion was too much for him—he sank into a fainting fit —the end was evidently near at hand; and the Bishop of Bangor, who was standing by the bedside of the dying man, struck perhaps by the scene which had just occurred, strongly exhorted him from the bottom of his heart to forgive all his enemies, and ask forgiveness of God and of men. The Prince replied, "I will." But the good Bishop was not so to be satisfied. Again he urged, " It suffices not to say only ' I will,' but where you have power, you ought to declare it in words, and to ask pardon." Again and again the Prince doggedly answered, " I will." The Bishop was deeply grieved, and, in the belief of those times, of which we may still admire the spirit, though the form, both of his act and expression, has long since passed away, he said, " An evil spirit holds his tongue—we must drive it away, or he will die in his sins." And so saying, he sprinkled holy water over the four corners of the room, and commanded the evil spirit to depart. The Prince *was* vexed by an evil spirit, though not in the sense in which the good Bishop meant it; he was vexed by the evil spirit of bitter revenge, which was the curse of

sense of his assistance on this and on all other occasions when I have had the pleasure of referring to him?

those feudal times, and which now, thank God, though it still lingers amongst us, has ceased to haunt those noble souls which then were its especial prey. That evil spirit did depart, though not perhaps by the means then used to expel it; the Christian words of the good man had produced their effect, and in a moment the Prince's whole look and manner was altered. He joined his hands, lifted up his eyes to heaven, and said, "I give thee thanks, O God, for all thy benefits, and with all the pains of my soul I humbly beseech thy mercy to give me remission of those sins I have wickedly committed against thee; and of all mortal men whom, willingly or ignorantly, I have offended, with all my heart I desire forgiveness." With these words, which seem to have been the last effort of exhausted nature, he immediately expired.[1]

It was at 3 P.M., on Trinity Sunday—a festival which he had always honoured with especial reverence—it was on the 8th of June, just one month before his birthday, in his forty-sixth year—the same age which has closed the career of so many illustrious men both in peace and war —that the Black Prince breathed his last.

Far and wide the mourning spread when the news was known. Even amongst his enemies, in the beautiful chapel of the palace of the French kings—called the Sainte Chapelle, or Holy Chapel—funeral services were celebrated by King Louis, son of that King John whom he had taken prisoner at Poitiers. Most deeply, of course, was the loss felt in his own family and circle, of which he had been so long the pride and ornament. His companion in arms, the Captal de Buch, was so heart-broken, that he refused to take any food, and in a few days died of starvation and grief. His father, already shaken in strength and years, never survived the blow, and lingered on only for one more year.

> "Mighty victor, mighty lord—
> Low on his funeral couch he lies.
> Is the sable warrior fled?
> Thy son is gone. He rests among the dead."

But most striking was the mourning of the whole

[1] Archæol. xxii. 229.

English nation. Seldom, if ever, has the death of one man
so deeply struck the sympathy of the English people.
Our fathers saw the mourning of the whole country over
the Princess Charlotte, and the great funeral procession
which conveyed the remains of Nelson to their resting-
place in St. Paul's—we ourselves have seen the deep grief
over the sudden death of our most illustrious statesman—
we know what is the feeling with which we should at this
moment [1] regard the loss of the great commander who,
perhaps more than any other single person, has filled in
our minds the place of the Black Prince. But in order to
appreciate the mourning of the people when Edward
Plantagenet passed away, we must combine all these
feelings. He was the cherished heir to the throne of
England, and his untimely death would leave the crown in
the hands of a child, the prey, as was afterwards proved,
to popular seditions, and to ambitious rivals. He was the
great soldier, " in whose health the hopes of Englishmen
had flourished, in whose distress they had languished, in
whose death they had died. In his life they had feared
no invasion, no encounter in battle ; he went against no
army that he did not conquer, he attacked no city that
he did not take," and now to whom were they to look ?
The last time they had seen him in public was as the
champion of popular rights against a profligate court, as
fearless in the House of Parliament as he had been on the
field of battle. And yet more, he died at a moment when
all was adverse and threatening—when all was blank in
the future, and that future was dark with cloud and storm.
That young student at Queen's, with whom we parted
thirty years ago, had already begun to proclaim those
great changes which shook every institution to its very
centre. There were mutterings, too, of risings in classes
hitherto never thought of—Wat Tyler and Jack Cade
were already on the horizon of Kent and of England ;
and in the rivalry of the King's sons, now left without an acknowledged chief, were already laid the seeds

[1] This was written in June, 1852, and
(with all that follows) has been left un-
altered. The coincidences with what
actually took place in the autumn of
that year, will occur to every one.

of the long and dreadful wars of the houses of York and Lancaster.

It is by remembering these feelings that we shall best enter into the closing scene, with which we are here so nearly connected.

For nearly four months—from the 8th of June to the 29th of September—the coffined body lay in state at Westminster, and then, as soon as Parliament met again, as usual in those times, on the Festival of Michaelmas, was brought to Canterbury. It was laid in a stately hearse, drawn by twelve black horses, and the whole court, and both Houses of Parliament, followed in deep mourning. The great procession started from Westminster Palace ; it passed through what was then the little village of Charing, clustered, in the midst of the open fields of St. Martin, round Queen Eleanor's Cross. It passed along the Strand, by the houses of the great nobles, who had so often fought side by side with him in his wars, and the Savoy Palace, where, twenty years before, he had lodged the French King as his prisoner in triumph. It passed under the shade of the lofty tower of the old Cathedral of St. Paul's, which had so often resounded with Te Deums for his victories. It descended the steep hill, overhung by the grey walls of his own Palace, above London Bridge, and over that ancient bridge, then the only bridge in London, it moved onwards on its road to Canterbury— that same road which at this very time had become so well known from Chaucer's " Canterbury Tales."

At the west gate of Canterbury—not the one which now stands there, which was built a few years later—but an older gateway, with the little chapel of Holycross at the top, surmounted by a lofty cross, seen far off, as the procession descended from Harbledown—at this gate they were met—so the Prince had desired in his will,[1]—by two chargers, fully caparisoned, and mounted by two riders in complete armour—one bearing the Prince's arms of England and France, the other the ostrich feathers—one to represent the Prince in his splendid suit as he rode in war, the other to represent him in black, as he rode to

---

[1] See Appendix, pp. 133, 140.

tournaments. Four black banners followed. So they passed through the streets of the city, till they reached the gate of the Precincts. Here, according to custom, the armed men[1] halted, and the body was carried into the cathedral. In the space between the high altar and the choir, a bier was placed to receive it, whilst the funeral services were read, surrounded with burning tapers, and with all the heraldic pomp which marked his title and rank. It must have been an august assemblage which took part in those funeral prayers. The aged king, in all probability, was not there, but we cannot doubt that the executors were present ; his rival brother, John of Gaunt, the famous Duke of Lancaster, and his long-tried friend, William of Wykeham, the great Bishop of Winchester, whose name is still dear to hundreds of Englishmen, old and young, from the two magnificent colleges which he founded at Winchester and at Oxford. Courtenay, too, the Bishop of London, would also be there, who now lies at the Prince's feet, and Simon of Sudbury, who had been Archbishop of Canterbury in the previous years—he whose magnificent bequests still appear in the gates and walls of the city—he whose fate it was to be the first to suffer in the troubles which the Prince's death would cause, who was beheaded by the rebels, under Wat Tyler, on Tower Hill, and whose burial was the next great funeral within the walls of the cathedral. And now, from the choir, the body was again raised up, and carried to the tomb.

We have seen, already, that as long as twelve years before, the Prince had turned his thoughts to Canterbury Cathedral as his last home, when in remembrance of his visit to the shrine of St. Thomas, and of the fact that the church was dedicated to the Holy Trinity, which, as we have seen, he had honoured with especial reverence, he founded the chapel in the crypt. In the centre of that crypt, on the spot where you now see the gravestone of Archbishop Morton, it had been his wish to be laid, as expressed in the will which he signed only the day before his death. But those who were concerned with the funeral had prepared for him a more magnificent resting-place : not in the

---

[1] See "Murder of Becket," pp. 63, 66, 77.

darkness of the crypt, but high aloft in the sacred space behind the altar, and on the south side of the shrine of St. Thomas, in the chapel itself of the Holy Trinity, on the festival of which he had expired, they determined that the body of the hero should be laid.   That space is now surrounded with monuments, then it was entirely, or almost entirely, vacant.[1] The gorgeous shrine stood in the centre on its coloured pavement, but no other corpse had been admitted within that venerated ground—no other, perhaps, would have been admitted but that of the Black Prince. It was twenty-seven years before the iron gates of the chapel would again be opened to receive the dead, and this too would be a royal corpse—the body of King Henry IV.— now a child of ten years old, and perhaps present as a mourner in this very funeral, but destined to overthrow the Black Prince's son, and then to rest by his side.

In this sacred spot—believed at that time to be the most sacred spot in England—the tomb stood in which "alone in his glory," the Prince was to be deposited, to be seen and admired by all the countless pilgrims who crawled up the stone steps beneath it on their way to the shrine of the Saint.

Let us turn to that tomb, and see how it sums up his whole life.   Its bright colours have long since faded, but enough still remains to show us what it was as it stood after the sacred remains had been placed within it.   There he lies : no other memorial of him exists in the world, so authentic. There he lies, as he had directed, in full armour, his head resting on his helmet, his feet with the likeness of "the spurs he won" at Cressy, his hands joined as in that last prayer which he had offered up on his death-bed. There you can see his fine face with the Plantagenet features, the flat cheeks, and the well-chiselled nose, to be traced perhaps in the effigy of his father in Westminster Abbey, and his grandfather in Gloucester Cathedral.   On his armour, you can still see the marks of the bright gilding with which the figure was covered

---

[1] The only exception could have been the tomb, which stands on the south-east side of the Trinity Chapel, and which, though not as early as Theobald to whom it is commonly ascribed, must be of the beginning of the thirteenth century.

THE TOMB OF THE BLACK PRINCE IN CANTERBURY CATHEDRAL.

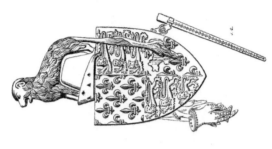

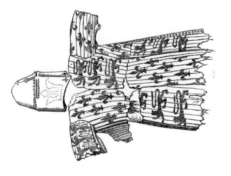

SURCOAT, HELMET, SHIELD, CREST, ETC., OF THE BLACK PRINCE, SUSPENDED OVER HIS TOMB.

G. A. *del.*

Page 121.

CANOPY OF THE BLACK PRINCE'S TOMB IN CANTERBURY CATHEDRAL.

from head to foot, so as to make it look like an image of pure gold. High above are suspended the brazen gauntlets, the helmet, with what was once its gilded leopard-crest, and the wooden shield, the velvet coat also, embroidered with the arms of France and England, now tattered and colourless, but then, blazing with blue and scarlet. There too, still, hangs the empty scabbard of the sword, wielded perchance at his three great battles, and which Oliver Cromwell, it is said, carried away. On the canopy over the tomb, there is the faded representation—painted after the strange fashion of those times—of the Persons of the Holy Trinity, according to the peculiar devotion which he had entertained. In the pillars you can see the hooks to which was fastened the black tapestry, with its crimson border and curious embroidery, which he directed in his will should be hung round his tomb and the shrine of Becket. Round about the tomb, too, you will see the ostrich feathers,[1] which, according to the old, but I am afraid doubtful, tradition, we are told he won at Cressy from the blind King of Bohemia, who perished in the thick of the fight : and interwoven with them, the famous motto,[2] with which he used to sign his name, " Houmout," " Ich diene." If, as seems most likely, they are German words, they exactly express what we have seen so often in his life, the union of " Hoch muth," that is, *high spirit*, with " Ich dien," *I serve*. They bring before us the very scene

---

[1] The Essay by the late Sir Harris Nicolas, in the Archæologia, vol. xxxii., gives all that can be said on this disputed question. The ostrich feathers are first mentioned in 1369, on the plate of Philippa, and were used by all the sons of Edward II., and of all subsequent kings, till the time of Arthur, son of Henry VII., after which they were appropriated as now to the Prince or Wales. The Black Prince had sometimes one ostrich feather, sometimes, as on the tomb, three. The old explanation given by Camden was that they indicated *fleetness* in discharge of duty. The King of Bohemia's badge was a Vulture.

[2] *Houmout—Ich-dien.* It occurs twice

as his autograph signature (see Appendix, 141.) But its first public appearance is on the tomb, where the words are written alternately above the coats of arms, and also on the quills of the feathers. It is said, though without sufficient proof, that the King of Bohemia had the motto " Ich dien" from his following King Philip as a stipendiary. The Welsh antiquaries maintain that it is a Celtic and not a German motto, " Behold the man," the words used by Edward I. on presenting his first born son to the Welsh, and from him derived to the subsequent Princes of Wales. "Behold the man," *i. e.* the male child.

itself after the battle of Poictiers, where, after having vanquished the whole French nation, he stood behind the captive king, and served him like an attendant.

And, lastly, carved about the tomb, is the long inscription, composed by himself before his death, in Norman French, still the language of the Court, written, as he begged, clearly and plainly, that all might read it. Its purport is to contrast his former splendour, and vigour, and beauty, with the wasted body which is now all that is left. A natural thought at all times, and increasingly so at this period, as we see from the further exemplification of it in Chichele's tomb, a hundred years later, where the living man and the dead skeleton are contrasted with each other in actual representation,— but singularly affecting here, if we can suppose it to have been written during the four years' seclusion, when he lay wasting away from his lingering illness, with the over- clouding of his high fortunes, and death full in prospect.

When we stand by the grave of a remarkable man, it is always an interesting and instructive question to ask— especially by the grave of such a man, and in such a place —what evil is there, which we trust is buried with him in his tomb ? what good is there, which may still live after him ? what is it, that taking him from first to last, his life and his death teach us ?

First, then, the thought which we most naturally connect with the name of the Black Prince, is the wars of the English and French—the victories of England over France. Out of those wars much noble feeling sprung, feelings of chivalry and courtesy and respect to our enemies, and (perhaps a doubtful boon) of unshaken confidence in ourselves. Such feelings are amongst our most precious inheritances, and all honour be to him who first inspired them into the hearts of his countrymen, never to be again extinct. But it is a matter of still greater thankfulness to remember, as we look at the worn-out armour of the Black Prince, that those wars of English conquest are buried with him, never to be revived. Other wars may arise in the unknown future still before us—but such wars as he and his father waged, we shall, we may thankfully hope, see no more again for ever. We shall never again see a King of England, or a Prince of Wales, taking advantage of a legal quibble to conquer a great neighbouring country, and laying waste with fire and sword a civilised kingdom, from mere self-aggrandisement. We have seen how, on the eve of the battle of Poitiers, one good man with a patience and charity truly heroic, did strive, by all that Christian wisdom and forbearance could urge, to stop that unhallowed warfare. It is a satisfaction to think that his wish is accomplished ; that what he laboured to effect almost as a hopeless project, has now well-nigh become the law of the civilised world. It is true, that the wars of Edward III. and the Black Prince were renewed again on a more frightful scale in the next century, renewed at the instigation of an Archbishop of Canterbury, who strove thus to avert the storm which seemed to him to be threatening the Church : but these were the last, and the tomb and college of Chichele are themselves lasting monuments of the deep remorse for his sin, which smote his declining years. With him finished the last trace of those bloody wars : may nothing ever arise, in our time or our children's, to break the bond of peace between England and France, which is the bond of the peace of the world !

Secondly, he brings before us all that is most characteristic of the ages of chivalry. You have heard of his courtesy, his reverence to age and authority, his generosity to his fallen enemy. But before I speak of this more at length, here also I must in justice remind you, that the evil as well as the good of chivalry was seen in him, and that this evil, like that which I spoke of just now, is also, I trust, buried with him. One single instance will show what I mean. In those disastrous years which ushered in the close of his life, a rebellion arose in his French province of Gascony, provoked by his wasteful expenditure. One of the chief towns where the insurgents held out, was Limoges. The Prince, though then labouring under his fatal illness, besieged and took it ;

and as soon as it was taken, he gave orders that his soldiers should massacre every one that they found; whilst he himself, too ill to walk or ride, was carried through the streets in a litter, looking on at the carnage. Men, women, and children, threw themselves on their knees, as he passed on through the devoted city, crying, "Mercy, mercy;" but he went on relentlessly, and the massacre went on, till struck by the gallantry of three French knights, whom he saw fighting in one of the squares against fearful odds, he ordered it to cease. Now, for this dreadful scene there were doubtless many excuses—the irritation of illness, the affection for his father, whose dignity he thought outraged by so determined a resistance, and the indignation against the ingratitude of a city on which he had bestowed many favours. But what is especially to be observed, is not so much the cruelty of the individual man, as the great imperfection of that kind of virtue which could allow of such cruelty. Dreadful as this scene seems to us, to men of that time it seemed quite natural. The poet who recorded it, had nothing more to say concerning it, than that—

> " All the townsmen were taken or slain
> By the noble Prince of price,
> Whereat great joy had all around,
> Those who were his friends ;
> And his enemies were
> Sorely grieved, and repented
> That they had begun the war against him."

This strange contradiction arose from one single cause. The Black Prince, and those who looked up to him as their pattern, chivalrous, kind, and generous as they were to their equals, and to their immediate dependents, had no sense of what was due to the poor, to the middle, and the humbler classes generally. He could be touched by the sight of a captive king, or at the gallantry of the three French gentlemen; but he had no ears to hear, no eyes to see, the cries and groans of the fathers, and mothers, and children, of the poorer citizens, who were not bound to him by the laws of honour and of knighthood. It is for us to remember, as we stand by his grave, that whilst he has left us the legacy of those noble and beautiful feelings, which are the charm and best ornaments of life, though not its most necessary virtues, it is our further privilege and duty to extend those feelings towards the classes on whom he never cast a thought; to have towards *all* classes of society, and to make them have towards each other, and towards ourselves, the high respect and courtesy, and kindness, which were then peculiar to one class only.

It is a well-known saying in Shakspeare, that—

> "The evil which men do lives after them;
> The good is oft interred with their bones."

But it is often happily just the reverse, and so it was with the Black Prince. His evil is interred with his bones; the good which he has done lives after him, and to that good let us turn.

He was the first great English captain, who showed what English soldiers were, and what they could do against Frenchmen, and against all the world. He was the first English Prince who showed what it was to be a true gentleman. He was the first, but he was not the last. We have seen how, when he died, Englishmen thought that all their hopes had died with him. But we know that it was not so; we know that the life of a great nation is not bound up with the life of a single man; we know that the valour and the courtesy, and the chivalry of England, are not buried in the grave of the Plantagenet Prince. It needs only a glance round the country, to see that the high character of an English gentleman, of which the Black Prince was the noble pattern, is still to be found everywhere; and has since his time been spreading itself more and more through classes, which in his time seemed incapable of reaching it. It needs only a glance down the nave of our own Cathedral; and the tablets on the walls, with their tattered flags, will tell you, in a moment, that he, as he lies up there aloft, with his head resting on his helmet, and his spurs on his feet, is but the first of a long line of English heroes—that the brave men who fought at Sobraon and Feroozeshah are the true descendants of those who fought at Cressy and Poitiers.

And not to soldiers only, but to all who are engaged in

the long warfare of life, is his conduct an example. To unite in our lives the two qualities expressed in his motto, " Hoch muth " and " Ich dien," " high spirit " and "reverent service," is to be, indeed, not only a true gentleman and a true soldier, but a true Christian also. To show to all who differ from us, not only in war but in peace, that delicate forbearance, that fear of hurting another's feelings, that happy art of saying the right thing to the right person, which he showed to the captive king, would indeed add a grace and a charm to the whole course of this troublesome world, such as none can afford to lose, whether high or low. Happy are they, who having this gift by birth or station, use it for its highest purposes; still more happy are they, who having it not by birth and station, have acquired it, as it may be acquired, by Christian gentleness and Christian charity.

And lastly, to act in all the various difficulties of our everyday life, with that coolness, and calmness, and faith in a higher power than his own, which he showed when the appalling danger of his situation burst upon him at Poitiers, would smooth a hundred difficulties, and ensure a hundred victories. We often think that we have no power in ourselves, no advantages of position, to help us against our many temptations, to overcome the many obstacles we encounter. Let us take our stand by the Black Prince's tomb, and go back once more in thought to the distant fields of France. A slight rise in the wild upland plain, a steep lane through vineyards and underwood, this was all that he had, humanly speaking, on his side; but he turned it to the utmost use of which it could be made, and won the most glorious of battles. So, in like manner, our advantages may be slight—hardly perceptible to any but ourselves —let us turn them to account, and the results will be a hundred-fold; we have only to adopt the Black Prince's bold and cheering words, when first he saw his enemies, *"God is my help, I must fight them as best I can;"* adding that lofty, yet resigned and humble prayer, which he uttered when the battle was announced to be inevitable, and which has since become a proverb, " *God defend the right.*"

APPENDIX.

ORDINANCE BY EDWARD THE BLACK PRINCE, FOR THE TWO CHAN-
TRIES FOUNDED BY HIM IN THE UNDERCROFT OF THE SOUTH
TRANSEPT, CHRIST CHURCH, CANTERBURY, RECITED IN THE
CONFIRMATION BY SIMON ISLIP, ARCHBISHOP OF CANTERBURY,
OF THE ASSENT AND RATIFICATION BY THE PRIOR AND
CHAPTER. DATED AUGUST 4, 1363.

(Orig. Charter in the Treasury, Canterbury, No. 145.) *

UNIVERSIS sancte matris ecclesie filiis ad quos presentes litere
provenerint, Prior et Capitulum ecclesie Christi Cantuariensis
salutem in omnium Salvatore. Ordinacionem duarum Cantariarum
in ecclesia predicta fundatarum, unius videlicet in honore Sancte
Trinitatis, et alterius in honore Virginis gloriose, inspeximus dili-
genter, Cujus quidem ordinacionis tenor sequitur in hec verba.
Excellencia principis a regali descendens prosapia, quanto in sua
posteritate amplius diffunditur et honorificencius sublimatur, tanto
ad serviendum Deo prompcior esse debet, et cum devota graciarum
accione capud suum sibi humiliter inclinare, ne aliter pro ingrati-
tudine tanti muneris merito sibi subtrahatur beneficium largitoris.
Sane nos, Edwardus, Princeps Wallie et serenissimi Principis ac
domini nostri, domini Edwardi illustris Regis Anglie, primogenitus,
pridem cupientes ad exaltacionem paterni solii nobis mulierem de
genere suo clarissimo recipere in sociam et uxorem, demum post
deliberaciones varias super diversis nobis oblatis matrimoniis, ad
nobilem mulierem, dominam Johannam Comitissam Kancie, consan-
guineam dicti patris nostri et nostram, ipsam videlicet in secundo,
et nos in tercio consanguinitatis gradibus contingentem, Dei pocius
inspirante gracia quam hominis suasione, convertimus totaliter
mentem nostram, et ipsam, de consensu dicti domini patris nostri
et aliorum parentum nostrorum, dispensacione sedis apostolice super
impedimento hujusmodi et aliis quibuslibet primitus obtenta, pre-
elegimus et assumpsimus in uxorem; Injuncto nobis etiam per
prius eadem auctoritate apostolica quod duas Cantarias quadraginta

---

* This document is copied in the
Registers B. 2, fo. 46, and F. 8, fo. 83,
vº, under this title,—Littera de Institu-
cione duarum cantariarum domini Principis. In the text here given the contracted
words are printed *in extenso.* I acknowledge with much gratification the privilege
liberally granted to me of examining the
ancient charters in the Treasury, amongst
which this unpublished document has
been found.

Marcarum obtentu dispensacionis predicte ad honorem Dei perpetuas faceremus.[1] Nos vero, in Deo sperantes firmiter per acceptacionem humilem Injunccionis hujus, et efficax ipsius complementum nupcias nostras Deo reddere magis placabiles, et paternum solium, per adeo sibi propinque sobolis propagacionem condecenter diffundere et firmius stabilire, ad honorem Sancte Trinitatis, quam peculiari devocione semper colimus, et beatissime Marie, et beati Thome Martyris, infra muros ecclesie Christi Cantuariensis, matris nostre precipue et metropolitis, ad quam a cunabilis[2] nostris devocionem mentis ereximus, in quodam loco ex parte australi ejusdem ecclesie constituto, quem ad hoc, de consensu reverendissimi in Christo patris, domini Simonis Dei gracia Cantuariensis Archiepiscopi, tocius Anglie Primatis et apostolice sedis Legati, et religiosorum virorum Prioris et Capituli ipsius ecclesie, designavimus, duas capellas, quarum una Sancte Trinitatis intitulabitur, et altera beate et gloriose Virginis Marie, sub duabus cantariis duximus con- struendas, ut sic ad dictam ecclesiam confluentes, et capellas nostras intuentes, pro conjugii nostri prosperitate animarumque nostrarum salute deum exorare propencius excitentur. In nostris vero Can- tariis ex nunc volumus et statuimus, quod sint duo sacerdotes idonei, sobrii et honesti, non contenciosi, non querelarum aut litium assumptores, non incontinentes, aut aliter notabiliter viciosi, quorum correccio, punicio, admissio et destitucio ad Archiepiscopum, qui tempore fuerit, loci diocesanum pertineat et debeat pertinere, eorem tamen statum volumus esse perpetuum, nisi per mensem et amplius a Cantariis suis hujusmodi absque causa racionabili et licencia a domino Cantuariensi Archiepiscopo, si in diocesi sua presens fuerit, vel aliter a Priore dicti monasterii, petita pariter et optenta, absentes fuerint ; vel nisi viciosi et insolentes trina moni- cione per temporum competencium intervalla, vel aliter trina correccione emendati, ab insolenciis suis desistere non curaverint ; quos tunc incorrigibiles seu intollerabiles censemus, et volumus per predictum ordinarium reputari, et propterea a dicta Cantaria penitus amoveri, nulla appellacione aut impetracione sedis Apostolice vel regis, aut alii[3] juris communis seu spiritualis remedio amoto hujus- modi aliqualiter valitura. Primum vero et principaliorem dominum Johannem Curteys, de Weldone, et dominum Willelmum Bateman, de Giddingg', secundarium, in eisdem nominamus et constituimus sacerdotes, quorum principalis in altari Sancte Trinitatis, et alter in altari beate Marie, cum per dominum Archiepiscopum admissi fuerint, pro statu salubri nostro, prosperitate matrimonii nostri, dum vixerimus, et animabus nostris, cum ab hac luce subtracti

---

[1] See the Bulls of Pope Innocent VI., concerning the marriage of the Prince with the Countess of Kent, Rymer, Fœd. deit. 1830, vol. iii., part ii., pp. 627, 632.

[2] *Sic* in orig.
[3] This word is contracted in original— *al.* The reading may be *alii* or *aliter.*

fuerimus, cotidie celebrabunt, nisi infirmitate aut alia causa racionabili fuerint prepediti. Cum vero alter eorum cesserit loco suo, vel decesserit, aut ipsum dimiserit, Nos, Edwardus predictus, in vita nostra, et post mortem nostram Rex Anglie, qui pro tempore fuerit, ad locum sic vacantem quem pro tunc secundum censemus quam cicius comode poterimus, saltem infra unius mensis spacium, dicto domino Archiepiscopo presentabimus et nominabimus ydoneum sacerdotem; et sic, quocienscunque vacaverit, imperpetuum volumus observari. Alioquin elapso hujusmodi tempore liceat Archiepiscopo illa vice loco sic vacante de sacerdote ydoneo providere, salvo jure nostro et successorum nostrorum in hac parte, ut prefertur, in proxima vacatione alterius sacerdotis. Volumus insuper et ordinamus quod dictus Archiepiscopus, qui fuerit, significata sibi morte per literas nostras aut successorum nostrorum hujusmodi vel aliter per literas Capellani qui supervixerit, aliquo sigillo autentico roboratas, statim absque inquisicione alia sive difficultate qualibet presentatum seu nominatum hujusmodi admittat, et literas suas suo consacerdoti et non alteri super admissione sua dirigat sive mittat. Dicent vero dicti sacerdotes insimul matutinas et ceteras horas canonicas in capella, videlicet sancte Trinitatis, necnon et septem psalmos penitenciales et quindecim graduales et commendacionem ante prandium, captata ad hoc una hora vel pluribus, prout viderint expedire. Et post prandium vesperas et completorium necnon placebo et dirige pro defunctis. Celebrabit insuper uterque ipsorum singulis diebus prout sequitur, nisi aliqua causa legitima sicut premittitur fuerint prepediti, unus eorum videlicet singulis diebus dominicis de die, si voluerit, vel aliter de Trinitate, et alter eorum de officio mortuorum, vel aliter de beata Virgine Maria. Feria secunda unus de festo novem lectionum, si acciderit, vel aliter de Angelis, et alius de officio mortuorum, vel de Virgine gloriosa. Feria tercia alter eorum de beato Thoma, et alius de beata Virgine vel officio mortuorum, nisi aliquod festum novem leccionum advenerit, tunc enim missa de beato Thoma poterit pretermitti. Feria quarta, si a festo novem leccionum vacaverit, unus de Trinitate et alter de beata Maria virgine vel officio mortuorum. Feria quinta unus de festo Corporis Christi, et alius de beata Virgine vel officio mortuorum, si a festo novem leccionum vacaverit. Feria sexta, si a festo novem leccionum vacaverit, unus de beata Cruce et alter de beata Virgine vel officio mortuorum. Singulis diebus sabbati, si a festo novem leccionem vacaverit, unus de beata Virgine et alter de officio mortuorum. Et hoc modo celebrabunt singulis diebus imperpetuum, et non celebrabunt simul et eadem hora, sed unus post alium, successive. Ante vero introitum misse quilibet rogabit et rogari publice faciat celebrans pro statu salubri utriusque nostrum dum vixerimus, et pro animabus nostris, cum ab hac luce

migraverimus, et dicet Pater et Ave, et in singulis missis suis
dum vixerimus de quocunque celebraverint collectam illam,—
"Deus cujus misericordie non est numerus," et, cum ab hac
miseria decesserimus,—"Deus venie largitor," cum devocione
debita recitabunt. Et volumus quod post missas suas vel ante,
secundum eorum discrecionem differendum vel anticipandum, cum
doctor aut lector alius in claustro monachorum more solito legerit
ibidem, nisi causa legitima prepediti fuerint, personaliter intersint,
et doctrine sue corditer intendant, ut sic magis edocti Deo devocius
et perfectius obsequantur. Principali vero sacerdote de medio
sublato, aut aliter loco suo qualitercumque vacante, socius suus, qui
tunc superstes fuerit, sicut prediximus locum Principaliorem occu-
pabit, et secundum locum tenebit novus assumendus. Ordinamus
etiam quod dicti sacerdotes singulis annis semel ad minus de eadem
secta vestiantur, et quod non utantur brevibus vestimentis sed
talaribus secundum decenciam sui status. Pro mora siquidem
dictorum sacerdotum assignavimus quemdam habitacionis locum
juxta Elemosinariam dicti Monasterii, in quo construetur ad usum
et habitacionem eorum una Aula communis in qua simul cotidianam
sument refeccionem, una cum quadam Camera per Cancellum divi-
denda, ita quod in utraque parte sic divisa sit locus sufficiens pro
uno lecto competenti, necnon et pro uno camino nostris sumptibus
erigendo. Ita tamen quod camera hujusmodi unicum habeat ostium
pro Capellanorum ingressu et egressu. Cujus locum divisum
viciniorem principaliori sacerdoti intitulari volumus et mandamus;
sub qua Camera officia eis utilia constituent prout eis magis videbitur
expedire. Coquinam etiam habebunt competentem; quas quidem
domus nostris primo sumptibus construendas prefati religiosi viri,
Prior et Capitulum, quociens opus fuerit, reparabunt ac eciam refor-
mabunt. De habitacione vero ipsorum hujusmodi liberum habebunt
ingressum ad dictas capellas, et regressum pro temporibus et horis
competentibus, ac retroactis temporibus pro ingressu secularium
consuetis. Comedent eciam insimul in Aula sua cum perfecta fuerit,
in ipsorum quoque cameris, et non alibi, requiescent. Ad hec dicti
sacerdotes vestimenta et alia ornamenta dicte Capelle assignanda
fideliter conservabunt, et cum mundacione aut reparacione aliqua
indigerint, predicti religiosi viri, Prior et Capitulum suis sumptibus
facient reparari, et alia nova quociens opus fuerit inveteratis et
inutilibus subrogabunt. Percipiet quidem uterque eorundem sacerdotum annis singulis de [1] Priore et Capitulo supradictis viginti
marcas ad duos anni terminos, videlicet, ad festa sancti Michaelis et
Pasche, per equales porciones, necnon ab eisdem Priore et Capitulo
ministrabitur ipsis Capellanis de pane, vino, et cera, ad sufficienciam,
pro divinis officiis celebrandis. Ita videlicet quod in matutinis,

---

[1] In the original—et Priore.

vesperis et horis sit continue cereus unus accensus, et missa quacumque duo alii cerei ad utrumque altare predictum. Quod si prefati Prior et Capitulum dictas pecunie summas in aliquo dictorum terminorum, cessante causa legitima, solvere distulerint ultra triginta dies ad majus, extunc sint ipso facto ab execucione divinorum officiorum suspensi, quousque ipsis Capellanis de arreragiis fuerit plenarie satisfactum. Pro supportacione vero predictorum onerum dictis Priori et Capitulo, ut premittitur, incumbencium, de licencia excellentissimi Principis domini patris nostri supradicti dedimus, concessimus et assignavimus eisdem Priori et Capitulo, eorumque successoribus, manerium nostrum de Faukeshalle juxta London', prout in cartis ejusdem patris nostri et nostris plenius continetur. Jurabit insuper uterque eorumdem sacerdotum coram domino Archiepiscopo, qui pro tempore fuerit, in admissione sua, quod hanc ordinacionem nostram observabit et faciet, quantum eum concernit et sibi facultas prestabitur, in omnibus observari. Jurabunt insuper iidem sacerdotes Priori dicti Loci obedienciam, et quod nullum dampnum inferent dicto monasterio vel personis ejusdem injuriam seu gravamen. Rursum, si in presenti nostra ordinacione processu temporis inveniatur aliquod dubium seu obscurum, illud interpretandi, innovandi, corrigendi et eidem ordinacioni nostre addendi, diminuendi et declarandi, nobis quamdiu vixerimus, et post mortem nostram reverendo patri, domino Archiepiscopo Cantuariensi, qui pro tempore fuerit, specialiter reservamus.[1] Cui quidem ordinacioni sic salubriter composite et confecte tenore presencium nostrum prebemus assensum, onera nobis in eadem imposita agnoscimus, et cetera in eadem ordinacione contenta, quantum ad nos attinet vel attinere in futurum poterit, approbamus, ratificamus, et eciam confirmamus. In quorum omnium testimonium sigillum nostrum commune presentibus est appensum. Datum in domo nostra Capitulari Cantuar' ije. Non' Augusti, Anno domini Millesimo Trescentesimo sexagesimo tercio. Et nos, Simon, permissione divina Archiepiscopus Cantuariensis, supradictus, premissa omnia et singula quatenus ad nos attinet autorizamus, approbamus, ratificamus et tenore presencium auctoritate nostra ordinaria confirmamus. In cujus rei testimonium sigillum nostrum fecimus hiis apponi. Datum eciam Cantuar' die, anno et loco supradictis, et nostre consecracionis anno quartodecimo.

(L.S. Seal lost.)

Endorsed.—Confirmacio Archiepiscopi et Conventus super Cantarias Edwardi principis Wallie in ecclesia nostra in criptis.[2] In a later hand,—Duplex.

---

[1] The word *jus* seems to be omitted in this sentence, of which the sense as it stands is incomplete. Here the recital of the Ordinance ends.

[2] This document bears the following numbers, by which it has been classed at various times :—45 (erased.)—Duplex vi. (erased) A.—C. 166.—C. 145, the latter being the right reference, according to the Indices now in use.

THE WILL OF EDWARD PRINCE OF WALES, A.D. 1376.[1]

COPIA TESTAMENTI PRINCIPIS WALL'.

(Register of Archbishop Sudbury, in the Registry at Lambeth, fol. 90 b, and 91 a and b.)

EN noun du Pere, du Filz, et de Saint Espirit, Amen. Nous, Eduuard, eisne filz du Roy d'Engletere et de Fraunce, prince de Gales, duc de Cornwaille, et counte de Cestre, le vij. jour de Juyn, l'an de grace mil troiscentz septantz et sisme, en notre chambre dedeyns le palois de notre tresredote seignour et pere le Roy à West'm esteantz en bon et sain memoire, et eiantz consideracion a le brieve duree de humaine freletee, et come non certein est le temps de sa resolucion à la divine volunte, et desiranz toujourz d'estre prest ove l'eide de dieu à sa disposicioun, ordenons et fesons notre testament en la manere qe ensuyt. Primerement nous devisons notre alme à Dieu notre Creatour, et à la seinte benoite Trinite et à la glorieuse virgine Marie, et à touz lez sainz et seintez; et notre corps d'estre enseveliz en l'eglise Cathedrale de la Trinite de Canterbirs, ou le corps du vray martir monseignour Seint Thomas repose, en mylieu de la chapelle de notre dame Under Crofte, droitement devant l'autier, siqe le bout de notre tombe devers les pees soit dix peez loinz de l'autier, et qe mesme la tombe soit de marbre de bone masonerie faite. Et volons qe entour la ditte tombe soient dusze escuchons de latone, chacun de la largesse d'un pie, dont les syx seront de noz armez entiers, et les autres six des plumez d'ostruce, et qe sur chacun escuchon soit escript, c'est assaveir sur cellez de noz armez et sur les autres des plumes d'ostruce,—Houmout.[2] Et paramont[3] la tombe soit fait un table-

---

[1] The following document was printed by Mr. Nichols in his "Collection of Royal Wills," p. 66. It is here given with greater accuracy, through careful collation of the transcript in Archbishop Sudbury's Register at Lambeth. The remarkable interest of the will as connected with the Prince's interment and tomb at Canterbury, may fully justify its reproduction in this volume.

[2] The escutcheons on the Prince's tomb are not in conformity with these directions. Over those charged with his arms appears the word *houmout*, on a little scroll, whilst over those bearing the three ostrich feathers is the motto—*ich diene.* There is probably an omission in the transcript of this passage in the Lambeth Register. The reading in the original document may have been — "sur cellez de noz armez—*ich diene*—et sur les autres des plumes d'ostruce — houmout." Representations of these escutcheons, as also of the altar tomb, showing their position, were given with the beautiful etchings of the figure of the Prince in Stothard's "Monumental Effigies." Representations on a larger scale will be found in the notes subjoined.—See p. 141.

[3] "Par-amont, en haut."—*Roquefort.*

ment de latone suzorrez de largesse et longure de meisme la tombe, sur quel nouz volons qe un ymage d'overeigne levez de latoun suzorrez soit mys en memorial de nous, tout armez de fier de guerre de nous armez quartillez et le visage mie, ove notre heaume du leopard mys dessouz la teste del ymage, Et volons qe sur notre tombe en lieu ou len le purra plus clerement lire et veoir soit escript ce qe ensuit, en la manere qe sera mielz aviz à noz executours :—

> Tu qe passez ove bouche close, par la ou cest corps repose
> Entent ce qe te dirray, sicome te dire la say,
> Tiel come tu es, Je au ciel [1] fu, Tu seras tiel come Je su,
> De la mort ne pensay je mie, Tant come j'avoy la vie.
> En terre avoy grand richesse, dont Je y fys grand noblesse,
> Terre, mesons, et grand tresor, draps, chivalx, argent et or.
> Mes ore su je povres et cheitifs, perfond en la terre gys,
> Ma grand beaute est tout alee, Ma char est tout gastee,
> Moult est estroite ma meson, En moy na si verite non,
> Et si ore me veissez, Je ne quide pas qe vous deeisez,
> Qe j'eusse onqes hom este, si su je ore de tout changee.
> Pur Dieu pries au celestien [2] Roy, qe mercy eit de l'arme [3] de moy.
> Tout cil qe pur moi prieront, ou à Dieu m'acorderont,
> Dieu les mette en son parays, [4] (sic) ou nul ne poet estre cheitifs. [5]

Et volons qe à quele heure qe notre corps soit amenez par my la ville de Canterbirs tantqe à la priorie, qe deux destrez covertz de noz armez, et deux hommez armez en noz armez et en noz heaumes voisent devant dit notre corps, c'est assavoir, l'un pur la guerre de noz armez entiers quartellez, et l'autre pur la paix de noz bages des plumes d'ostruce ove quatre baneres de mesme la sute, et qe chacum de ceux qe porteront lez ditz baneres ait sur sa teste un chapeu de noz armes. Et qe celi qe sera armez pur la guerre ait un homme armez portant a pres li un penon de noir ove plumes d'ostruce. Et volons qe le herce soit fait entre le haut autier et le cuer, dedeyns lc quel nous voloms qe notre corps soit posee, tantqe les vigiliez, messes et les divines services soient faites; lesquelx services ensi faitez, soit notre corps portes en l'avant dite chappelle de notre dame ou il sera ensevillez. Item, nous donnons et devisoms al haut autier de la dite eglise notre vestement de velvet vert enbroudez d'or,

[1] Thus in the MS. On the tomb the reading here is *autiel*, doubtless the word intended. "Auteil ; pareil, de même."—*Roquefort*.

[2] The correct reading may be *celestieu*. Roquefort gives both *celestiau* and *celestien*.

[3] Thus written, as likewise on the tomb. Roquefort gives "Arme; ame, esprit," &c.

[4] Mr. Nichols printed this word—*paradys*, as Weever, Dart, Sandford and others had given it. On the tomb the reading is—*paray*, which usually signifies in old French, *paroi, mur*, Lat. *paries*. Compare Roquefort,—"Paradis, *parehuis*, parvis, place qui est devant une eglise, &c. en bas Lat. parvisius."

[5] The inscription as it actually appears on the tomb is not literally in accordance with the transcript here given, but the various readings are not of importance. The inscription is given accurately by Mr. Kempe in the account of the tomb, Stothard's Monumental Effigies.

avec tout ce qe apperptient (*sic*) au dit vestement. Item, deux bacyns
d'or, un chalix avec le patyn d'or, noz armez graves sur le pie, et
deux cruetz d'or, et un ymage de la Trinite à mettre sur le dit
autier, et notre grande croix d'argent suzorrez et enamellez, c'est
assavoir la meliour croix qe nous avons d'argent; toutes lesqueles
chosez nouz donnons et devisons au dit autier à y servir perpetuelement, sainz jammes le mettre en autre oeps pur nul mischiefs.   Item,
nous donnons et devisons al autier de notre dame en la chappelle
surdite notre blank vestiment tout entier diapree d'une vine[1]
d'azure, et auxi le frontel qe l'evesqe d'Excestre nous donna, q'est de
l'assumpcion de notre dame en mylieu severee d'or et d'autre
ymagerie, et un tabernacle de l'assumpcioun de notre dame, qe le
dit evesqe nous donna auxi, et deux grandez chandelabres d'argent
qe sont tortillez, et deux bacyns de noz armez, et un grand chalix
suzorre et enameillez des armez de Garrenne, ove deux cruetz taillez
còme deux angeles, pur servir à mesme l'autier perpetuelement,
sainz jamez le mettre en autre oeps pur nul meschief.   Item, nous
donnons et devisons notre sale[2] des plumes·d'ostruce de tapicerie
noir et la bordure rouge, ove cignes ove testez de dames, cest
assavoir un dossier, et huyt pieces pur les costers, et deux banqueres,
à la dit esglise de Canterbirs.   Et volons qe le dossier soit taillez
ensi come mielz sera avis à noz executours pur servir devant et
entour le haut autier, et ce qe ne busoignera à servir illec du remenant du dit dossier, et auxi les ditz banqueres, volons qe soit
departiz à servir devant l'autier la ou monseignour saint Thomas
gist, et à l'autier la ou la teste est, et à l'autier la ou la poynte de
l'espie est, et entour notre corps en la dite chappelle de notre dame
Undercrofte, si avant come il purra suffiere.   Et voloms qe les
costres de la dit Sale soient pur pendre en le quer tout du long
paramont les estallez, et en ceste manere ordenons à servir et estre
user en memorial de nous, à la feste de la Trinite, et à toutz lez
principalez festes de l'an, et à lez festes et jour de Monseignour
saint Thomas, et à toutez lez festes de notre dame, et les jours auxi
de notre anniversaire perpetuelement, tant come ils purront durer
sainz jamez estre mys en autre oeps.   Item, nous donnons et
devisons à notre chappelle de ceste notre dite dame Undercrofte,
en la quele nous avoms fondes une chanterie de deux chapellayns à
chanter pur nous perpetuelement, nostre missal et nostre portehors,
lesquelx nous mesmes avons fait faire et enlimyner de noz armures
en diversez lieux, et auxi de nos bages dez plumes d'ostruce; et
ycelx missal et portehors ordenons à servir perpetuelement en la

---

[1] This word is printed by Mr. Nichols—
viue.   The white tissue was probably
diapered with a trailing or branched
pattern in azure, in form of a vine.
[2] A complete set of hangings for a
chamber was termed a Hall, *salle*, and
by analogy a large tent or pavilion
formed of several pieces was called a Hall;
the hangings, *aulœa*, were also called
Hallynges.

dite chappelle sainz james le mettre en autre oeps pur nul meschief; et de toutez cestes choses chargeons les armes des Priour et Couvent de la dite eglise, sicome ils vorront respondre devant Dieu. Item, nous donnons et devisons à la dite chappelle deux vestementz sengles, cest assavoir, aube, amyt, chesyble, estole et fanon, avec towaille covenables à chacum des ditz vestementz, à servir auxi en la dite chapelle perpetuelement. Item, nous donnons et devisons notre grand table d'or et d'argent tout pleyn dez precieuses reliques, et en my lieu un croiz *de ligno sancte crucis,* et la dite table est garniz de perres et de perles, c'est assavoir, vingt cynq baleis, trent quatre safirs, cinquant oyt perles grosses, et plusours autres safirs, emeraudes et perles petitz, à la haut autier de notre meson d'Assherugge q'est de notre fundacioun,[1] à servir perpetuelement au dit autier, sanz jamez le mettre en autre oeps pur nul meschief; et de ce chargeons les armes du Rectour et du Couvent de la dite meson à respondre devant Dieu. Item, nous donnons et devisons le remenant de touz noz vestimentz, draps d'or, le tabernacle de la Resurreccioun, deux cixtes[2] d'argent suzorrez et enameillez d'une sute, croix, chalix, cruetz, chandelabres, bacyns, liveres, et touz noz autrez ornementz appertenantz à seinte eglise, à notre chapelle de saint Nicholas dedeynz notre chastel de Walyngforde,[3] à y servir et demurer perpetuelement, sanz jamez le mettre en autre oeps; et de ceo chargeons les armes des doien et souz doyen de la dite chapelle à respondre devant Dieu, horspris toutesfoiz le vestement blu avec rosez d'or et plumes d'ostruce, liquel vestement tout entier avec tout ce qe appertient à ycelle nous donnons et devisons à notre fitz Richard, ensemble avec le lit qe nous avons de mesme la sute et tout l'apparaille du dit lit, lequele notre tresredote seignour et pere le Roy nous donna. Item, nous donnons et devisons à notre dit filz notre lit palee de baudekyn et de camaca rouge q'est tout novel, avec tout ce qe appertient au dit lit. Item, nous donnons et devisons à notre dit filz notre grand lit des angeles enbroudez, avec les quissyns, tapitz, coverture, linceaux et tout entierement l'autre apparalle appertienant au dit lit. Item, nous donons et devisons à notre dit filz la Sale d'arras du pas de Saladyn, et auxi la Sale de Worstede embroudez avec mermyns de mier, et la bordure de rouge de noir pales et embroudes de cignes ove testez de dames et de plumes d'ostruce, lesqueles Sales nous volons qe notre dit filz ait avec tout

[1] Mr. Nichols supposes this to be the Augustine College at Ashridge, Bucks, founded by Edmund, Earl of Cornwall, about 1283, but he was unable to trace any part taken by the Black Prince in the affairs of that house. In the last edition of Dugdale's "Monasticon," vol. vi., p. 515, it is stated that a copy of the statutes given to this house about a century after the foundation is preserved at Ashridge House. These therefore may have been given in the times of the Black Prince.

[2] *Cistes, cistæ,* shrines.

[3] Of this collegiate chapel, see the last edition of Dugdale's Monast. vol. vi., p. 1330. In 1356, the Prince had granted to it the advowson of the church of Hare-well, Berkshire.

ce qe appartient à ycelle. Et quant à notre vesselle d'argent,
porce qe nous pensons qe nous receumes avec notre compaigne la
princesse au temps de notre mariage, jusqes à la value de sept centz
marcs d'esterlinges de ļa vesselle de notre dit compaigne, Nous
volons qe elle ait du notre tantqe à la dite value ; et du remenant
de notre dit vesselle nous volons qe notre dit filz ait une partie
covenable pur son estat, solonc l'avis de noz executours. Item,
nous donnons et devisons à notre dit compaigne la princesse la Sale
de Worstede rouge d'egles et griffons embroudez, avec la bordure de
cignes ove testes de dames. Item, nous devisoms à Sire Roger de
Claryndone¹ un lit de soie solonc l'avis de noz executours, avec
tout ce qe appertient au dit lit. Item, nous donnons et devisons
à Sire Robert de Walsham notre confessour un grand lit de rouge
camoca avec noz armes embroudes à checum cornere, et le dit
Camaka est diapreez en li mesmes des armes de Hereford, avec le
celure entiere, curtyns, quissyns, traversin, tapitz de tapiterie, et
tout entierment l'autre apparaille. Item, nous donons et devisons à
mons'r Alayn Cheyne notre lit de camoca blank poudres d'egles
d'azure, c'est assavoir, quilte, dossier, celure entiere, curtyns,
quissyns, traversyn, tapiz, et tout entierement l'autre apparaille. Et
tout le remenant de noz biens et chateux auxi bien vessel d'or et
joialx come touz autere biens ou q'ils soient, outre ceux qe nous
avons dessuz donnes et devisez come dit est, auxi toutez maneres
des dettes à nous duez, en queconqe manere qe ce soit, ensemble
avec touz les issuez et profitz qe purront sourdre et avenir de touz
nos terrez et seignouries, par trois ans a pres ce qe dieux aura fait
sa volunte de nous, lesquelx profitz notre dit seignour et pere nous
a ottroiez pur paier noz dettz, Nous ordenons et devisoms si bien
pur les despenz funerales qe convenront necessairement estre faites
pur nostre estat, come pur acquiter toutez noz dettez par les mains
de noz executours, siqe ils paient primerement les dis despencz
funerales, et apres acquiptent principalement toutez les debtes par
nous loialement dehues. Et cestes choses et perfourmez come dit est
si rien remeint de noz ditz biens et chateux, nous volons qe adonqes
noz ditz executours solonc la quantite enguerdonnent noz povres
servantz egalement selonc leur degreez et desertes si avant come ils
purront avoir informacione de ceux qe en ont melliour cognissance,
si come ils en vorront respondre devant Dieu au jour de Juggement,
ou nul ne sera jugge qe un seul. Et quant à les annuytes qe nous
avons donnes à noz chivalers, esquiers, et autres noz servitours, en
gueredon des services q'ils nous ont fait et des travalx q'ils ont eeu

---

¹ Sir Roger was a natural son of the
Prince, born probably at Clarendon, and
thence named. See Sandford, Geneal.
Hist., p. 189. He was made one of the
knights of the chamber to his half-brother,
Richard II., who granted to him an
annuity of 100*l.* per ann., in 1389. He
bore, *Or*, on a bend *Sa*, three ostrich
feathers *Arg.*, the quills transfixed
through as many scrolls of the first.

entour nous, notre entiere et darriene volunte est qe les dictes
annuytees estoisent, et qe touz ceux asquelx nous les avons donnes
en soient bien et loialement serviz et paiez, solonc le purport de
notre doun et de noz letres qels en ont de nous. Et chargeoms
notre filz Richard sur notre beneson de tenir et confermer à checum
quantqe nous lour avons ensi donnez, et si avant come Dieu nous a
donnez poair sur notre dit filz nous li donnons notre malison s'il
empesche ou soeffre estre empesches en quantqe en il est notre dit
doun. Et de cest notre testament, liquel nous volons estre tenuz et
perfourmez pur notre darreine volunte, fesons et ordenons noz
executors notre trescher et tresame frere d'Espaigne, Duc de
Lancastre, les reverenz peres en Dieu, William Evesqe de
Wyncestre,[1] Johan Evesqe de Bathe,[2] William Evesqe de Saint
Assaphe,[3] notre trescher en Dieu sire Robert de Walsham notre
confessour, Hughe de Segrave Senescal de noz terres, Aleyn de
Stokes, et Johan de Fordham; lesquelx nous prioms, requerons et
chargeoms de executer et acomplir loialment toutez les choses
susdites. En tesmoignance de toutez et checunes les choses susdites
nous avons fait mettre à cest notre testament et darreine volunte
nous prive et secree sealx,[4] et avons auxi commandez notre notair
dessous escript de mettre notre dite darriere volunte et testament en
fourme publique, et de soy souz escriere et le signer et mercher de
son signe acustumez, en tesmoignance de toutez et checunes les
choses dessusdictes.

Et ego, Johannes de Ormeshevede, clericus Karliolensis diocesis
publicus autoritate apostolica Notarius, premissis omnibus et singulis
dum sic ut premittitur sub anno Domini Millesimo, ccc. septua-
gesimo sexto, Indictione quartadecima, pontificatus sanctissimi in
Christo patris et domini nostri domini Gregorii, divina providentia
pape, undecimi, anno sexto, mense, die et loco predictis, predictum
metuendissimum dominum meum principem agerentur et fierent,
presentibus reverendo in Christo patre domino Johanne Herefordensi
Episcopo, dominis Lodewico de Clifford, Nicholao Bonde, et
Nicholao de Scharnesfelde, militibus, et domino Willelmo de

[1] William of Wykeham, Bishop of Winchester, 1367-1404.
[2] John Harewell, Chancellor of Gascony and Chaplain to the Prince, was Bishop of Bath, 1366-1386.
[3] William de Springlington, appointed Bishop of St. Asaph, Feb. 4, 1376, in the same year as the Prince's will is dated.
[4] This expression deserves notice, as showing the distinction between the *Sigillum privatum* and the *secretum*. The seals of the Black Prince are numerous; eight are described by Sir H. Nicolas in his Memoir, Archæologia, vol. xxxi., p. 361, but none of them are identified with the seals above mentioned. The *secree seal* was doubtless the same kind of seal described in other instances as the Privy Signet. The will of Edward III. was sealed "sigillo privato et signeto nostris," with the Great Seal in confirmation. Richard II. on his deposition took from his finger a ring of gold of his own Privy Signet, and put it on the Duke of Lancaster's finger. The will of Henry V. was sealed with the Great and Privy Seals and the Privy Signet.

Walsham clerico, ac aliis pluribus militibus, clericis et scutiferis,
unacum ipsis presens fui eaque sic fieri vidi et audivi, et de mandato
dicti domini mei principis scripsi, et in hanc publicam formam redegi,
signoque meis et nomine consuetis signavi rogatus in fidem et
testimonium omnium premissorum, constat michi notario predicto
de interlinear' harum dictionum—*tout est,* per me fact' superius
approbando.

Probatio dicti Testamenti coram Simone Cantuar' Archiepiscopo, iv. Idus Junii, M.CCC.lxxvj. in camera infra scepta domus
fratrum predicatorum conventus London'.   Nostre Translationis
anno secundo.

A marginal note records that John, Bishop of Durham, and
Alan Stokes, executors of the will, had rendered their account of
the goods, and have a full acquittance, as also another acquittance
from the Prior and Chapter of Christ Church, Canterbury, for the
legacies bequeathed to that church, as appears in the Register of
William (Courtenay) Archbishop of Canterbury, under the
year 1386.

NOTES ON THE WILL OF EDWARD PRINCE OF WALES.

In perusing the foregoing document, so characteristic of the
habitual feelings and usages of the times, and of deep interest in
connection with the history of the Prince, we cannot fail to remark
with surprise the deviation from his last wishes, in regard to the
position of his tomb.   The instructions here minutely detailed were
probably written, from his own dictation, the day previous to his
decease ;[1] and it were only reasonable to conclude, that injunctions,
so solemnly delivered, would have been fulfilled with scrupulous
precision by the executors, even in the most minute particulars.
We are unable to suggest any probable explanation of the deviations
which appear to have taken place : neither the chronicles of the
period, nor the records of the Church of Canterbury, throw light
upon the subject.
        According to the instructions given by the Prince, the corpse on

---

[1] The day given in the printed text of
Walsingham, Hist. Angl. p. 190, as that
of the Prince's death, namely, July 8, is
obviously incorrect.   It is singular that
Mr. Nichols should have followed this
inadvertent error.   Royal Wills, p. 77.
Trinity Sunday in the year 1376 fell on
June 8, and that is the day stated in the
inscription on the tomb to have been that
on which the Prince died.

reaching the church was for a time to be deposited on a hearse, or temporary stage of framework, to be constructed between the high altar and the choir, namely, in that part of the fabric designated by Professor Willis as the presbytery, parallel with the eastern transepts. There it was to remain, surrounded doubtless by the torches and all the customary funeral pageantry of the hearse, until the vigils, masses and divine services were completed. The remains of the Prince were then to be conveyed to the Chapel of our Lady Under Croft and there interred: it is further enjoined that the foot of the tomb should be ten feet from the altar. If, therefore, it may be assumed, as appears highly probable, that the position of that chapel and altar at the period in question was identical with that of the Lady Chapel, of which we now see the remains in the centre of the crypt, it would appear that the site selected by Edward as his last resting-place was situate almost precisely below the high altar in the choir above. It is obvious that the screen-work and decorations of the Chapel, now existing in a very dilapidated condition, are of a period subsequent to that of the Prince's death, and some have attributed the work to Archbishop Morton, towards the close of the fifteenth century. This, it will be remembered, is the Chapel of Our Lady, the surprising wealth of which is described by Erasmus, who, by favour of an introduction from Archbishop Warham, was admitted within the iron screens by which the treasure was strongly guarded.[1]

Here, then, in the obscurity of the crypt, and not far distant from the chantries which the Prince at the time of his marriage had founded in the Under Croft of the south transept, was the spot where Edward enjoined his executors to construct his tomb. It were vain to conjecture, in default of any evidence on the subject, to what cause the deviation from his dying wishes was owing; what difficulties may have been found in the endeavour to carry out the interment in the crypt, or what arguments may have been used by the prior and convent to induce the executors to place the tomb in the more conspicuous and sightly position above, near the shrine of Saint Thomas, in the Chapel of the Trinity, where it is actually to be seen.[2]

[1] Pilgrimage to St. Thomas of Canterbury, translated by John G. Nichols, p. 56. An interior view of this chapel is given by Dart, plate 9, showing also the large slab in the pavement, once encrusted with an effigy of brass, sometimes supposed to cover the burial-place of Archbishop Morton.

[2] The supposition that the tomb of the Prince might have been originally placed in the crypt, and removed subsequently into the Chapel of the Trinity, may appear very improbable. Yet it may be observed, that the iron railings around the monuments of Edward and of Henry IV., are apparently of the same age, and wrought by the same workman, as shown by certain ornamental details. This might seem to sanction a conjecture that the two tombs had been placed there simultaneously, that of the Prince having possibly been moved thither from the Under Croft when the memorial of Henry was erected.

The instructions given by the Prince for the solemn pageant present a striking and characteristic picture of his obsequies, as the procession passed through the West Gate and along the High Street towards the Cathedral. He enjoined that two chargers (*dextrarii*), with trappings of his arms and badges, and two men accoutred in his panoply and wearing his helms, should precede the corpse. One *"cheval de dule"* is often mentioned in the splendid funerals of former times. In this instance there were two; one of them bearing the equipment of war, with the quarterly bearings of France and England, as seen upon the effigy of Edward and upon the embroidered surcoat still suspended over it. The array of the second was directed to be *"pur la paix, de noz bages des plumes d'ostruce;"* namely, that which the Prince had used in the lists and in the chivalrous exercises of arms distinguished from actual warfare, and termed *hastiludia pacifica*, or "justes of peas."[1] Four sable banners of the same suit, with the ostrich plumes, accompanied this noble pageant, and behind the war-horse followed a man armed, bearing a penon, likewise charged with ostrich plumes. This was the smaller flag, or streamer, attached to the warrior's lance, and it may here, probably, be regarded as representing that actually carried in the field by the Prince.[2]

There can be little doubt that on the beam above the Prince's tomb at Canterbury there were originally placed two distinct atchievements, composed of the actual accoutrements, *"pur la guerre"* and *"pur la paix,"* which had figured in these remarkable funeral impersonations. It was the custom, it may be observed, when the courser and armour of the deceased formed part of a funeral procession, that the former was regarded as a mortuary due to the church in which the obsequies were performed, but the armour was usually hung up near the tomb. There may still be noticed two iron standards on the beam above mentioned, now bearing the few remaining reliques of these atchievements. One of these standards probably supported the embroidered armorial surcoat, or "coat of worship," by which Edward had been distinguished in the battle-field, charged with the bearings of France and England, his helm, his shield of war, likewise displaying the same heraldic ensigns, and the other appliances of actual warfare. The second trophy was doubtless composed of his accoutrements for the joust, characterised not by the proper charges of heraldry, but by

[1] See the curious documents and memoir relating to the peaceable Justs or Tiltings of the Middle Ages, by Mr. Douce, Archæologia, vol. xvii., p. 290.

[2] A remarkable illustration of these instructions in Edward's Will is supplied by an illumination in the Metrical History of the Deposition of Richard II., where that king appears with a black surcoat powdered with ostrich plumes, his horse in trappings of the same, and a penon of the like badge carried behind him. Richard is represented in the act of conferring knighthood on Henry of Monmouth. Archæologia, vol. xx., p. 32, Plate II.

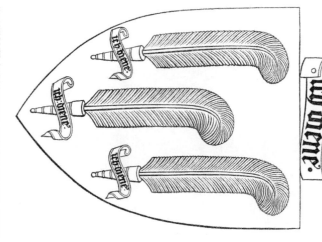
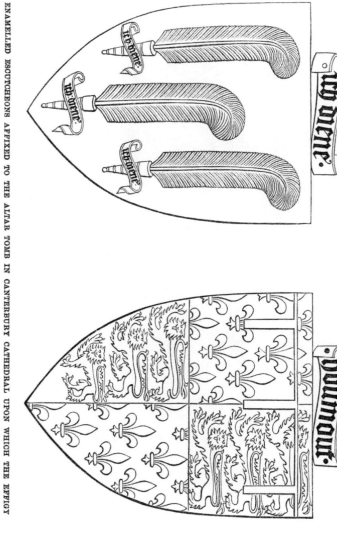

ENAMELLED ESCUTCHEONS AFFIXED TO THE ALTAR TOMB IN CANTERBURY CATHEDRAL UPON WHICH THE EFFIGY

OF EDWARD THE BLACK PRINCE IS PLACED.

To face p. 141.

REPRESENTATION OF EDWARD THE BLACK PRINCE, KNEELING IN VENERATION
OF THE HOLY TRINITY.

From a metal plate preserved in the British Museum.
(Of the same dimension as the original.)

his favourite badge of the ostrich feather, the origin of which still perplexes the antiquary. Conformably, moreover, to such arrangement of the twofold atchievements over the tomb, the escutcheons affixed to its sides are alternately of war and peace; namely, charged with the quarterly bearing, and with the feathers on a sable field.

In regard to these richly enamelled escutcheons the Prince's instructions were given with much precision. They were to be twelve in number, each a foot wide, formed of latten or hard brass; six being "*de nos armez entiers,*" and the remainder of ostrich feathers; "*et qe sur chacun escuchon soit escript, c'est assaveir sur cellez de noz armez et sur les autres des plumes d'ostruce,—Houmout.*" Here, again, the tomb presents a perplexing discrepancy from the letter of the will, which Sir Harris Nicolas, Mr. Planché, and other writers have noticed. The escutcheons of arms are actually surmounted by labels inscribed "*houmout,*" whilst those with ostrich feathers have the motto, "*ich diene,*" not mentioned in the Prince's injunctions. It must, however, be considered that the text of his will has not been obtained from the original instrument, (no longer, probably, in existence,) but from a transcript in Archbishop Sudbury's Register, and the supposition seems probable that the copier may have inadvertently omitted the words, "*ich diene,*" after "*noz armez,*" and the sentence as it now stands appears incomplete. Still, even if this conjecture be admitted, the mottos over the alternate escutcheons are transposed, as compared with the Prince's directions.

The origin and import of these mottos have been largely discussed: it may suffice to refer to the arguments advanced by the late Sir Harris Nicolas and by Mr. Planché, Archæologia, vol. xxxi. pp. 357, 372 and vol. xxxii., p. 69.[1] The most remarkable fact connected with this subject is that the Prince actually used these mottos as a sign manual; thus, "*De par homout Ich dene,*" the mottos being written one over the other, and enclosed within a line traced around them. This interesting signature was first noticed in a communication to the Spalding Society, some years since, and a facsimile engraved in Mr. Nichols' "Bibliotheca Topographica." Another document thus signed, and preserved in the Tower, was communicated by Mr. Hardy to the late Sir Harris Nicolas. It has been published in his "Memoir on the Badges and Mottos of the Prince of Wales," before cited.[2] I am indebted to the obliging courtesy of the Viscount Mahon,

[1] See also Mr. Planché's "History of British Costume," p. 178.

[2] Archæologia, vol. xxxi. pp. 358, 381. The document in the Tower which bears this signature is dated April 25, 1370, being a warrant granting to John de Esquet fifty marks per annum out of the Exchequer of Chester. The document given in Bibl. Topog. vol. iii. p. 90, seems not to have been noticed by Sir Harris Nicolas. It is described as a grant of twenty marks per ann. to John de Esquet, dated 34 Edw. III. (1360-61.)

President of the Society of Antiquaries, whose kindness enables me to place before the reader of these notes a faithful representation of the Prince's signature, as also the accompanying illustrations of the subject under consideration, being woodcuts prepared for the Memoirs, by Sir Harris Nicolas, in the Archæologia.

A brief notice of the interesting reliques which still remain over the tomb may here be acceptable.[1]   The chief of these is the gamboised jupon of one pile crimson velvet, with short sleeves, somewhat like the tabard of the herald, but laced up the back ; the foundation of the garment being of buckram, stuffed with cotton, and quilted in longitudinal ribs. The sleeves, as well as both front and back, of this coat display the quarterly bearing, the *fleurs-de-lys* (*semées*) and lions being embroidered in gold.   Recently it has been lined with leather, for its better preservation.   The shield is of wood, covered with moulded leather, or *cuir bouilli*, wrought with singular skill, so that the *fleurs de lys* and lions of the quarterly bearing which it displays preserve the sharpness of finish and bold relief in remarkable perfection.   The iron conical-topped helm is similar in form to that placed under the head of the effigy; its original lining of leather may be seen, a proof of its having been actually intended for use ; it has, besides the narrow *ocularia,* or transverse apertures for sight, a number of small holes pierced on the right side in front, probably to give air ; they are arranged in form of a crown.   Upon the red chapeau, or cap of estate, lined with velvet, with the ermined fore-part turned up, was placed the gilded lion which formed the crest.   This is hollow, and constructed of some light substance, stated to be pasteboard, coated with a plastic composition, on which the shaggy locks of the lion's skin were formed by means of a mould.   The chapeau and crest were, it is said, detached from the helm some years since, on the occasion of a visit by the Duchess of Kent to Canterbury.   The scabbard of red leather, with gilt studs, and a fragment of the belt of thick cloth, with a single

[1] I regret much that I was unable to examine these highly interesting reliques. The following particulars are from the notes by Mr. Kempe in the letterpress of Stothard's Effigies, where admirable representations of these objects are given : a short account by Mr. J. Gough Nichols, in Gent. Mag. xxii. p. 384, and Mr. Hartshorne's Memoir on Mediæval Embroidery, Archæological Journal, vol. iii. pp. 326, 327.

buckle, alone remain; it has been stated, on what authority I have not been able to ascertain, that the sword was carried away by Cromwell. The gauntlets are of brass, differing only from those of the effigy in having been ornamented with small lions riveted upon the knuckles; the leather which appears on the inside is worked up the sides of the fingers with silk.[1] The fact that these gauntlets are of brass may deserve notice, as suggesting the probability that the entire suit which served as a model for the effigy of the Prince was of that metal.

A representation has happily been preserved of another relique, originally part of the funeral atchievements of the Black Prince, and which may have formed a portion of the accoutrements "*pur la paix.*" Edmund Bolton, in his "Elements of Armories," printed in 1610, remarks that the ancient fashion of shields was triangular, namely, that of the shield still to be seen over the Prince's tomb, but that it was not the only form, and he gives two examples, one being the "honorary" shield belonging to the most renowned Edward, Prince of Wales, whose tomb is in the Cathedral Church in Canterbury. "There (beside his quilted coat-armour with halfe-sleeves, taberd-fashion, and his triangular sheild, both of them painted with the royall armories of our kings, and differenced with silver labels) hangs this kinde of Pavis or Targat,[2] curiously (for those times) embost, and painted, the scucheon in the bosse beeing worne out, and the Armes (which it seems were the same with his coate-armour, and not any peculiar devise) defaced, and is altogether of the same kinde with that, upon which (Froisard reports) the dead body of the Lord Robert of Duras, and nephew to the Cardinall of Pierregourt was laid, and sent unto that Cardinall, from the battell of Poictiers, where the Blacke Prince obtained a victorie, the renowne whereof is immortall."

The form of this Pavis is ovoid, that is, an oval narrowing towards the bottom: in the middle is a circle, apparently designated by Bolton as "the bosse," the diameter of which is considerably more than half the width of the shield at that part; this circle encloses an escutcheon of the arms of France and England quarterly, with a label of three points. All the rest of the shield around this circle is

---

[1] It is to be regretted that the curious lioncels on the Prince's gauntlets should have been detached by "Collectors." One was shown me at Canterbury, now in private hands, which I much desire were deposited in the Library, in Dr. Bargrave's cabinet of coins and antiquities, or in some other place of safe custody. Another was in the possession of a Kentish collector, whose stores were dispersed by public auction a few years since.

[2] A wood-cut is introduced here in the description. "Elements of Armories," p. 67. It has been copied in Brayley's "Graphic Illustrator," p. 128. It is remarkable that Bolton should assert that the arms both on the quilted coat and triangular shield were differenced by a label of silver; none is now to be seen; the silver may possibly have become effaced. The label appears on the shield figured by Bolton, as also on the effigy.

diapered with a trailing or foliated ornament.[1] Unfortunately, Bolton has not recorded the dimension of this shield, but it may probably be concluded from his comparing it with the *"targe,"* mentioned by Froissart, upon which the corpse of Duras was conveyed, that it was of larger proportions than the ordinary triangular war-shield.

The Holy Trinity, it has been remarked, was regarded with especial veneration by the Black Prince. In the Ordinance of the chantries founded at Canterbury, printed in this volume, p. 128, the Prince states his purpose to be—*" ad honorem Sancte Trinitatis, quam peculiari devocione semper colimus."* On the wooden tester, beneath which his effigy is placed, a very curious painting in distemper may still be discerned, representing the Holy Trinity; according to the usual conventional symbolism the Supreme Being is here pourtrayed seated on the rainbow and holding a crucifix, the foot of which is fixed on a terraqueous globe. The four angles contain the Evangelistic symbols. An interesting illustration of the Prince's peculiar veneration for the Holy Trinity is supplied by the curious metal badge, preserved in the British Museum, and of which Sir Harris Nicolas has given a representation in his "Observations on the Institution of the Order of the Garter."[2] On this relique the Prince appears kneeling before a figure of the Almighty, holding a crucifix, almost identical in design with the painting above mentioned. His gauntlets lie on the ground before him, he is bare-headed, the crested helm being held by an angel standing behind, and above is seen another angel issuing from the clouds, and holding his shield, charged with the arms of France and England, differenced by a label. The whole is surrounded by a Garter, inscribed ᚻonp soot ke mal p pense. It is remarkable that on this plate, as also in the painting on the tester of the tomb, the dove, usually introduced to symbolise the third person of the Holy Trinity, does not appear.

There are other matters comprised in this remarkable Will to which time does not now allow me to advert. It appeared very desirable to give with greater accuracy than had hitherto been done, the text of a document so essential to the illustration of the History of Edward, as connected with the Cathedral Church of Canterbury.[3]

A. W.

---

[1] A jousting-shield in the Goodrich Court Armory is decorated with gilt foliage in very similar style. See Skelton's Illustrations, vol. i., pl. xii.

[2] Archæologia, vol. xxxi., p. 141. This object is a casting in pewter or mixed white metal, from a mould probably intended for making badges, which may have been worn by the Prince's attendants affixed to the dress.

[3] It is with pleasure that I here acknowledge the courtesy of the Rev. J. Thomas, Librarian to the Archbishop, in giving facilities for the collation of the transcript of the Prince's Will preserved amongst the Records at Lambeth Palace.

THE SHRINE

S. THOMAS OF CANTERBURY.

The authorities for the subject of the following Essay are—besides the chroniclers and historians of the time, and the ordinary text-books of Canterbury antiquities, Somner, Batteley, Hasted, and Willis :—(I.) Erasmus's Pilgrimage to Canterbury and Walsingham, as edited with great care and copious illustrations by Mr. Nichols; (II.) Tyrwhitt's Chaucer, and the Supplementary Tale, edited by Mr. Wright, in the twenty-sixth volume of the Percy Society. To these I have added, in an Appendix, extracts from sources less generally accessible. (1.) A MS. history of Canterbury Cathedral, in Norman French, entitled "Polistoire," now in the British Museum, of the time of Edward II. (2.) The Narrative of the Bohemian Embassy, in the reign of Edward IV. (3.) The MS. Defence of Henry VIII., by William Thomas, of the time of Edward VI., in the British Museum. (4.) Some few notices of the Shrine in the Archives of Canterbury Cathedral; which last have been collected and annotated by Mr. Albert Way, who has also added notes on the Pilgrims' Road, and on the Pilgrimage of John of France. I have also appended in this edition a note, by Mr. George Austin, of Canterbury, on the crescent above the Shrine, and on the representation of the story of Becket's miracles in the stained glass of the Cathedral.

THE SHRINE OF BECKET.

AMONGST the many treasures of art and of devotion, which once adorned or which still adorn the metropolitical Cathedral, the one point to which, for more than three centuries, the attention of every stranger who entered its gates was directed, was the Shrine of St. Thomas of Canterbury. And although that Shrine, with the special feelings of reverence of which it was once the centre, has long passed away, yet there is still sufficient interest around its ancient site—there is still sufficient instruction in its eventful history—to require a full narrative of its rise, its progress, and its fall, in any historical records of the great Cathedral of which in the eyes of England it successively formed the support, the glory, and the disgrace. Such a narrative, worthily told, would be far more than a mere investigation of local antiquities. It would be a page in one of the most curious chapters of the history of the human mind —it would give us a strange insight into the interior working of the ancient monastic and ecclesiastical system, in one of the aspects in which it least resembles anything which we now see around us, either for good or for evil ; it would enable us to be present at some of the most gorgeous spectacles and to meet some of the most remarkable characters of mediæval times ; it would help us to appreciate more comprehensively and more clearly, some of the main causes and effects of the Reformation.

In order to understand this singular story, we must first go back to the state of Canterbury and its Cathedral in the times preceding not only the Shrine itself, but the event of which it was the memorial. Canterbury, from

the time of Augustine, had been the chief city of the
English Church. But it had not acquired an European
celebrity ; and the comparative splendour which it had
enjoyed during the reign of Ethelbert as capital of a
large part of Britain, had entirely passed away before the
greater claims of Winchester and of London. And even
in the city of Canterbury, the Cathedral was not the chief
ecclesiastical edifice. There was, we must remember,
close outside the walls, the great Abbey and church of
St. Augustine ; and we can hardly doubt that here, as in
many foreign cities, the church of the patron saint was
regarded as a more sacred and important edifice than
the church attached to the episcopal see. St. Zeno at
Verona, and St. Apollinaris at Ravenna, outshine the
cathedrals of both those ancient cities. The Basilica of
St. Mark at Venice, though only the private chapel of the.
Ducal Palace, has, ever since its claim to possess the relics of
the Evangelist of Alexandria, thrown into the most distant
shade the seat of the Patriarchate, in the obscure church
of St. Peter in the little island beyond the Arsenal. The
Basilica of St. John Lateran, though literally the metropolitan Cathedral of the metropolitan city of Christendom,
though containing the see and chair of the Roman Pontiffs,
though the mother and head of all the churches, with the
princes of Europe for the members of its Chapter, has
been long superseded in grandeur and in sanctity by the
august dome which in a remote corner of the city rises
over the grave of the Apostle St. Peter. In two celebrated
instances the Cathedral has, as in the case of Canterbury,
from accidental causes, overtaken the church of the original
saint. Milan Cathedral has, from Galeazzo Visconti's
efforts to expiate his enormous crimes, and from the
popular devotion to St. Carlo Borromeo, more than
succeeded in eclipsing the ancient church of St. Ambrose.
Rheims—the Canterbury of France—furnishes a still more
exact parallel. The Abbey Church of St. Remy and the
Cathedral at the two extremities of the city, are the
precise counterparts of Christ Church and of St. Augustine's Abbey in the first Christian city of England.
The present magnificence of Rheims Cathedral as its

architecture at once reveals, dates from a later period
than the simple but impressive edifice which encloses
the shrine of the patron saint, and shows that there was
a time when the distinction conferred on the Cathedral
by the coronation of the French kings, had not yet rivalled
the glory of St. Remigius, the Apostle of the Franks.
These instances, to which many more might be added,
exemplify the feeling which, in the early days of
Canterbury, placed the monastery of St. Augustine above
the monastery of Christ Church. The former was an
Abbey, headed by a powerful dignitary who, in any
gathering of the Benedictine Order, ranked next after the
Abbot of Monte Casino. The latter was but a Priory,
under the superintendence of the Archbishop, whose
occupations usually made him a non-resident, and therefore not necessarily bound up with the interests of the
institution, of which he was but the nominal head.

Besides this natural pre-eminence, so to speak, of the
original church of Augustine over that in which his see
was established by Ethelbert, there was another peculiarity
which seemed at one time likely to perpetuate its superiority. We have seen how the position of the abbey as
the burial-place of Augustine was determined by the usages
which he brought with him from Italy.[1] It was outside
the walls, and within its extra-mural precincts alone the
bodies of the illustrious dead could be deposited. To our
notions this would seem, perhaps, of trifling importance
in considering the probable fortunes either of an edifice or
of an institution. But it was not so then; and we shall
but imperfectly understand the history not only of the
particular subject on which we are now engaged, but of
the whole period of the Middle Ages, unless we bear in mind
the vast importance which, from the fifth century onwards
till the fifteenth, was ascribed to the possession of relics.

No doubt this feeling had a just and natural origin, so
far as it was founded on the desire to retain the memorials
of those honoured in former times. And it is almost as
unreasonable to deprive our great cathedrals of this
legitimate source of interest, where no sanitary objections

[1] See "Landing of Augustine," p. 24.

exist, as it was formerly to insist upon promiscuous interment within every church to the manifest injury of the living. But, however excellent this sentiment may be in itself, it was in the Middle Ages exaggerated beyond all due bounds, by the peculiar reverence which at that time attached to the corporeal elements and particles (so to speak) of religious objects. To this, too, we must add, as has been well remarked by a sagacious observer of ancient and modern usages, the concentration of all those feelings and tastes which now expend themselves on collections of pictures, of statues, of books, of manuscripts, of curiosities of all kinds, but which then found their vent in this one only department. It became a mania, such as never was witnessed before or since. The traces which still exist in some Roman Catholic countries are mere shadows of what is past. In the times preceding or immediately following the Christian era, it hardly existed at all. But at the time of the foundation of the two monasteries of Canterbury, and nearly through the whole period which we have now to consider, its influence was amongst the most powerful motives by which the mind of Europe was agitated. Hence the strange practice of dismembering the bodies of saints,—a bone here, a heart there, a head here—which painfully neutralises the religious and historical effect of even the most authentic and the most sacred graves in Christendom. Hence the still stranger practice of the invention and sale of relics, which throws such doubt on the genuineness of all. Hence the monstrous incongruities, often repeated, of the same relics in different shrines. Hence, the rivalry, the thefts, the commerce, of these articles of sacred merchandise, especially between institutions whose jealousy was increased by neighbourhood, as was the case with the two monasteries of Canterbury.

According to the rule just noticed, no King of Kent, no Archbishop of Canterbury, however illustrious in life or holy in death, could be interred within the precincts of the Cathedral, enclosed as it was by the city walls. Not only Augustine and Ethelbert, but Laurence, the honoured successor of Augustine, who had reconverted the apostate Eadbald, and Theodore of Tarsus, fellow-townsman of the

Apostle of the Gentiles, and first teacher of Greek learning in England, were laid beneath the shadow of St. Augustine's Abbey. As far as human prescience could extend, a long succession of sainted men was thus secured to the rival monastery, and the inmates of the Cathedral were doomed to lament the hard fate that made over to their neighbours treasures that seemed peculiarly their own. Thus passed away the eight first primates. At last an Archbishop arose, in whom the spirit of attachment to the monastery of which he was the authorised head prevailed over the deference due to the usages and example of the founder of his see. Cuthbert, the ninth Archbishop, determined by a bold stroke to break through the precedent by leaving his bones to his own Cathedral. Secretly during his lifetime he prepared a document, to which he procured the sanction of the King of Kent, and of the Pope, authorising this important deviation. And when at last he felt his end approaching, he gathered the monks of Christ Church round him, delivered the warrant into their hands, and adjured them not to toll the Cathedral bell till the third day after his death and burial. The order was gladly obeyed ; the body was safely interred within the Cathedral precincts, and not till the third day was the knell sounded which summoned the monks of St. Augustine's Abbey, with ther Abbot Aldhelm at their head, to claim their accustomed prey. They were met at the gates of the Priory with the startling intelligence that the Archbishop was duly buried, and their indignant remonstances were stopped by the fatal compact. There was one more attempt made under Jambert, the next Abbot, to carry off the body of the next Archbishop at the head of an armed mob. But the battle was won, and from that time, with the single exception of Jambert, who was afterwards himself raised from the Abbacy of St. Augustine's to the archiepiscopal see, and who could not but remember the claims which he had himself so strongly defended, no Primate has been interred within the walls of St. Augustine's, and, till the epoch of the Reformation, not more than six outside the precincts of the Cathedral.[1]

[1] Thorn, 1773.

It has been thought worth while to relate at length this curious story, partly as an illustration of the relic-worship of the time, partly also as a necessary step in the history of the Cathedral, and of that especial portion of it now before us. But for the intervention of Cuthbert, the greatest source of power which the Cathedral was ever to claim, would never have fallen to its share. The change indeed immediately began to tell. Hitherto the monks of the Cathedral had been compelled to content themselves with such fragments as they could beg or steal from other churches, but now the vacant spaces were filled with a goodly array, not only of illustrious prelates, but even of canonised saints. Not only did the Cathedral cover the graves of ancient Saxon primates, and of Lanfranc, the founder of the Anglo-Norman hierarchy—but also those of the confessor St. Dunstan, of the martyr St. Alphege, of the great theologian, St. Anselm. To those three tombs —now almost entirely vanished—the monks of Christ Church would doubtless have pointed in the beginning of the reign of Henry II. as the crowning ornaments of their Cathedral, and the monks of St. Augustine would have confessed with a sigh that the artifice of Cuthbert had to a certain extent succeeded.

Still there was yet no decided superiority of one over the other,—and neither edifice could be said to possess a shrine of European, hardly even of British celebrity. It is probable that St. Cuthbert at Durham, St. Wilfrid at Ripon, St. Edmund in East Anglia, equalled in the eyes of most Englishmen the claims of any saints buried in the metropolitical city. But the great event of which Canterbury was the scene on the 29th of December, 1170, at once rivetted upon it the thoughts, not only of England, but of Christendom. A Saint—so it was then almost universally believed—a saint of unparalleled sanctity had fallen — in the church of which he was Primate, a martyr for its rights ; and his blood, his remains, were in the possession of that church, as an inalienable treasure for ever. It was believed that a new burst of miraculous powers, such as had been suspended for many generations, had broken out at the tomb ; and the contemporary monk Benedict fills a volume with extraordinary cures, real or imaginary, wrought within a very few years after the "Martyrdom." Far and wide the fame of "St. Thomas of Canterbury" spread. Other English saints, however great their local celebrity, were for the most part not known beyond the limits of Britain. No churches in foreign parts knew the names even of St. Cuthbert of Durham or St. Edmund of Bury. But there is probably no country in Europe which does not exhibit traces of Becket. In Rome, the chapel of the English College marks the site of the ancient church dedicated to him, and the relics attesting his martyrdom are laid up in the Basilica of St. Maria Maggiore beside the cradle of Bethlehem. In Verona, the Church of San Thomaso Cantuariense contains a tooth, and did contain till recently part of his much contested skull. A portion of an arm is still shown to inquiring travellers in a convent at Florence : at Lisbon, in the time of Fuller, both arms were exhibited in the English nunnery. In France, the scene of his exile, his history may be tracked again and again. On the heights of Fourvières, overlooking the city of Lyons, is to be seen the chapel of which it is told, that it was dedicated to St. Thomas of Canterbury ; because when there, four years before his death, being asked as he walked on the terraced bank of the river underneath, to whom the chapel should be dedicated, he replied, "To the next martyr," on which his companion remarked, "Perhaps then to you." The same story with the same issue is also told at St. Lo in Normandy. In Sens the vestments in which he officiated [1] and an ancient altar at which he said mass, are exhibited in the Cathedral ; and the old convent at St. Colomb, where he resided, is pointed out in the city. In the magnificent windows of Chartres, of Sens, and of St. Ouen, the story of his life holds a conspicuous place. Even far away in Syria, "St. Thomas" was not forgotten by the crusading army. His name was inscribed on the banner of Archbishop Baldwin, at Acre. William, chaplain of the Dean

[1] These vestments are curious in one point of view, as confirming the account of his great stature. (See " Murder of Becket," p. 54.) On the feast of " St. Thomas" they are worn for that one day by the officiating priest. The tallest priest is always selected—and, even then, they have to be pinned up.

of St. Paul's, on his voyage thither, made a vow that if he entered the place in safety, he would build there a chapel to the "Martyr," with an adjoining cemetery to bury the departed.   The city was taken, and the vow accomplished. William passed his life within the precincts of his church, engaged as Prior in the pious work of interring the dead. King Richard, at the same time and place, founded an Order of St. Thomas under the jurisdiction of the Templars. And from these circumstances, one of the names by which the Saint henceforward was most frequently known, was "Thomas Acrensis," or "St. Thomas of Acon or Acre." [1]

To trace his churches and memorials through the British dominions would be an endless labour.   In Scotland, within seven years from the murder, the wild rocks of Aberbrothock were crowned by the stately abbey dedicated to his memory by William the Lion, partly, it would seem, from an early friendship contracted with the Archbishop at Henry's court, partly from a lively sense of the Martyr's power in bringing about his defeat and capture at Alnwick.[2]   In the rough border-land between the two kingdoms, no oath was considered so binding in the thirteenth century, as one which was sworn upon "the holy mysteries" and "the sword of St. Thomas."   This, in all probability, was the sword which Hugh de Moreville wore on the fatal day, and which, being preserved in his native province, thus obtained the same kind of honour in the north as that of Richard Le Bret in the south, and was long regarded as the chief glory of Carlisle Cathedral.[3] In England there was hardly a county which did not possess some church or convent connected with his name. At Derby, at Warwick, at St. Albans, were portions of his dress ; at Chester his girdle, at Alnwick his cup, at Bury his penknife and boots, at Windsor and Peterborough drops of his blood.[4]

[1] Maitland's London, p. 885; Diceto, 654 ; Mills' Crusades, vol. ii. p. 89.

[2] See "Murder of Becket," pp. 92, 93.   The authorities for William's motives in the foundation of the Abbey are given in the "Registrum vetus de Aberbrothoc," printed by the Bannatyne Club, Pref., p. 12.

[3] See "Murder of Becket," p. 81, and the account of the oath of Robert

Bruce at Carlisle, in Holinshed, ii., 523, and the brief "History of Carlisle Cathedral," by its present excellent Dean, p. 30.   The above statement is, no doubt, the mode of reconciling the difficulty about the two swords stated in Pegge, Beauchief Abbey, p. 6.

[4] See Pegge's Beauchief, p. 3; Nichols' Erasmus, 229.

The priory of Woodspring on the Bristol Channel, the Abbey of Beauchief in Derbyshire, were direct expiations of the crime.[1] The very name of the latter was traced by popular, though probably erroneous belief, to its connexion with the "Bellum caput," or "Beautiful head" of the slaughtered Archbishop.[2] London was crowded with memorials of its illustrious citizen. The chapel of St. Thomas of Acre, now merged in the Mercers' Hall, marked the place of his birth, and formed one of the chief stations in the procession of the Lord Mayor.[3] The chapel which guarded the ancient London Bridge was dedicated to St. Thomas. The solitary vacant niche, which is seen in the front of Lambeth Palace facing the river, was once filled by a statue of the great Primate, to which the watermen of the Thames doffed their caps as they rowed by in their countless barges.

But Canterbury was of course the centre of all. St. Augustine's still stood proudly aloof, and was satisfied with the glory of Ethelbert's baptism, which appears on its ancient seals; but the arms of the City and of the Chapter represented "the Martyrdom;" and the very name of "Christ Church" or of "the Holy Trinity," by which the Cathedral was properly designated, was in popular usage merged in that of "The Church of St. Thomas."[4]

For the few years immediately succeeding his death, there was no regular shrine. The popular enthusiam still clung to the two spots immediately connected with the murder. The transept in which he died, within five years from that time acquired the name by which it has ever since been known, "The Martyrdom."[5] This spot, and its subsequent alterations, have been already described. The flagstone on which his skull was fractured, and the solid corner of masonry in front of which he fell, are probably the only parts which remain unchanged. But against that corner may still be seen the marks of the space where was erected the wooden altar, which continued in its original simplicity through all the sub-

[1] See "Murder of Becket," pp. 80, 83.
[2] See Pegge's Beauchief Abbey, pp. 6—20. He proves that the ground on which the abbey stands was called Beauchief, or the *Beautiful Headland*, prior to the building of the convent.
[3] Maitland's London, 885.
[4] See Nichols' Erasmus, p. 110; Somner's Canterbury, p. 18.
[5] See Garnier, 76, and "Murder of Becket," p. 64.

sequent magnificence of the church till the time of the
Reformation, probably the identical memorial erected in
the first haste of enthusiasm after the reopening of the
Cathedral for worship in 1172. It was called the altar
of "The Martyrdom," or more commonly, the altar of
"The Sword's point," ("Altare ad Punctum Ensis,") from
the circumstance that in a wooden chest placed upon
it was preserved the fragment of Le Bret's sword, which
had been left on the pavement after accomplishing its
bloody work. There was also a portion of the brains
kept under a piece of rock crystal [1] surmounting this
shrine. To this altar a regular keeper was appointed
from among the monks, under the name of "Custos
Martyrii." In the first fervour of enthusiam for the relics
of St. Thomas, even this guarantee was inadequate. Two
memorable acts of plunder are recorded within the first
six years, curiously illustrative of the prevalent passion
for such objects. The first was accomplished by Benedict,
a monk of Christ Church, probably the most distinguished of his body ; who was in 1176 appointed Abbot
of Peterborough. Finding that great establishment almost
entirely destitute of relics, he returned to his own cathedral and carried off with him the flagstones immediately
surrounding the sacred spot, with which he formed two
altars in the conventual church of his new appointment,
besides two vases of blood and parts of Becket's clothing.[2]
The other instance is still more remarkable. The keeper
of the "Altar of the Martyrdom" at that time was Roger.
The monks of St. Augustine's Abbey offered to him (and
their chronicler [3] is not ashamed to boast of the success
of the experiment, though affecting to despise any addition to their own ancient store), no less an inducement
than the vacant abbacy, in the hope of obtaining through
his means for their church a portion of the remains of
the sacred skull, which had been specially committed to
his trust. He carried off the prize to the rival establishment, and was rewarded accordingly.

---

[1] See note F.

[2] Robert of Swaffham in Hist. Anglic.,
p. 101. Benedict also built a chapel to
St. Thomas, by the gateway of the Precincts of Peterborough. This still remains, and is now used as the Cathedral
school.

[3] Thorne, 1176.

Next to the actual scene of the murder, the object which this event invested with especial sanctity was the tomb in which his remains were deposited in the crypt [1] behind the Altar of the Virgin. It was to this spot that the first great rush of pilgrims was made when the church was reopened in 1172, and it was here that Henry performed his penance.[2]   Hither, on the 21st of August, 1179, came the first King of France who ever set foot on the shores of England, Louis VII., having, as he believed, received his son back from a dangerous illness through the Saint's intercession.   He knelt by the tomb, and offered upon it the celebrated jewel, of which more shall be said hereafter, as also his own rich cup of gold.   To the monks he gave a hundred measures of wine, to be payed yearly at Poissy, as well as exemption of toll, tax, and tallage,[3] on going to or from his domains, and was himself, after passing a night in prayers at the tomb, admitted to the fraternity of the monastery in the Chapter House.   It was on this occasion (such was the popular belief of the Dover seamen) that he asked and obtained from the Saint (" because he was very fearful of the water,"), that " neither he nor any others that crossed over from Dover to Witsand, should suffer any manner of loss or shipwreck."[4]   Richard's first act on landing at Sandwich, after his return from Palestine, was to walk all the way to Canterbury to give thanks " to God and St. Thomas " for his deliverance.[5]   There also came John in great state immediately after his coronation.[6]   The spot was always regarded with reverence, and known by the name of " The Tomb," with a special keeper, and it would probably have invested the whole crypt with its own peculiar sacredness, and rendered it,—like that of Chartres in old times,—the most important part of the church, but for an accidental train of circumstances which led to the erection of the great Shrine whose history is now to be unfolded.

[1] See "Murder of Becket," p. 73. On one occasion the body was removed to a wooden chest in fear of an assault from the old enemies of Becket, who were thought to be lurking armed about the church for that purpose. But they were foiled by the vigilance of the monks, and by a miraculous storm.— Benedict de Mirac. i. 50.
[2] See " Murder of Becket," p. 91.
[3] Diceto, 604; Gervase, 1455; Stow, 155; Holinshed, ii. 178.
[4] Lambard's Kent, p. 129.
[5] Brompton, 1257.   [6] Diceto, 706.

It was nearly four years after the murder, on the 5th of September, 1174, that a fire broke out in the Cathedral which reduced the choir—hitherto its chief architectural glory—to ashes. The grief of the people is described in terms which (as has been before observed[1]) show how closely the expressions of mediæval feeling resembled what can now only be seen in Italy or the East—" They tore their hair ; they beat the walls and pavement of the Church with their shoulders and the palms of their hands ; they uttered tremendous curses against God and his saints,—even the patron saint of the Church ; they wished they had rather have died than seen such a day." How far more like the description of a Neapolitan mob in disappointment at the slow liquefaction of the blood of St. Januarius, than of the citizens of a quiet cathedral town in the county of Kent. The monks, though appalled by the calamity for a time, soon recovered themselves ; workmen and architects, French and English, were procured ; and, amongst the former, William, from the city of Sens, so familiar to all Canterbury at that period as the scene of Becket's exile. No observant traveller can have seen the two cathedrals without remarking how closely the details of William's workmanship at Canterbury were suggested by his recollections of his own church at Sens, built a short time before. The forms of the pillars, the vaulting of the roof, even the very bars and patterns of the windows are almost identical. It is needless to go into the story of the restoration, thoroughly worked out as it has been by Professor Willis in his " Architectural History of Canterbury Cathedral ;" but it is important to observe, in the contemporary account preserved to us,[2] how the position and the removal of the various relics is the principal object, if not in the mind of the architect, at least of the monks who employed him. It was so even for the lesser and older relics—much more then for the greater and more recent treasure for which they were to provide a fitting abode, and through which they were daily obtaining those vast pecuniary resources that alone could have enabled them to rebuild the church on its

[1] See "Murder of Becket," p. 56.
[2] Gervase, in the "Decem Scriptores,"
and Professor Willis's "History of Canterbury Cathedral," c. 3.

present splendid scale. The French architect had unfortunately met with an accident which disabled him from continuing his operations. After a vain struggle to superintend the works by being carried round the Church in a litter, he was compelled to surrender the task to a namesake, an Englishman, and it is to him that we owe the design of that part of the Cathedral which was destined to receive the sacred Shrine.

To those who are unacquainted with the fixed concatenation of ideas, if one may so speak, which guided the arrangement of these matters at a time when they occupied so prominent a place in the thoughts of men, it might seem a point of comparative indifference where the Tomb of the Patron Saint was to be erected. But it was not so in the age of which we speak. It is important to observe, that in this respect, a marked difference prevailed between the ancient and southern practice on the one hand, and the mediæval and northern practice on the other hand. In Italy the bones of a saint or martyr were almost invariably deposited either beneath or immediately in front of the altar. Partly, no doubt, this arose from the Apocalyptic image of the souls crying from beneath the altar; chiefly from the fact, that in the original burial-places of the catacombs, the altar, or table of the Eucharistic feast, was erected over the grave of some illustrious saint, so that they might seem, even in death, to hold communion with him. Eminent instances of this practice may be seen in the vaults of St. Peter's at Rome, of St. Carlo Borromeo in the Cathedral of Milan, and of St. Ambrose in the Church of S. Ambrogio in the same city. But in the Gothic nations this original notion of the burial-place of the Saints became obscured, in the increasing desire to give them a more honourable place. According to the precise system of orientation, almost unknown south of the Alps, the eastern portion of the church was by German nations regarded as pre-eminently sacred. Thither the high altar was gradually moved, and to it the eyes of the congregation were specially directed. And in the eagerness to give a higher and holier even than the highest and holiest place to any great Saint, on whom popular devotion was fastened, there sprung up in most of the larger churches during the 13th century a fashion of throwing out a still further eastern end, in which the shrine or altar of the Saint might be erected,—and to which, therefore, not merely the gaze of the whole congregation, but of the officiating priest himself, even as he stood before the high altar, might be constantly turned. This notion happened to coincide in time with the great burst of devotion towards the Virgin Mary, which took place under the Pontificate of Innocent III., during the first years of the 13th century ; and, therefore, in all cases where there was no special local saint, this eastern end was dedicated to " Our Lady," and the chapel thus formed was called " The Lady Chapel." Such was the case in the Cathedrals of Salisbury, Norwich, and Chester. But when the popular feeling of any city or neighbourhood had been directed to some indigenous object of devotion, this at once took the highest place, and the Lady Chapel, if any there were, was thrust down to a less honourable position. Of this arrangement, the most notable instances in England are, or were (for in many cases the very sites have perished), the shrines of St. Alban in Hertfordshire, St. Edmund at Bury, St. Edward in Westminster Abbey, St. Cuthbert at Durham, and St. Etheldreda at Ely.

It was this which determined the space to be allotted to the Shrine of St. Thomas in the reconstruction of Canterbury Cathedral. This space was the site of an earlier chapel, now destroyed, where there had stood an altar of the Holy Trinity,[1] where Becket had been accustomed to say mass. Partly for the sake of preserving the two old Norman towers of St. Anselm and St. Andrew, which stood on the north and south side of this part of the Church—but chiefly for the sake of fitly joining in with this new appendage to the Church, the pillars of the choir were contracted with that singular curve which attracts the eye of every spectator, as Gervase foretold that it would, when, in order to explain this peculiarity, he stated the two aforesaid reasons.[2] The eastern end of the

---

[1] Gervase (in Willis's Canterbury Cathedral, p. 56).   [2] *Ibid.*, p. 60.

Cathedral was thus enlarged, as at Ely, for the sake
of a more spacious receptacle for the honoured remains ;
the new Trinity Chapel reaching considerably beyond the
extreme limit of its predecessor, and opening, beyond, into a
yet further chapel, popularly called Becket's Crown. High
in the tower of St. Anselm, on the south side of the destined
site of so great a treasure was prepared—a usual accompaniment of costly shrines—the Watching Chamber. One
such exists beside the vacant space once occupied by St.
Frideswide's Shrine in the Cathedral of Christ Church
Oxford. That at Canterbury may still be seen in the rude
chamber just indicated, with the fire-place where the
watcher could warm himself during the long winter nights,
and the narrow gallery between the pillars, whence he
could overlook the whole platform of the shrine, and at
once detect any sacrilegious robber who was attracted by
the immense treasures there collected. The windows were
duly filled with the richest painted glass of the period, and
amongst those on the northern side may still be traced
elaborate representations of the miracles wrought at the
subterraneous tomb, or by visions and intercessions of the
mighty Saint.

When the Cathedral was thus duly prepared, the time
came for what, in the language of those days, was termed
the "Translation" of the relics.

It was the year 1220 : in every sense—so the contemporary chronicler observes [1]—an auspicious moment. It
seemed to the people of the time as if the long delay had
been interposed in order that a good king and a good
archbishop might be found together to solemnise the great
event. The wild Richard and the wicked John had gone
to their account ; and there was now seated on the throne
the young Henry III. ; his childhood (for he was but a
boy of thirteen), his unpretending and inoffensive character,
won for him a reputation which he hardly deserved, but
which might well be granted to him after such a predecessor : the first troubled years of his reign were finished—
the later calamities had not begun : he had just laid the

---

[1] Robert of Gloucester, who observes all the coincidences in his metrical Life
of Becket, 2820.

first foundation of the new Abbey Church of Westminster, and all recollection of his irregular coronation at Gloucester had been effaced by his solemn inauguration on May 17, the Whitsunday of this very year. The Primate to whose work the lot fell, was one whose name commands far more unquestioned respect than the weak King Henry ; it was the Cardinal Archbishop, the great Stephen Langton, whose work still remains amongst us in the familiar division of the Bible into chapters, and in the Magna Charta, which he was the chief means of wresting from the reluctant John. He was now advanced in years, recently returned from his long exile, and had just assisted at the coronation of the king at Westminster. The year also and the day in that age of ceremonial observance of times and seasons, seemed providentially marked out for such an undertaking. The year was the 50th year from the murder, which thus gave it the appearance of a jubilee ; and it was a bissextile or leap-year, and this seemed an omen that no day would be wanting for the blessings to be procured through the Martyr's intercession. The day also was marked by the coincidences which had made a lasting impression on the minds of that period, Tuesday, the 7th of July ;—Tuesday, the fatal day of Becket's life : the 7th of July also, the same day of the month on which, thirty years before, the remains of his royal adversary, Henry II., had been carried to the vault of the Abbey of Fontevraud.[1] There must have been those living who remembered the mournful spectacle, the solitary hearse descending from the stately castle of Chinon, where the unhappy king had died deserted by friends and children,—the awful scene, when the scanty procession was met at the entrance of the abbey by Richard,—when the face of the dead corpse was uncovered as it lay on the bier marked with the expression of the long agony of death,—when (according to the popular belief), blood gushed from the nostrils, as if to rebuke the unnatural son for his share in having thus brought his father's gray hairs in sorrow to the grave.

[1] All these coincidences are noticed by Langton in a tract or sermon circulated by him in the following year, to keep up the memory of the Translation, published in Giles' Collection, vol. ii., p. 276.

The contrast of that scene with the funeral, which now took place on the anniversary of the day, in 1220, must have been, even to indifferent bystanders, most striking. It was indeed a magnificent spectacle. Such an assemblage had never been collected in any part of England before ; [1] all the surrounding villages were filled—

> " Of bishops and abbots, priors and parsons,
> Of earls, and of barons, and of many knights thereto ;
> Of serjeants, and of squires, and of husbandmen enow
> And of simple men eke of the land—so thick thither drew.[2]

The Archbishop had given two years' notice in a proclamation, circulated not only throughout England, but throughout Europe ; and through the range of his episcopal manors, had issued orders for maintenance to be provided for the vast multitude, not only in the city of Canterbury itself, but on the various roads by which they would approach.[3] During the whole celebration, along the whole way from London to Canterbury, hay and provender was given to all who asked,[4] and at each gate of Canterbury,[5] in the four quarters of the city, and in the four licensed cellars, were placed tons of wine, to be distributed gratis ; and on the day of the festival, wine ran freely through the gutters of the streets.[6]

On the eve of the appointed day the Archbishop, with Richard, Bishop of Salisbury, and the whole body of monks, headed by their Prior, Walter, entered the crypt by night with psalms and hymns, and after prayer and fasting, at midnight solemnly approached the tomb and removed the stones which closed it, and saw for the first time the remains of the Saint with tears of joy.[7] Four priests, distinguished for the sanctity of their lives, took out the relics—first the head (then, as always, kept separate), and offered it to be kissed ; the bones were then deposited in a chest well studded with iron nails and closed with iron locks, and laid in a secret chamber.

The next day a long procession entered the Cathedral. It

---

[1] Waverley Annals; Gale's Scriptores, iii. 185. [2] Robert of Gloucester, 2848.
[3] Waverley Annals, *ib.*
[4] Polistoire. See Note A.

[5] Knyghton, 2430.
[6] Archæologia, ix. 42; Polistoire. See Note A.
[7] Robert of Gloucester, 2374.

was headed by the young king, " King Henry, the young child." Next was the Italian Pandulf, Bishop of Norwich, and Legate of the Holy See ; and Archbishop Langton, accompanied by his brother primate of France, the Archbishop of Rheims. With them was Hubert de Burgh, the Lord High Justiciary and greatest statesman of his time, and " four great lordlings, noble men and tried." On the shoulders of this distinguished band the chest was raised, and the procession moved forward. The King, on account of his tender age, was not allowed to take any part in bearing the sacred load : onwards it was borne, and up the successive stages of the Cathedral, till it reached the Shrine awaiting its reception, eastward of the Patriarchal Chair ; [1] and there it was deposited. Mass was celebrated by the French Primate, in the midst of nearly the whole [2] episcopate of the province of Canterbury. The day was enrolled amongst the great festivals of the English Church as the " Feast of the Translation of St. Thomas." The expenses incurred by the See of Canterbury were hardly paid off by Langton's fourth successor.[3]

And now began the long succession of pilgrimages which for three centuries gave Canterbury a place amongst the great resorts of Christendom, and which, through Chaucer's poem have given it a lasting hold on the memory of Englishmen as long as English literature exists. Let us endeavour through the means of that poem, and through other incidental notices, to reproduce the picture of a mode of life which has now entirely passed away from England, though it may still be illustrated from some parts of the Continent. There were during this period three great approaches to Canterbury.

For Pilgrims who came from the eastern parts of Europe, Sandwich was the ordinary place of debarcation. From this point, the Kings of England, on their return from France, and the Kings of France on their way to England, must commonly have made their journey. One record of this route is preserved by the companions of a Bohemian ambassador who paid a visit to England in the reign of

---

[1] Polistoire, note A.
[2] Three only were absent. Note A.   [3] Knyghton, 2730.

Edward IV., and their impressions are worth recording as probably representing those of most foreign pilgrims.[1] In one respect the travellers of that age and this were on a level. As they crossed the Channel, they were dreadfully sea-sick, and "lay on the deck as if they were dead;" but they had still life enough left to observe the various objects of the strange land that they were approaching. The white cliffs of Dover, as they rose into view above the sea, seemed "like mountains of snow:" of Dover Castle they speak as we might speak of Sebastopol—"the strongest fortress in Christendom." Sailing by this tremendous place, the work, they were told, of evil spirits, they arrived at Sandwich. It is striking to perceive the impression which that now decayed and deserted haven produced on their minds: they speak of it as we might speak of Liverpool or Portsmouth—the resort of ships from all quarters—vessels of every size—now seen by them for the first time; and most of all, the agility of the sailors in running up and down the masts—one especially, absolutely incomparable. From this busy scene they advanced along the Stour to Canterbury. Their expectations had been highly raised by its fame in foreign parts; at a distance, however, the point that chiefly struck them, was the long line of leaden roof, unlike the tiled covering of the continental cathedrals.[2] What they saw at the Shrine of "St. Thomas of Kandelberg," as they had called him in their own country, shall be seen as we proceed.

Another line of approach was along the old British track which led across the Surrey downs from Southampton; it can still be traced under the name[3] of the Pilgrim's-way, or the Pilgrim's-lane, marked often by long lines of Kentish yews,—usually creeping half-way up the hills immediately above the line of cultivation, and under the highest crest,—passing here and there a solitary chapel or friendly monastery, but avoiding for the most part the towns and villages and the regular roads, probably for the same reason as "in the days of Shamgar, the son

---

[1] See note B.

[2] "Desuper stanno totum contegitur." Leo von Rotzmital, pp. 39, 44. They observe the same of Salisbury, p. 46.

[3] See Mr. Way's account of the Pilgrims' Road in note D.

of Anath, the highways were unoccupied, and the travellers
walked through byeways."[1]

This must have been the usual route for Pilgrims from
Normandy and from the west of England. But no doubt
the most frequented road was that from London, celebrated in Chaucer's poem of the "Canterbury Tales."
It would be out of place here to enter on any general
review of that remarkable work. All that can here be
proposed is to examine how far the poem illustrates, or
is illustrated by, the Canterbury pilgrimage which suggested it.

In the first place we may observe that every element
of society except the very highest and lowest was represented—the knight, the yeoman, the prioress, with her
attendant nuns and three priests,—the monk, the friar,
the merchant, the Oxford scholar, the lawyer, the squire,
the five tradesmen, the cook, the shipman, the physician,
the great clothier of Bath, the parish priest, the miller, the
reeve, the manciple, the apparitor of the law-courts, the
seller of indulgences, and the poet himself. These no
doubt are selected as the types of the classes who would
ordinarily have been met on such an excursion. No one
can read the account of their characters, still less the
details of their conversation, without being struck by the
extremely miscellaneous nature of the company—without
seeing, on the one hand, how widely the passion for
pilgrimages extended, how completely it swept into its
vortex all the classes who now travel together in excursion
trains, or on Rhine steam-boats ; and, on the other hand,
how very light a touch it laid on the characters of those
concerned,—how much of levity, how little of gravity was
thought compatible with an object professedly so serious.
As relics took the place of all the various natural objects
of interest which now occupy the minds of religious, literary, or scientific men, so pilgrimages took the place of
modern tours. A pilgrim was a traveller with the same
adventures, stories, pleasures, pains, as travellers now ;
the very names by which we express the most listless

[1] Compare Arnold's Lectures on Modern History (Lecture 2), where the
same observation is made on ancient
roads generally.

wanderings are taken from pilgrimages to the most solemn places : if, indeed, we may trust the etymology which makes a "*Roamer*" to have been one who had visited the Apostles' graves at Rome ; and a "*saunterer*" one who had wandered through the "Sainte terre," or Holy Land.   Let us be thankful for it in this instance for having given us in Chaucer's prologue such an insight into the state of society in the fourteenth century as nothing else can furnish.

In the second place, the mere fact of his selecting such a company and such a time as the vehicle of his tales, indicates the fame of Canterbury as the resort of English pilgrims.   Every reader, he felt, would at once understand the scene, and that he felt truly is shown by the immense popularity of his work at the time. And further, though the particular plan laid out in his prologue, and the regulation of the whole by the host, is evidently the poet's own creation ; yet the practice of telling stories on the journeys to and from Canterbury must have been common in order to give a likelihood to such a plan.   It was even a custom for the bands of pilgrims to be accompanied by hired minstrels and story-tellers, as the friends of the practice maintained, that "with such solace the travail and weariness of pilgrims might be lightly and merrily borne out ; " as their enemies said, "that they might sing wanton songs, and then if these men and women be half a month out in their pilgrimage, many of them shall be, half a year after, great jugglers, story-tellers, and liars." [1] And, in point of fact, the marvels that were related on these occasions, probably on the return from the wonder-working shrine, were such as to have given rise to the proverbial expression of a "Canterbury Tale," as identical with a fabulous story.   It is noticed as such even as late as the time of Fuller,[2] and although it is now probably extinct in England, it travelled with many other old provincialisms across the Atlantic ; and our brethren of the United States, when they come to visit our metropolitical city, are struck by the strange familiarity with

[1] Dialogue of Archbishop Arundel and William Thorpe.—Nichols' Erasmus, 188.
[2] Fuller's Worthies, Kent (Proverbs).

which its name recurs to them, having from their earliest
years been accustomed to hear a marvellous story, followed by the exclamation, "What a Canterbury!"[1] In
conceiving the manner in which these tales were related,
a moment's reflection will show us that they were not
told, as we often imagine, to the whole company at once.
Every one who has ridden in a cavalcade of travellers
along a mountain pathway—and such, more or less, were
the roads of England at the time of Chaucer—will see at
once that this would be impossible. Probably they were
in point of fact related in the midday halts or evening
meals of the party. In the present instance the poet
represents the host as calling the story-teller out of
the ranks to repeat the tale to him as the judge. "Do
him come forth," he cries to the cook, and to the monk,
"Ride forth, mine own Lord;"[2] and the rest hear or not,
according to their curiosity or their nearness—a circumstance which to some extent palliates the relation of
some of the coarser stories in a company which contained
the prioress, the nuns, the parson, and the scholar.

Finally we cannot fail to mark how thoroughly the
time and season of the year falls in with the genius
and intention of the poet. It was, he tells us, the month
of April. Every year, as regularly as "April with his
showers sweet" "the drought of March hath pierced to
the root," came round again the Pilgrims' start—

> " When Zephyrus eke with his sweet breath
> Inspired hath in every holt and heath,
> The tender crops . . . .
> And small fowls are making melody
> That sleepen all night with open eye . . . .
> Then longen folk to go on pilgrimages.
> And specially from every shire's end
> Of England, to Canterbury they wend
> The holy blissful martyr for to seek,
> That them hath holpen when that they were sick."

These opening lines give the colour to Chaucer's whole
poem; it is in every sense the spring of English poetry :
through every line we seem to feel the freshness and vigour
of that early morning start—as the merry cavalcade winds

[1] This observation I derived from an intelligent American clergyman, on a visit
to Canterbury.   [2] Chaucer, 16960, 13930.

its way over the hills and forests of Surrey or of Kent. Never was the scene and atmosphere of a poem so appropriate to its contents, so naturally sustained and felt through all its parts.

When we pass from the general illustrations which the poem receives from the Canterbury pilgrimage to its details, there is unfortunately but little light thrown by one upon the other. Not only are the stages of the route indistinctly marked, but the distances are so roughly calculated as to introduce into the geography, though on a small scale, incongruities almost as great as those which disfigure the "Winter's Tale" and "The Two Gentlemen of Verona." The journey, although at that time usually occupying three or four days, is compressed into the hours between sunrise and sunset on an April day : an additional pilgrim is made to overtake them within seven miles of Canterbury, by galloping hard for "three miles ;" and the tales of the last two miles occupy a space equal to an eighth part of the whole journey of fifty miles. Still such as the local notices are, they must be observed.

It was at the Tabard Inn in Southwark that the twenty-nine pilgrims met ; its site is still marked by a humble tavern, the Talbot Inn, No. 75, High-street, Borough-road : a modern front faces the street, but at the back of a long passage a court-yard opens, surrounded by an ancient wooden gallery, not dating, it is said, beyond the 16th century ; but still, probably, preserving some likeness of the older arrangements, and commemorating its former celebrity, by a large picture or sign, hung from its balustrade, representing in faded colours the Cavalcade of the Pilgrims. Its ancient sign must have been the coat or jacket, now only worn by heralds, but then by noblemen in war ; and it was no doubt selected as the rendezvous of the Pilgrims, as the last inn on the outskirts of London before entering on the wilds of Surrey. Another inn, long since disappeared, entitled "The Bell," was close by. It was doubtless then one of the most flourishing hotels, as we should now say, in London.

"The chambers and the halls were wide.

The host was a man of consideration :

"A fairer burgess was there none in Cheep,"

that is, Cheapside, then the abode of the wealthiest citizens of London. He seems to have been a well-known character, and his name, Henry Bailey, was remembered even till the time of Elizabeth.[1]

It was on the morning of the 28th of April, " when the day began to spring," that the company set forth from the inn, headed by the host who was to act as guide, and who " gathered them together in a flock." Those who have seen the move of an Eastern caravan of European travellers can best form a notion of the motley group of grave and gay, old and young, that must have often been then gathered on the outskirts of London ; and the halt which took place " a little more than a pace " at the second milestone, at the spring, called from this circumstance " the Waterings of St. Thomas," [2] corresponds to the well-known halt which caravans make a few miles from Cairo, on the first day's march, to see whether all the party are duly assembled, and all the necessaries for the long journey duly provided.

At half-past seven A.M. they reached Deptford and Greenwich.

"Lo Deptford, and it is half way prime ;
Lo Grenewich, there many a shrew is in."

By midday,

" Lo Rochester standeth here fast by." [3]

Sittingbourne was probably the place for refreshment :

" Before I come to Sidenbourne,"

implies that it was a point to be looked for as a halt.[4]

And now they were approaching the steep hills of the forest of Blean, when, probably anxious to join them before that long ascent, " at Boughton under Blee," the village which lies at the western foot of the hill—a new companion overtook them, the servant of the rich canon —so powerful an alchymist, that they are assured as they

[1] Tyrwhitt. Preface to Chaucer, § 5.   [3] Chaucer, 1390, 3950.
[2] Chaucer, 828.   [4] Chaucer, 6428.

go up the steep paved road, as it then was, now within seven miles from their destination,

> "That all the ground on which we be riding,
> Till that we come to Canterbury town,
> He could all clean turn upside down,
> And pave it all of silver and of gold." [1]

They now passed the point where all travellers along that road must have caught the welcome sight of the central tower of Canterbury Cathedral, with the gilded Angel then shining on its summit. For a moment the tower is seen, and then disappears, as the road sinks again amidst the undulations of the wild country which still retains the traces of what was the great forest of Blee, or Blean,—famous in recent times as the resort of the madman or fanatic, who rallied round him, in 1838, the rude peasants of the neighbouring villages in the thicket of Bosenden Wood. But they were now at the last halting-place ; just where the forest ends,—just where the hilly ascent rises and falls for the last time,

> "Wist ye not where standeth a little town,
> Which that ycleped is Bob up and down,
> Under the Blee in Canterbury way." [2]

There can be little doubt that this "little town" was the old village of Harbledown, clustered round the ancient lazar-house of Lanfranc,[3] whose situation on the crest of the hill, under the forest of Blean, suggested to the pilgrims the familiar name by which it is here called. They had but to go "up and down" once more, and the Cathedral burst upon them. It was now, according to the Poet's calculation, four in the afternoon, and they would easily reach Canterbury before sunset.

Unfortunately, he

> "who left half told
> The story of Cambuscan bold,"

---

[1] Chaucer, 16024, 16066. It is an ingenious conjecture of Tyrwhitt that a great confusion has been here introduced ; that the Nun's tale was intended to be on the return from Canterbury ; and hence the otherwise difficult expression of the "five miles" silence before she begins, and of the "three miles" gallop of the canon's servant to overtake them. As the text stands in Tyrwhitt's edition, it must be as I have represented it, but the order of the MSS. of Chaucer is evidently very doubtful.

[2] Chaucer, 16950.

[3] It was sometimes called the *Hospitale de bosco de Blean.* Dugdale, vol. i., part 2, p. 653.

has left unfinished the story of his travellers. The plan was to have embraced the arrival at Canterbury, and the stories of their adventures there as they rode back to London, and the supper at the Tabard, when the host was to award the prize to the best. For lovers of Chaucer's simple and genial poetry this is much to be lamented ; but for historical purposes the gap is in a great measure filled by a Supplementary Tale,[1] evidently written within a short time after the poet's death, which relates the story of their arrival, and a few of their adventures in the city. By the help of this, and whatever other light can be thrown on the subject, we may endeavour to reproduce the general aspect which Canterbury and its pilgrims presented on their arrival.

It would doubtless have made a great difference whether we entered Canterbury with such an occasional group of pilgrims as might visit the Shrine at ordinary seasons, or on the great festivals of St. Thomas ; either the winter festival of his " Martyrdom," on the 29th of December, or the summer festival of the Translation of his relics, on the 7th of July, which (as falling in a more genial season) was far more frequented. Still greater would have been the difference if we were to have been there at one of the jubilees, that is, one of the fiftieth anniversaries of the Translation ; when indulgences were granted to all who came, and the festival lasted for a fortnight, dating from midnight on the vigil of the Feast. There were from the first consecration of the Shrine to its final overthrow, six such anniversaries, 1270, 1320, 1370, 1420, 1470, 1520. What a succession of pictures of English history and of the religious feeling of the time, would be revealed if we could but place ourselves in Canterbury as those successive waves of pilgrimage rolled through the place, with all the various impressions they would bring with them of the state of the world at that time. On one of those occasions, in 1420, no less than a hundred thousand persons

---

[1] The Supplementary Tale is printed in Urry's edition of Chaucer from a MS. which is now lost; and is reprinted from thence in Wright's edition of haucer, Percy Society, vol. xxvi., pp. 191—318, from whom I have quoted it, modernising the spelling to make it intelligible.

were thus collected : they came from all parts, but chiefly from the British dominions at that time, immediately after the great battle of Agincourt, extending far over the neighbouring continent. Englishmen, with their language just struggling into existence—Scotch, Irish, and Welsh, with their different forms of Celtic—Frenchmen and Normans, and the inhabitants of the Channel Islands, pouring forth their questions in French,—are amongst those expressly stated to have been present.[1] How various too the motives—some, such as Kings and ministers of state, from policy and ancient usage,—others, merely for the excitement of a long journey with good companions,—others, travelling from shrine to shrine, as men now travel from watering-place to watering-place, for the cure of some obstinate disorder,—some from the genuine feeling of religion, that expresses itself in lowly hearts, under whatever is the established form of the age,—some from the grosser superstition of seeking to make a ceremonial and local observance the substitute for moral acts and holy thoughts. What a sight, too, must have been presented, as all along the various roads through the long summer day, these heterogeneous bands—some on horseback, some on foot—moved slowly along, with music, and song, and merry tales, so that "every town they came thro', what with the noise of their singing, and with the sound of their piping, and with the jangling of their Canterbury bells, and with the barking of the dogs after them, they made more noise than if the King came there with all his clarions and many other minstrels" . . . "And when one of the pilgrims that goeth barefoot striketh his toe upon a stone, and hurteth him sore, and maketh him bleed," then "his fellow sings a song, or else takes out of his bosom a bagpipe to drive away with wit and mirth the hurt of his fellow."[2] Probably at the first sight of the Cathedral this discordant clamour would be exchanged for more serious sounds, hymns, and exhortations, and telling of beads ; even Chaucer's last tale between Harbledown and Canterbury is a sermon : and

[1] Somner, part i. App., No. xliv.
[2] William Thorpe's Examination, in Nichols' Erasmus, p. 188.

thus the great masses of human beings would move into the city.

Their first object would be to find lodgings. It is probable, that to meet this want, there were many more inns at Canterbury than at present. At the great sanctuary of Einsiedlen in Switzerland, almost every house in the long street of the straggling town which leads up to the monastery is decorated with a sign, amounting altogether to no less than fifty. How many of the present inns at Canterbury date from that time cannot perhaps be ascertained. One, the Star Inn, in St. Dunstan's parish, which is supposed to have been the receptacle of the pilgrims who there halted on their entrance into the town, has long since been absorbed in the surrounding houses. But the site and, in part, the buildings of the lodgings which, according to the Supplementary Tale, received the twenty-nine pilgrims of Chaucer, can still be seen, although its name is gone and its destination altered.[1] "The Chequers of the Hope" occupied the antique structure, which, with its broad overhanging eaves, forms so picturesque an object at the corner of High Street and Mercery Lane. Its vicinity to the great gate of the Precincts naturally pointed it out as one of the most eligible quarters for strangers, whose main object was a visit to the Shrine ; and the remains which can be traced in the houses that for more than two centuries have been occupied by the families of the present inhabitants,[2] amply justify the tradition. It was a venerable tenement, entirely composed, like houses in Switzerland, of massive timber, chiefly oak and chestnut. An open oblong court received the pilgrims as they rode in. In the upper story, approached by stairs from the outside, which have now disappeared, is a spacious chamber, supported on wooden pillars, and covered by a high pitched wooden roof—traditionally known as "the Dormitory of the Hundred Beds." Here the mass of the pilgrims slept ; and many must have been the prayers, the tales, the jests, with

[1] "At Chekers of the Hope that every man doth know."
Suppl. Tale, 14.

[2] To the obliging attention of the present occupants I owe the information here given.

which those old timbers have rung,—many and deep the
slumbers which must have refreshed the wearied travellers
who by horse and foot had at last reached the sacred
city.—Great, too, must have been the interest with which
they walked out of this crowded dormitory at break of
day on the flat leads which may be still seen running
round the roof of the court ; and commanding a full view
of the vast extent of the southern side of the Cathedral.
With the Cathedral itself a communication is said to
exist by means of a subterraneous gallery, of which the
course can be in part traced under the houses on the
western side of Mercery Lane.

Besides the inns, were many other receptacles for
the pilgrims, both high and low.   There were various
hospitals or convents, of St. John, St. Gregory, St. Laurence,
and St. Margaret ; of the Gray, of the Black, and of the
Austin Friars, not to speak of the great abbey of St.
Augustine, where the Kings usually lodged ;—on one, the
Hospital of Eastbridge, they had a double claim, both as
tracing its foundation to St. Thomas, whose name it bore,
and as having been intended for the reception of pilgrims ;[1]
twelve of whom were, especially if sick, to be provided with
beds[2] and attendance.   Above all, the Priory attached to
the Cathedral would feel bound to provide for the reception of guests on whose contributions and support its
fame and wealth so greatly depended.   It is by bearing
this in mind that we are enabled to understand how so
large a part of conventual buildings was always set aside
for strangers.   Thus, for example, by far the greater portion of the gigantic monastery of the Grande Chartreuse
was intended to be occupied by guests—" Aula Burgundiæ
—Aula Franciæ—Aula Aquitaniæ," still marking the
assignment of the vast, and now vacant halls, to the numerous pilgrims from all parts of feudal, and, at that time, still
divided France, who, swarming from the long galleries
opening into their private chambers, were there to be
entertained in common.   So on a lesser scale at Canterbury : the long edifice of old grey stone, long apportioned
as the residence of " the eleventh canon," overlooking " the

Dugdale, vol. i., pt. 2, p. 91.

Oaks," then the garden of the convent, was the receptacle for the greater guests,[1]—that at the south-west corner of the "Green-court," for the ordinary guests, who were brought through the gate of the court, thence under the old wooden cloister, which still in part remains; and then lodged in the Strangers' Hall, with a steward appointed to look after all their wants.[2]

In the city, there were many preparations made for the chief Festival of St. Thomas. A notice was placed on a post in the "King's Street," opposite the "Court Hall," ordering the provision of lodging for pilgrims. Expensive pageants were got up, in which "The Martyrdom" was enacted, on the eve of the festival.[3] Accounts are still preserved of payments for "St. Thomas' garment," and the "knights' armour," and gunpowder for fireworks, and "staves and banners," to be carried out before the "morris pykes" and the gunners.[4]

From these various receptacles the pilgrims would stream into the Precincts. The outside aspect of the cathedral can be imagined without much difficulty—standing out of the wide cemetery, which, with its numerous gravestones, as on the south side of Peterborough Cathedral, occupied the vacant space still called the Churchyard, divided from the garden beyond by the old Norman arch since removed. In the cemetery were interred such pilgrims as died during their stay in Canterbury. Excepting this, and the numerous statues that then filled its now vacant niches, the general appearance of the Church must have been much what it is now. Not so its interior. Bright colours on the roof, on the windows, on the monuments; hangings suspended from the rods which may still be seen running from pillar to pillar; chapels, and altars, and chantries intercepting the view, where now all is clear, must have rendered it so different, that at first we should hardly recognise it to be the same building.

At the church door the miscellaneous company of

---

[1] Somner, Appendix, p. 13, No. xvii.
[2] Somner, p. 93.
[3] Archæol. xxxi. 207—209. Such plays were probably general on this Festival. There is a record of their performance on the Eve of St. Thomas, at the ancient Chapel of St. William, the patron Saint of Norwich, on Mousehold Heath.
[4] Hasted, iv., 573.

pilgrims had to arrange themselves "every one after his degree"—

> " The courtesy gan to rise
> Till the knight, of gentleness that knew right well the guise,
> Put forth the prelate, the parson, and his fere." [1]

Here they encountered a monk, who, with the "sprengel," sprinkled all their heads with holy water. After this,

> " The knight went with his compeers round the holy shrine,
> To do that they were come for, and after for to dine."

The rest are described as waiting for a short time behind, the friar trying to get the 'sprengel' as a device to see the nun's face ; whilst the others, the "pardoner, and the miller, and other lewd sots," amused themselves with gaping at the fine painted windows, of which the remnants in the choir are still a chief ornament of the Cathedral, but which then filled the nave also. Their great difficulty was—not unnaturally—to make out the subjects of the pictures.

> " ' He beareth a ball-staff,' quoth the one, ' and also a rake's end ;'
> ' Thou failest,' quoth the miller, ' thou hast not well thy mind ;
> It is a spear, if thou cans't see, with a prick set before,
> To push adown his enemy, and through the shoulder bore.' "

"Peace," quoth the host of Southwark (breaking in upon this idle talk)—

> " ' Let stand the window glazed ;
> Go up and do your offerings, ye seemeth half amazed.' " [2]

At last, therefore, they fall into the tide of pilgrims, and we have now to follow them through the Church. There were two courses adopted ; sometimes they were taken to the Shrine first, and to the lesser objects afterwards ; sometimes to the Shrine last. The latter course will be most convenient to pursue for ourselves. [3]

The first object was the Transept of the Martyrdom. To this they were usually taken through the dark passage under the steps leading to the choir. It was greatly altered since the time of the murder: the column by which Becket had taken his stand had been removed to clear the view

---

[1] Supp. Tale, 134.
[2] Supp. Tale, 150.
[3] The following account is taken chiefly from Erasmus' Pilgrimage, with such occasional illustrations as are furnished from other sources.

of the wooden altar which stood by the spot where he fell ;
the steps up which he was ascending were removed, and
a wall, part of which still remains,[1] was drawn across the
transept to facilitate the arrangements of the entrance of
great crowds.   The Lady Chapel, which had then stood
in the nave, had now taken the place of the chapels of
St. Benedict and St. Blaise, which were accommodated to
their new destination.   The site, however, of the older
Lady Chapel in the nave was still marked by a stone
column, on which had stood a statue of the Virgin,
which—such was the story told to foreign pilgrims—had
often conversed with St. Thomas as he prayed before it.
The statue itself now stood in the choir, covered with
pearls and precious stones.[2]   An inscription [3] over the
door, which was still legible in the 17th century,

> " Est sacer intra locus venerabilis atque beatus
> Præsul ubi Sanctus Thomas est martyrisatus,"

rudely indicated the event of which the chapel was the
scene.   Those who visited the spot in the close of the
15th century, might have seen the elaborate representation
of the " Martyr " in the great window of gorgeous painted
glass, of which all has now perished except one band,
giving the figures of the donors, King Edward IV. and his
queen, the princesses his daughters, and the two unhappy
children that perished in the Tower.

Before the wooden altar the pilgrims knelt, and its
guardian priest exhibited to them the various relics con-
fided to his especial charge.   But the one which surpassed
all others was the rusty fragment of Le Bret's sword, which
was presented to each in turn to be kissed.   The foreign
pilgrims, by a natural mistake, inferred from the sight of
the sword, that the martyr had suffered death by behead-
ing.[4]   They were next led down the steps on the right to
the crypt, where a new set of guardians received them.   On
great occasions the gloom of the old Norman aisles was

---

[1] The rest was removed in 1734.
Hasted, iv. 520.
[2] Leo von Rotzmital, Note B., p. 154.
On the whole it seems more likely that
the Lady Chapel in the nave is meant,
than that in the crypt. But this is
doubtful.
[3] Somner, 91.
[4] See Leo von Rotzmital. Note B.

broken by the long array of lamps suspended from the rings still seen in the roof, each surrounded by its crown of thorns.   Here were exhibited some of the actual relics of St. Thomas—part of his skull, cased in silver, and also presented to be kissed ; and hanging aloft the celebrated shirt [1] and drawers of hair-cloth, which had struck such awe into the hearts of the monks on the night of his death. [2] This was all that ordinary pilgrims were allowed to see ; but, if they were persons of rank, or came with high recommendations, they were afterwards permitted to return, and the Prior himself with lights exhibited the wonders of the Chapel of Our Lady Undercroft, carefully barred with iron grates, but within glittering with treasures beyond any other like shrine in England.   Some portion of the stars of bright enamel may still be seen on the roof.

Emerging from the crypt the pilgrims mounted the steps to the choir, on the north side of which the great mass of general relics were exhibited.   Most of them were in ivory, gilt, or silver coffers.   The bare list of these occupies eight folio pages, and comprises upwards of four hundred items ; [3] some of these always, but especially the arm of St. George, [4] were offered to be kissed,

> " The holy relics each man with his mouth
> Kissed, as a goodly monk the names told and taught."

Those who were curious in the gorgeous altar-cloths, vestments, and sacred vessels, were also here indulged with a sight of these treasures in the grated vault beneath the altar.

Leaving the choir, they were brought to the sacristy in the northern aisle, in St. Andrew's tower.   Here again the ordinary class of pilgrims was excluded ; but to the privileged were shown, besides the vast array of silk vestments

---

[1] So it was seen by Erasmus.   (See Nichols, p. 47.)   In 1465 it seems to have been suspended (much as the Black Prince's coat) over the lid of the Shrine. Leo von Rotzmital, p. 154, Note B.   A fragment apparently of the original tomb was here shown, namely, a slip of lead inscribed with the title by which he was sometimes known, *Thomas Acrensis.* See Nichols, pp. 47, 120.

[2] See "Murder of Becket," pp. 75-76.
[3] As given in an inventory of 1315. See Nichols' Erasmus, pp. 124, 155., Dart's Antiquities of Canterbury, Appendix, pp. iv.—xviii.
[4] The name is not given by Erasmus (p. 48), but the prominence given in Leo's account to the right arm of " our dear Lord, the Knight St. George," (p. 154, Note B.), seems to fix it.

and golden candlesticks, what were far more valuable in their eyes, the rude pastoral staff of pear-wood, with its crook of black horn, the rough cloak and the bloody handkerchief of the "Martyr" himself.   There was too a chest cased with black leather, and opened with the utmost reverence on bended knees, containing scraps and rags of linen, with which (the story must be told throughout) the Saint wiped his forehead and blew his nose.[1]

And now they have reached the holiest place.   Behind the altar, as has been already observed, was erected the Shrine itself.   What seems to have impressed every pilgrim who has left the record of his visit, as absolutely peculiar to Canterbury, was the long succession of ascents, by which " Church seemed," as they said, " to be piled upon church," and " a new Temple entered as soon as the first was ended." [2]   This unrivalled elevation of the sanctuary of Canterbury was partly necessitated by the position of the   original crypt, partly by the desire to construct the Shrine immediately above the place of the Saint's original grave, that place itself being beautified by the noble structure which now encloses it. Up these steps the Pilgrims mounted, many of them probably on their knees, and the long and deep indentations in the surface of the stones, even now bear witness to the devotion and the number of those who once ascended to the sacred platform of the eastern chapel.   The popular hymn to St. Thomas, if it was not suggested, must at least have been rendered doubly impressive, by this continual ascent,—

> Tu, per Thomæ sanguinem
> Quem pro te impendit,
> Fac nos Christo *scandere*
> Quo Thomas *ascendit.*
> Gloriâ et honore coronasti eum Domine
> Et constituisti eum *supra opera* manuum tuarum
> Ut ejus meritis et precibus a Gehennæ incendiis liberemur.[3]

Trinity Chapel in the thirteenth century, immediately

---

[1] Nichols' Erasmus, 49, 57, 156.   I quote the original words :—"Fragmenta linteorum lacera plerumque mucci vestigium servantia.   His ut aiebant, vir pius extergebat sudorem è facie, sive collo, pituitam à naribus, aut si quid esset, similium sordium quibus non vacent humana corpuscula."

[2] Note B, and Nichols' Erasmus, p. 50.

[3] Wharton, Anglia Sacra, i. p. 121.

The forme and figure of the Shrine of Tho
Becket of Canterbury

Siluergilt 60 ounces

It. 80.

Siluergilt 60 ounces

Tom H 8.

As aboue the stone worke was first of wod Iewels if gold set with stone
wrought vppon with gold men then agayn with Iewells of gold as from
10, or 12 togyther cramped with gold into the ground of gold the g
chest such as 5. or 8. men could not convay owt of the churchat
an Anyell of gold poynting ther with offred ther by a king of france
into a ring. and wear it on his thomb.

this chest of Iron con
bones of Thomas Bec
soll with at me
the pise

BECKET'S SHRINE.

NOTE

TO THE ENGRAVING OF THE SHRINE OF BECKET.

———◆———

THE accompanying engraving is a fac-simile of a drawing of the Shrine in ink, on a folio page of the Cottonian MS., Tib. E, viii. fol. 269. It has been already engraved in Dugdale's Monasticon, vol. i. p. 10, and partially in Nichols' Erasmus, pp. 118, 165, but with several deviations from the original. It is here given exactly as it appears in the MS., even to the bad drawing of the end of the Shrine, and the effects of the fire which partially destroyed the MSS. in 1731, visible in the mutilated engravings of the page. It will be observed on a comparison with the appearance in Dugdale and Nichols, that the skull and the bones on the lid of the iron chest are not (as there represented) raised, but lie flat on the surface; and are therefore, in all probability, not meant to pourtray the actual relics (which were inside), but only a carving or painting of them on the lid. The piece of the skull is also here exhibited in a form much more conformable to the written accounts, than would be inferred from Dugdale's inexact copy.

The burnt inscriptions may be restored thus, from Dugdale's Latin translation of them, and from Stow's Annals (Anno 1538), whose description of the Shrine is evidently taken from this MS., before it had been mutilated by the fire of 1731 :—

The form and figure of the Shrine of Tho : Becket of Canterbury.

Then a statement respecting the three finials of the Canopy :—

Silver gilt 60 *ounces.* [*Silver gi*]*lt* 80 *ounces.* *Silver gilt* 60 *ounces.*

Then the description of the Shrine :—

Tem : H. 8. *All above the stone work was first of wood, jewels of gold set with stone,* [covered with plates of gold] *wrought upon with gold wier, then again with jewells, gold, as bro*[oches, images, angels, rings] 10 *or* 12 *together, cramped with gold into the ground of gold, the s*[poils of which filled two] *chests such as* 6 *or* 8 *men could but convey on out of the church. At* [one side was a stone with] *an Angell of gold poynting therunto, offered ther by a king of France,* [which King Henry put] *into a ring, and wear it on his* [1] *thumb.*

Then the description of the chest (not a table, as Mr. Nichols, p. 118, erroneously infers, from Dugdale's Latin translation of the inscription, but the identical iron chest deposited by Langton within the golden Shrine) :—

This chest of iron con[tained the] *bones of Thomas Beck*[et, skull and] *all, with the wounde* [of his death] *and the pece cut* [out of his skull laid in the same wound].

---

[1] Dugdale, in his Latin translation (p. 10) inserts here the word *rapacious*, " *rapaci* pollice."

after the erection of the Shrine, must have presented a very different aspect from that which it wore a few generations later. The Shrine then stood entirely alone ; no other mortal remains had yet intruded into the sacred solitude. Gradually this rule was broken through, and the pilgrim of the fifteenth century must have beheld the Shrine, flanked on the right hand and the left, by the tombs of the Black Prince and of Henry IV., then blazing with gold and scarlet. Why Archbishop Courtenay was brought into so august a company, is not clear; it was against his own wish, and is said to have been at the express command of King Richard II., who was at Canterbury at the time.[1] These, however, were the only exceptions.

The Pilgrims were first led beyond the Shrine to the easternmost apse, where was preserved a golden likeness of the head of the Saint,[2] richly studded with jewels. This either contained, or had contained, the scalp or crown of the Saint, severed by Le Bret's sword, and this probably was the altar often mentioned in offerings as " the Altar of the Head,"[3] and gave its name to the eastern apse, called from this, " Becket's Crown."

We now arrive at the Shrine. Although not a trace of it remains, yet its position is ascertainable beyond a doubt, and it is easy from analogy and description to imagine its appearance. A rude representation of it still exists in one of Sir Robert Cotton's MSS.[4] in the British Museum, from which it appears that it strongly resembled the Shrine of St. Cuthbert of Durham, of which an accurate

[1] See "Edward the Black Prince," pp. 119, 120.

[2] This must have been the *corona*, from which the apse derived its name of "Becket's crown." The expression, *ad coronam*, used of the two shrines of Odo and St. Wilfrid, on its north and south side, could not have been used if the whole building had been the Corona; in which case, "*in* corona" would have been the expression. (See Willis, p. 56, who, it must be said, takes a different view.)

[3] See Nichols, pp. 115, 116, 118. There is a confusion about the position of this relic, but, on the whole, there can be little doubt that it must at times have been exhibited in this place. When the Shrine was opened, so much of the skull was found with the rest of the bones, that a doubt naturally arose whether the large separate portion of the skull shown elsewhere was not an imposture. See Declaration of Faith, 1539 ; Nichols, p. 236, and the notes in the Appendix.

[4] Copies of this drawing are to be seen in Dugdale's Monasticon, and Nichols' Erasmus, but both are so inaccurate, that I have thought it worth while to publish an exact fac-simile of the original.

description has been preserved.[1]   One shrine also still remains comparatively uninjured, the only one in England,[2] that of Edward the Confessor, in Westminster Abbey. The space which it covered may still be traced by the large purple stones which surround the vacant square. Above its eastern extremity was fixed in the roof the mysterious gilded crescent, of uncertain origin, but apparently brought back by some crusading pilgrim from the dome of an Oriental mosque. Round it probably hung a group of Turkish flags and horsetails, which waved from the roof over the Shrine beneath—like the banners of St. George's Chapel, Windsor.[3]   At its western extremity, separating[4] it from the Patriarchal Chair, which stood where the Communion Table is now placed, extended the broad pavement of Mosaic with its border of circular stones, ornamented with fantastic devices, chiefly of the signs of the Zodiac, similar to that which surrounds the contemporary tombs of Edward the Confessor and Henry III. at Westminster. Immediately in front of this Mosaic was placed "the Altar of St. Thomas" at the head of the Shrine, and before this the pilgrims knelt, where the long furrow in the purple pavement still marks the exact limit to which they advanced. Before them rose the Shrine, secure within its strong iron rails, of which the stains and perhaps the fixings can still be traced in the broken pavement around. For those who were allowed to approach still closer, there were iron grates which opened. The lower part of the Shrine was of stone, supported on arches ; and between these arches the sick and lame pilgrims were allowed to ensconce themselves, rubbing their rheumatic backs or diseased legs and arms against the marble which brought them into the nearest contact with the wonder-working body within.[5]   The

---

[1] See Willis's Cant. Cath., p. 100.

[2] In Chester Cathedral the shrine of St. Werburga remains, but the body is removed, and the shrine converted into the episcopal throne. In foreign churches, the shrine of the Three Kings at Cologne, of St. Ferdinand at Seville, and of St. Remigius at Rheims, are, perhaps, the nearest likenesses.

[3] See the grounds for this explanation

in note G. communicated by Mr. George Austin, in the Appendix.

[4] There is also a fragment of this "Opus Alexandrinum" from Rome in Wilton Church. See "Gentleman's Magazine," November, 1854.

[5] This is expressly stated with regard to St. Cuthbert's shrine. Willis's Canterbury Cathedral, p. 100; Raine's Account of Durham Cathedral, pp. 52—55.

Shrine, properly so called, rested on these arches, and was at first invisible. A wooden canopy, probably painted outside with sacred pictures, suspended from the roof, concealed it; at a given signal this canopy was drawn up by ropes, and the Shrine then appeared blazing with gold and jewels; the wooden sides were plated with gold and damasked with gold wire, and embossed with innumerable pearls and jewels and rings, cramped together on this gold ground.[1]

As soon as this magnificent sight was disclosed, every one dropped on his knees, and probably the tinkling of the silver bells attached to the canopy would indicate the moment to all the hundreds of pilgrims in whatever part of the Cathedral they might be.[2] The body of the Saint in the inner iron chest was not to be seen except by mounting a ladder, which would be but rarely allowed. But whilst the votaries knelt around, the Prior, or some other great officer of the monastery, came forward, and with a white wand touched the several jewels, naming the giver of each, and for the benefit of foreigners, adding the French name of each, with a description of its value and marvellous qualities. A complete list of them[3] has been preserved to us, curious, but devoid of general interest. There was one, however, which far outshone the rest, and indeed was supposed to be the finest in Europe. It was the great carbuncle or diamond, said to be as large as a hen's egg, and commonly called "The Regale of France." The attention of the spectators was rivetted by the figure of an angel pointing to it. It had been given to the original tomb in the crypt by Louis VII. of France, when here on his pilgrimage; but the donation was enhanced in the eyes of the pilgrims of the 15th century by a marvellous legend, quite unknown to earlier chroniclers. "The King," so ran the story, "had come thither to discharge a vow made in battle, and knelt at the Shrine with the stone set

---

[1] This account is taken from Stow's Chronicle, 1538, and the Cotton MS. description of the shrine. Both are given in Nichols' Erasmus, pp. 166, 167.

[2] Compare Raine's "Durham," p. 54. At St. Cuthbert's Shrine were "fine sounding silver bells attached to the ropes, which at the drawing up of the ropes made such a goodly sound, that it stirred all the people's heart in the church."

[3] The list of jewels (from the Inventory of 1315) is given in Nichols' Erasmus, p. 169.

in a ring on his finger.   The Archbishop, who was present, entreated him to present it to the Saint.   So costly a gift was too much for the royal pilgrim, especially as it ensured him good luck in all his enterprises.   Still, as a compensation, he offered 100,000 florins for the better adornment of the Shrine.   The Primate was fully satisfied ; but scarcely had the refusal been uttered when the stone leapt from the ring, and fastened itself to the Shrine, as if a goldsmith had fixed it there."   The miracle of course convinced the king, who left the jewel, with the 100,000 florins as well ; and it remained, the wonder of the church, so bright that it was impossible to look at it distinctly, and at night burning like fire : so costly, that it would suffice for the ransom of a king of England, almost of England itself.[1]

The lid once more descended on the golden ark ; the pilgrims,

> " telling heartily their beads,
> Prayed to St. Thomas in such wise as they could," [2]

and then withdrew, down the opposite flight of steps from that which they had ascended.   Those who saw the long files of pilgrims at Trèves, at the time of the exhibition of the " Holy Coat," in 1844, can best form a notion of this part of the scene at Canterbury.   There, as at Canterbury, the long line of pilgrims ascended and descended the flights of steps which led to the space behind the high altar, muttering their prayers, and dropping their offerings into the receptacles which stood ready to receive them at the foot of either staircase.

Where these offerings were made at Canterbury we are not told, but probably at each of the three great places of devotion—the " Point of the Sword," "the Head," or " Crown," and "the Shrine."   Ordinary pilgrims presented " silver brooches and rings," Kings and princes gave jewels or money, magnificent drapery, spices, tapers, cups, and statues of themselves in gold or silver.[3]

And now the hour arrived for departure.   The hour of

[1] The account of the exhibition of the shrine is taken from Erasmus (see Nichols, p. 55) ; Stow, and the Cotton MS. See Nichols. p. 166, 167 ; and the Bohemian Travellers, who give the story of the Regale of France, (see Note B.)   [2] Supp. Tale, 168.
[3] See Nichols' Erasmus, p. 108, 160.

" the dinner," which had been carefully prepared by the host of Southwark, now approaching—

"They drew to dinner-ward, as it drew to noon." [1]

But, before they finally left the Precincts, one part of their task still remained, namely, to carry off memorials of the visit. Of these, the most important was furnished within the monastery itself. The story of the water mixed with the martyr's blood [2] has been already mentioned ; and the small leaden bottles or " ampulles " in which this was distributed were the regular marks of Canterbury pilgrims. But to later generations the wonder was increased by showing a well in the Precincts, into which, as the story ran, the dust and blood from the pavement had been thrown immediately after the murder, and called forth an abundant spring where before there had been but a scanty stream ; and this spring turned, it was said, both at the time and since, four times into blood and once into milk. With this water miracles were supposed to be wrought ; and, from the beginning of the 14th to the close of the 15th century, it was one of the greatest marvels of the place. [3] Absurd as the story was, it is worth recording, as being one of which the comparatively late origin can be traced by us, though wholly unsuspected by the pilgrims, and perhaps by the monks who profited by its wonders ; and thus an instance, even to the most credulous, of the manner in which the fables of miraculous springs have in all countries been originated. But besides these leaden bottles, the pilgrims usually procured more common reminiscences on their way back to the inn. Mercery Lane, the narrow street which leads from the Cathedral to the

[1] Supp. Tale, 190.
[2] See "Murder of Becket," p. 74.
[3] The story of the well is given in the Polistoire, of the time of Edward II.; by the Bohemian Travellers, in the time of Edward IV.; and by William Thomas, in the time of Henry VIII. (See Notes A, B, and C). It is unknown to Gervase and the earlier chroniclers. The well was probably that which is in the old plans of the monastery marked *Puteus*, immediately on the north side of the choir, of which all traces have now disappeared. Two remarkable instances of miraculous springs may be mentioned, of which, as in this case, the later story can be discovered. One is that in the Mamertine Prison, said to have been called forth for the baptism of St. Peter's gaoler; though it really existed there in the days of the Roman Republic. The other is the Zemzem at Mecca, commonly believed to have been the well of Ishmael, although it is known to have been really dug by Abd-ul-Motallib. (Sprenger's Mahomet, pp. 31, 54.)

"Chequers," in all probability takes its name from its
having been the chief resort of the shops and stalls where
objects of ornament or devotion were clamorously offered
for sale to the hundreds who flocked by, eager to carry
away some memorial of their visit to Canterbury. At
that time the street was lined [1] on each side with arcades,
like the "Rows" at Chester, underneath which the
pilgrims could walk, and turn in to the stalls on either
side. Such a collection of booths—such a clamour of
vendors—is the first sight and sound that meets every
traveller who visits Loretto or Einsiedlen. The objects, as
in these modern, so in those ancient resorts of pilgrimage,
were doubtless mostly of that flimsy and trivial character
so expressively designated by a word derived from a place
of this very kind—*tawdry*, that is, like the lace sold at
the fair of *St. Awdrey*, or *Etheldreda*, the patron saint of
the Isle of Ely. But what they chiefly looked for were
"signs," to indicate where they had been.

> "As manner and custom is, signs there they bought,
> For men of contrè to know whom they had sought,
> Each man set his silver in such thing as they liked." [2]

These signs they fastened on their caps or hats, or hung
from their necks, and thus were henceforth distinguished.
As the pilgrims from Compostella brought home the
scallop-shells, which still lie on the sea-shores of Gallicia—
as the "palmers" from Palestine brought the palm-branches
still given at the Eastern pilgrimage, in the tin-cases which,
slung behind the mules or horses, glitter in long succession
through the cavalcade as it returns from Jerusalem to Jaffa
—as the roamers from Rome brought models of St. Peter's
keys, or a "vernicle," that is, a pattern of Veronica's handkerchief, sewed on their caps—so the Canterbury pilgrim
had his hat thick set with a "hundred ampulles," or with
leaden brooches representing the mitred head of the saint,
with the inscription, "*Caput Thomæ*." [3] Many of these are
said to have been found in the beds of the Stour and the
Thames, dropped as the vast concourse departed from
Canterbury or reached London.

[1] Hasted, iv. 423.
[2] Supp. Tale, 194.
[3] See Piers Ploughman and Giraldus, as quoted by Nichols, p. 70, who over-
looks the fact that the "ampullæ" were
Canterbury signs.

At last, after all these sights and purchases, came the dinner, "at noon."

> "Every man in his degree took his seat,
> As they were wont to do at supper and at meat." [1]

The remains of the vast cellars under the Chequers Inn still bear witness to the amount of good cheer which could be provided.

After the repast, they all dispersed to see the town.

> "All that had their changes with them
> They made them fresh and gay,"

And—

> "They sorted them together,
> As they were more used travelling by the way."

The knight—

> "With his menee went to see the wall
> And the wards of the town, as to a knight befall—"

the walls of Simon of Sudbury, which still in great part exist round the city—

> "Devising attentively the strength all about,
> And pointed to his son both the perill and the dout,
> For shot of arblast and of bow, and eke for shot of gun,
> Unto the wards of the town, and how it might be won." [2]

The monk of the party took his clerical friends to see an acquaintance—

> "that all these years three,
> Hath prayed him by his letters that I would him see." [3]

The wife of Bath induced the Prioress to walk into the garden or "herbary,"

> "to see the herbs grow,
> "And all the alleys fair and pavid and raylid, and y-makid,
> The savige and the ysope y-fretted and y-stakid,
> And other beddis by and by fresh y-dight,
> For comers to the host, right a sportful sight." [4]

Such were the ordinary amusements of the better class of Canterbury pilgrims. The rest are described as employing themselves in a less creditable manner.

On the morrow they all start once again for London, and the stories on the road are resumed. At Dartford,

[1] Supp. Tale, 230—240.
[2] Supp. Tale, 194.
[3] Supp. Tale, 270.
[4] Supp. Tale, 290. This last expression seems to imply that the Herbary was in the garden of the inn. A tradition of such a garden still exists in the tenements on the north-west side of Mercery Lane.

both on going and returning, they laid in a stock of pilgrims' signs.[1] The foreign pilgrims sleep at Rochester, and it is curious to note that the recollections of Canterbury have so strong a hold on their minds, that the first object which they visit on their arrival in London is the chapel of St. Thomas,[2] the old chapel built over the place of his birth, and the graves of his parents, Gilbert and Matilda.

Besides the mass of ordinary pilgrims, there were those who came from the very highest ranks of life. Probably there was no king, from the second to the eighth Henry, who did not at some time of his life think it a matter of duty or of policy to visit the Shrine of St. Thomas. Before the period of the Translation, we have already seen the visits of Louis VII. of France, and Richard and John of England. Afterwards, we have express records of Isabella,[3] Queen of Edward II., of Edward I., and of John, the captive king of France. Edward I., in the close of his reign (1299), offered to the Shrine no less a gift than the golden crown of John Baliol ;[4] and in the same year he celebrated, in the Chapel of the Martyrdom, his marriage with his second wife, Margaret.[5] John of France was at Canterbury both on his arrival and on his return from his captivity.[6] The last acts of his long exile were to drop an alms of ten crowns into the hands of the nuns of Harbledown, to offer ten nobles at the three sacred places of the Cathedral, and to carry off as a reminiscence from the Mercery stalls, a knife for the Count of Auxerre. A Sunday's ride brought him to Dover ; and thence, after a dinner with the Black Prince in Dover Castle, he once more embarked for his native country. Distinguished members of the great Scottish families also came, from far over the Border ; and special licenses and safe-conducts were granted to the Bruces, and to the Abbot of Melrose,[7] to enable them to perform their

[1] Dunkin's History of Dartford.
[2] See note B.
[3] Archæologia, xxxvi. 461. She was four days on the road, and made offerings at the tomb, the head, and the sword. Mary, daughter of Edward I., accompanied her. (Green's Princesses of England, vol. ii.)
[4] See Hasted, iv. 514.
[5] See note A.
[6] See note E.
[7] Hasted, iv. 514.

journeys securely through those troubled times. The great barons of the Cinque Ports, too, came here after every coronation, to present the canopies of silk and gold which they held, and still hold, on such occasions over our kings and queens, and which they receive as their perquisites.[1]

We have seen the rise of the Shrine of St. Thomas—we now come to its decline. From the very beginning of its glory, there had been contained within it the seeds of its own destruction. Whatever there may have been of courage or nobleness in Becket's life and death, no impartial person can now doubt that the ages which followed regarded his character and work with a reverence exaggerated beyond all reasonable bounds. And whatever feelings of true religion were interwoven with the devotion of those who came over land and sea to worship at his shrine, it is impossible to overlook the groundless superstition with which it was inseparably mingled, or the evil results, social and moral, to which the Pilgrimage gave birth. Even in the first beginnings of this localisation of religion, there were purer and loftier spirits (such as Thomas à Kempis in Germany)[2] who doubted of its efficacy, and in the 14th century, when it reached its height, there had already begun a strong reaction against it in a large part of the national mind of England. Chaucer's narrative leads us to infer, and the complaints of contemporary writers, like Piers Plowman and William Thorpe, prove beyond doubt, that the levity, the idleness, the dissoluteness,[3] produced by these promiscuous pilgrimages, provoked that sense of just indignation which was one of the most animating motives of the Lollards, and was one of the first causes which directly prepared the way for the Reformation. Even the treasures of the Cathedral and of St. Augustine were not deemed quite secure ; and the Lord Warden of the Cinque Ports, in the reign of Richard II., advised that they should be moved "for

---

[1] Hasted, iv. 514.

[2] " There are few whom sickness really amends, as *there are few whom* *pilgrimage really sanctifies.*" (Imitatio Christi, i. 23, 4.)

[3] See the very instructive quotations in Nichols' Erasmus, pp. 182—189.

more safety" to Dover Castle[1]—just as, in the wars of the
Palatinate, the Holy Coat of Treves was for many years
shut up in the fortress of Ehrenbreitstein.

Nor was it only persons of humble life and narrow
minds that perceived these evils, and protested against
them. In the year of the fourth Jubilee, 1370, the
pilgrims were crowding as usual along the great London
road to Canterbury, when they were overtaken by Simon
of Sudbury, at that time Bishop of London, but afterwards
Primate, and well known for his munificent donations to
the walls and towers of the town of Canterbury. He
was a bold and vigorous prelate ; his spirit was stirred
within him at the sight of what he deemed a mischievous
superstition, and he openly told them that the plenary
indulgence which they hoped to gain by their visit to
the holy city would be of no avail to them. Such
a doctrine from such an authority fell like a thunderbolt
in the midst of the vast multitude. Many were struck
dumb ; others lifted up their voices and cursed him to
his face, with the characteristic prayer that he might
meet with a shameful death. One especially, a Kentish
gentleman—by name, Thomas of Aldon—rode straight up
to him, in towering indignation, and said : " My Lord
Bishop, for this act of yours, stirring the people to sedition
against St. Thomas, I stake the salvation of my soul that
you will close your life by a most terrible death," to
which the vast concourse answered, " Amen, Amen." The
curse, it was believed, prevailed. The "*vox populi*," so the
chronicler expressly asserts, turned out to be the " *vox
Dei*." Eleven years from that time, the populace of London
not unnaturally imagined that the rights of St. Thomas
were avenged, when they saw the unfortunate Primate
dragged out of the Tower, and beheaded by the Kentish
rebels under Wat Tyler.[2] The tomb is to be seen on the
south side of the choir of the Cathedral, to which his
remains were brought ; and not many years ago, when
it was accidentally opened, the body was seen within,
wrapped in cerecloth, a leaden ball occupying the vacant
space of the head.

[1] Lambard's Kent, p. 293.   [2] Birchington's Annals.

But Sudbury was right, after all, and the end was not far off. It was between the years 1511 and 1513,[1] that there appeared within the Precincts of the Cathedral the two most illustrious strangers that had visited the spot since Chaucer. The one was John Colet, first scholar of his time in England, Dean of St. Paul's Cathedral, and founder of St. Paul's Grammar School. The other was Desiderius Erasmus, the prince and patriarch of the learning and scholarship of Europe, then just reviving from the slumber of a thousand years. They had made the journey from London together ; they had descended the well-known hill, and gazed with admiration on the well-known view. Long afterwards, in the mind of Erasmus, lived the recollection of " the majesty with which the Church rises into the sky, so as to strike awe even at a distant approach ; the vast towers,[2] saluting from far the advancing traveller; the sound of the bells, sounding far and wide through the surrounding country." They were led the usual round of the sights of pilgrims. They speculated on the figures of the murderers over the south porch ; they entered the nave, then, as now, open to all comers, and were struck by its " spacious majesty," then comparatively new from the works of Prior Chillenden. The curious eye of Erasmus passed heedlessly over the shrine[3] of Archbishop Wittlesey, but fixed on the books fastened to the columns, and noted, with his caustic humour, that amongst them was a copy of the apocryphal Gospel of Nicodemus. They were taken to the Chapel of the Martyrdom, and reverently kissed the rusty sword, and then, in long succession, as already described, were exhibited to them the wonders of the crypt, the choir, the sacristy, and the Shrine. Their acquaintance with Warham, the gentle and learned Primate, secured their admission even to the less accessible regions of the crypt and sacristy. The Prior, who received them at the shrine, was Goldstone, the last great benefactor to the Cathedral, who had just built the Christ Church gate, and the central tower.[4] Erasmus saw enough

---

[1] The date is fixed by the events of Erasmus' life, (see Nichols, p. viii.)

[2] He says " two," by an oversight.

[3] " Sepulcrum nescio cujus."

[4] Hasted, iv. 556.

to find out not only that he was a pious and sensible man, but that he was well acquainted with the philosophy—now trembling to its ruin—of Duns Scotus and the schoolmen. Even if no record were left, it would have been impossible not to inquire and to imagine with deep interest what impression was produced by these various objects, at this critical moment of their history, on two such men as Colet and Erasmus. We are not left to conjecture. Every line of the narrative, dry and cautious as it is, marks the feelings awakened in the hearts of these two friends. The beauty of the edifice, as we have seen, touched them deeply. But when they come to the details, two trains of thought are let loose which carry away every other consideration. First, the vast display of wealth, which in former ages would have seemed the natural accompaniment of so sacred a spot, awakens in the mind of Erasmus only a sense of incongruity and disproportion. He dwells with pleasure on the "wooden altar" of the "martyrdom," as "a monument of antiquity, rebuking the luxury of this age ; " he gladly kisses the "rough cloak" and "napkin" of Becket, as "memorials of the simplicity of ancient times." But the splendid stores of the treasury, "before which Midas or Crœsus would have seemed beggars," rouse only the regret —the sacrilegious regret, as he confesses, for which he begged pardon of the saint before he left the Church— that none of these gifts adorned his own homely mansion. His friend took, as was his wont, a more serious view of the matter ; and, as they were standing before the gilded head in Becket's Crown, broke in with the unseasonable suggestion, that if St. Thomas had been devoted to the poor in his lifetime, and was now unchanged, unless for the better, he would far rather prefer that some portion of this vast treasure should be expended on the same objects now. The verger knit his brows, scowled, pouted, and, but for Warham's letter of introduction, would have turned them out of the church. Erasmus, as usual, took the milder side ; hinted that it was but his friend's playful way, and dropped a few coins into the verger's hand for the support of the edifice. But he was not the less convinced of the substantial truth of the good Dean's complaint. On the next point, there was more difference between them. The natural timidity of Erasmus led him to shrink from an open attack on so wide-spread a feeling as the worship of relics. Colet had no such scruple, and the objects of reverence which had held enthralled the powerful minds of Henry Plantagenet and of Stephen Langton, excited in the devout and earnest mind of the theologian of the 16th century sentiments only of disgust and contempt. When the long array of bones and skulls were produced, he took no pains to disguise his impatience; he refused the accustomed kiss due to the arm of St. George; and when the kind Prior offered one of the filthy rags torn from one of the saint's robes, as a choice present, he held it up between his fingers, and laid it down with a whistle of contempt, which distracted Erasmus between shame for his companion's bad manners and a fear for the consequences. But the Prior pretended not to see; perhaps such expressions were now not so rare as in the days of Sudbury : at any rate, the courtesy of his high office prevailed ; and, with a parting cup of wine, he bade them farewell.

There was to be yet one more trial of Erasmus's patience. They were to return to London. Two miles from Canterbury, they found themselves in a steep descent through a steep and narrow lane, with high banks on either side ; on the left rose an ancient almshouse. We recognise at once without a word the old familiar lazar-house of Harbledown, so often mentioned in these pages, so picturesque even now in its decay, and in spite of the modern alterations, which have swept away almost all but the ivy-clad chapel of Lanfranc ; the road, still steep, though probably wider than at that time ; the rude steps leading from the doorway, under the shade of two venerable yews, one now decayed and withered, the other still stretching its dark branches over the entrance. Down those steps came, according to his wont, an aged almsman ; and as the two horsemen approached, he threw his accustomed shower of holy water, and then pressed forward, holding the upper-leather of a shoe, bound in a brass rim, with a crystal set in the centre. Colet was the left-hand horseman thus confronted. He bore the shower of holy water

o

with tolerable equanimity, but when the shoe was offered
for him to kiss, he sharply asked the old man what he
wanted. " The shoe of St. Thomas," was the answer.
Colet's anger broke all bounds.   Turning to his companion, " What ! " he said ; " Do these asses expect us to
kiss the shoes of all good men that have ever lived ? Why,
they might as well bring us their spittle or their dung to
be kissed ! "   The kind heart of Erasmus was moved for
the old almsman ; he dropped into his hand a small coin,
and the two travellers pursued their journey to the
metropolis.   Three hundred years have passed, but the
natural features of the scene remain almost unchanged ;
even its minuter memorials are not wanting.   In the old
chest of the almshouse still remain two relics, which no
reader of this story can see without interest.   The one is
an ancient maple bowl, bound with a brazen rim, which
contains a piece of rock crystal, so exactly reminding us of
that which Erasmus describes in the leather of St. Thomas's
shoe, as to suggest the conjecture that when the shoe was
lost, the crystal was thus preserved.   The other is a rude
box, with a chain to be held by the hand, and a slit for
money in the lid, at least as old as the 16th century.
In that box, we can hardly doubt, the coin of Erasmus
was deposited.
   Trivial as these reminiscences may be, they are not
without importance, when they bring before us an incident
so deeply illustrative of the characters and fortunes of the
two pilgrims who thus passed onwards, soon to part and
meet no more, but not soon to lose their influence on the
world in which they lived ; Colet, burning with his honest
English indignation against a system of which the overthrow, though not before his eyes were closed in death,
was near at hand ; Erasmus, sharing his views, yet by
a natural weakness and timidity of nature, unable to carry
them out into rude practice—chafing against the vehemence of Colet, as he afterwards chafed against the
mightier vehemence of Luther, shrinking from the shock
to the feelings of the old almsman of Harbledown, as he
afterwards shrunk from the collision into which his own
convictions would have driven him with the ancient

churches of Christendom. In the meeting of that old
man with the two strangers in the lane at Harbledown,
how completely do we read, in miniature, the whole
history of the coming revolution of Europe.

Still, however, with that strange unconsciousness of
coming events, which often precedes the overthrow of the
greatest of institutions, the tide of pilgrimage and the pomp
of the Cathedral continued apparently unabated almost to
the very moment of the final crash. Almost at the very
time of Erasmus's visit, the offerings at the shrine still
averaged between 800*l.* or 1000*l.*, that is, in our money,
at least 4000*l.*, a year.[1] Henry VII. had in his will left a
kneeling likeness of himself, in silver gilt, to be "set before
St. Thomas of Canterbury, and as nigh to the Shrine of
St. Thomas as may well be." Prior Goldstone, who had
shown Erasmus and Colet the wonders of the Shrine, had
erected its noble central tower, and the stately entrance to
the Precincts. The completion of Becket's Crown was in
contemplation. Great anxiety was still expressed for the
usual privileges and indulgences, on the last Jubilee in
1520 ; it was still pleaded at Rome that, since the death
of St. Peter, there was never a man that did more for the
liberties of the Church than St. Thomas of Canterbury.[2]
Henry VIII., in that same year, had received the Emperor
Charles V. at Canterbury, immediately before the meeting
of the Cloth of Gold. They rode together from Dover, on
the morning of Whitsunday, and entered the city through
St. George's Gate. Under the same canopy were seen
both the youthful sovereigns; Cardinal Wolsey was directly
in front ; on the right and left were the proud nobles of
Spain and England ; the streets were lined with clergy,
all in full ecclesiastical costume. They lighted off their
horses at the west door of the Cathedral ; Warham was
there to receive them ; together they said their devotions
—doubtless before the Shrine.[3] So magnificent a meeting
had probably never been assembled there, nor such an

---

[1] Nichol's Erasmus, p. 110, quotes
Cardinal Morton's Appeal. There is
a similar passage often quoted from
Somner's Canterbury.

[2] Appendix to Battely's Canterbury,
No. 6, xxi.

[3] Battely ; Somner, Part II., App.,
No. x.; Holinshed, 1520.

entertainment given, as Warham afterwards furnished at
his palace, since the days of Langton.   We would fain ask
what the Emperor, fresh from Luther, thought of this,—
the limit of his tour in England ; or how Henry did the
honours of the Cathedral, of which, but for his elder
brother's death, he was destined to have been the Primate.
But the chronicles tell us only of the outward show ;
regardless of the inevitable doom which, year by year,
was drawing nearer and nearer.

   Events moved on.   The Queen, who had greeted[1] her
Imperial nephew with such warmth at Canterbury, was
now divorced.   In 1534 the Royal supremacy and separation from the see of Rome, was formally declared.   The
visitation of the monasteries began in 1535.   The lesser
monasteries were suppressed in 1536.   For a short space
the greater monasteries with their gorgeous shrines and
rituals still remained erect.   In the close of 1536 was
struck the first remote blow at the worship of St. Thomas.
Royal injunctions were issued, abrogating all superfluous
holidays which fell in term-time, or in the time of
harvest : the Festival of the Martyrdom on the 29th of
December escaped ; but the far greater festival of the
Translation of the Relics, falling as it did in the season of
harvest, which extended from the 1st July to the 29th of
December, was thus swept away.   The vast concourse
of pilgrims or idlers from the humble classes, who had
hitherto crowded the Canterbury roads, were now for the
first time detained in their usual occupations ; those from
the higher classes were still free to go ; but one significant
circumstance showed what was to be expected from them.

   Ever since the Festival of the Translation had been
established, its eve, or vigil—that is, the evening of the 6th
of July—had been rigidly observed as a fast by the
Primates of the English Church : on that day the usual
festivities in the palace at Canterbury or Lambeth, as the
case might be, had always been suspended ; the poor,
who usually came to the gates to be fed, came not ; the
fragments of meat which the vast retinue of domestics
gathered from the tables of the spacious hall, were

Holinshed 1520.

withheld. But it was with no wavering spirit that Archbishop Cranmer carried out the Royal injunctions. In a letter written to Thomas Cromwell, from Ford, in the August of this year (1537)—for the most part by his secretary—he had with his own hand inserted a strong remonstrance against the inconsistency of the royal practice and profession :—" But, my lord, if in the court you do keep such holidays and fasting-days as be abrogated, when shall we persuade the people to cease from keeping of them ? for the king's own house shall be an example to all the realm to break his own ordinances." [1] He was determined at any rate that "the Archbishop's own house" should on this, the most important of all the abrogated days, set a fitting precedent of obedience to the new law. On that eve, for the first time for more than three hundred years, the table was spread as usual in the palace-hall [2] for the officers of his household, with the large hospitality then required by custom as almost the first duty of the primate. And then the archbishop " ate flesh " on the Eve of St. Thomas, and " did sup in his hall with his family," as the monk of St. Augustine's Abbey who relates the incident, drily observes, " which was never seen before." [3]

In the spring of the next year (1538), the fatal blow at last began to descend. The names of many of the saints whose festivals had been discontinued remained, and still remain, in the English calendar. But Becket's memory was open to a more grievous charge than that of having given birth to idleness and superstition. We must remember that the mind of the King, and, with a few exceptions, of the government, of the hierarchy, of the nation itself, was possessed with one master idea—that of establishing the Supremacy of the Crown over all causes, ecclesiastical as well as civil, within the dominions of England. It has now in practice been interwoven with all our institutions ; it has in theory been defended and adopted by some of our ablest statesmen, divines, and

---

[1] Strype's Cranmer, Appendix, No. xix.
[2] Ibid., p. 16.
[3] " Annals by an Augustine Monk,"

Harleian MSS., 419, fol. 112. It is somewhat inaccurately quoted by Strype.

philosophers : however liable to be perverted to worldly
or tyrannical purposes, there is a point of view from which
it has been justly regarded as the largest and noblest
opportunity which outward institutions can furnish for
the realisation of the kingdom of God upon earth.   But,
be it right or wrong, it was at that time held to be the
one great question of the English people, and it is therefore not surprising that the story of Becket's career
should have seemed to contain a direct contradiction to
the doctrine of the new reign.   Doubtless philosophical
historians might have drawn distinctions between the
times of the second and the eighth Henry—might have
shown that the truths and feelings represented by the civil
and ecclesiastical powers at these two epochs were widely
different.   But in that age of indiscriminating partisanship,
of half-formed knowledge, of passionate impulses, such a
view of past events could not be found.   Even King John,
whom we now justly account one of the worst of men,
was exalted into a hero, as striving, though in vain, to
resist the encroachments of the Papacy.   The recent
memory of the two great opponents of the new doctrine,
More and Fisher, whose virtues every party now acknowledges, was then set aside with the summary question,
" Should the King's highness have suffered those traitors
to live, Thomas More, 'the jester,' and Fisher, the 'glorious
hypocrite ? ' " [1]   It is necessary to enter into these feelings
to understand in any degree the events which followed.

On the 24th of April, 1538 (such, at any rate, was
the story reported all over the continent of Europe),
a summons was addressed in name of King Henry VIII.,
" to thee, Thomas Becket, sometime Archbishop of Canterbury," charging him with treason, contumacy, and rebellion.
It was read within the walls of the Cathedral, by the side
of the Shrine : thirty days were allowed for his appearance ;
and when, at the expiration of that period, the canopy, and
ark, and iron chest remained unmoved, and the dead man
had not risen to answer for himself, the case was formally
argued at Westminster by the Attorney-General, on the part
of Henry II., on the part of the accused by an advocate

[1] Declaration of Faith, 1539. (Collier, Ecc. Hist, vol. ii. Appendix, No. xlvii.)

granted at the public expense by the King. The arguments
of the Attorney-General prevailed, and on the 10th of
June sentence was pronounced against the Archbishop,
that his bones should be publicly burnt, to admonish the
living of their duty by the punishment of the dead ; and
that the offerings made at the Shrine should be forfeited
to the Crown.[1]

Such, at least, was the belief at Rome, and though
the story has of late years been doubted, there is nothing
in it, which is of itself incredible. It would, if true,
be but one instance of the strange union of violent self-
will with rigid adherence to law,[2] which characterises
all the Tudor family, but especially Henry VIII. It is
but an instance of the same scrupulous casuistry, which
furnished him with his original argument from the Levitical
law for annulling his marriage with Catherine ; and which
then induced him, instead of gratifying his passions as
would most princes of equal power and equal licentious-
ness, to sacrifice one wife after another by regular legal
forms. It is but an instance of the way in which every
act of that most arbitrary reign was performed in due
course of law ; and thus, as if by a Providence working
good out of evil, all the stages of the Reformation received
all the sanction which the combined will of the sovereign
and the nation could give them. And it must be
remembered that in this process there was nothing contrary to the Roman Catholic religion, which Henry still
professed. However absurd to us may seem the proceedings of citing a dead man from his grave, and burning
his bones to ashes because he does not appear, it was the

[1] The grounds for doubting this
story, as related by Sanders, Pollini, and
by Pope Paul III., (Wilkins's Concilia,
ii. 835), are given in Nichols' Erasmus,
p. 233. There are mistakes in detail :
the shrine was not destroyed in August,
as Pollini states ; the Narrative of
Thomas (see note C,) as well as the
Declaration of Faith, (539,) suggests
a doubt, whether any of the bones,
except the head, were burnt. (See
Jenkyns's Cranmer, i. 262). But against
the story generally, there is nothing but
negative evidence, and it is slightly

confirmed by the language of the Proclamation, 1538, the Declaration of
1539, "Forasmuch as it now appeareth
clearly." . . . "By approbation it appeareth clearly."

[2] This is specially put forward in his
defence in the Declaration of Faith,
(1539). "The King's Highness hath
never put any man to death, but by
ordinary process. . . . who can find in
his heart, knowing this, to think the
same prince that so hath judgment
ministered by the law, to be a tyrant?"
(Collier, Eccl. Hist., ii., App. No. xlii.)

exact copy of what had been before enacted in the case of Wycliffe at Lutterworth; and of what was shortly afterwards enacted by Queen Mary in the case of Bucer and Fagius at Cambridge. But, whatever might be the precise mode in which the intentions of Henry and Cranmer were expressed, a ·Royal Commission was duly issued for their execution.

One more visit is recorded in this strange interval of suspense. In August the Shrine was still standing. On the last day of that month, 1538, a great French lady passed through Canterbury, Madame de Montreuil, who had just been attending Mary of Guise to Scotland. She was taken to see the wonders of the place, and " marvelled at the great riches thereof," and said, " that if she had not seen it, all the men in the world could never 'a made her to believe it." But it was mere wonder : the ancient spirit of devotion, which had compelled respect from Colet and Erasmus, had now no place : cushions were set for her to kneel both at the " Shrine " and " Head ; " and thrice the Prior, opening " St. Thomas' head, offered her to kiss it, but she neither kneeled nor would kiss it, but still viewing the riches thereof. . . . . So she departed and went to her lodging to dinner ; and after the same to entertain her with honest pastimes. And about 4 of the clock, the said Prior did send her a present of coneys, capons, chickens, with diverse fruits—plenty—insomuch that she said 'What shall we do with so many capons ? Let the Lord Prior come, and eat, and help us to eat them to-morrow at dinner,' and so thanked him heartily for the said present." [1] This was the last recorded present that the " Lord Prior" of Canterbury gave, and the last recorded pilgrim who saw the Shrine of St. Thomas.

In the course of the next month [2] the Royal Commission for the destruction of shrines, under Dr. Leyton, arrived at Canterbury. Unfortunately, every authentic record of the final catastrophe has perished : and the precise manner of the devastation is involved in obscurity

---

[1] State Papers, vol. i. 583, 584.
[2] Stow gives the proceedings under "September, 1538," which agrees with the date of Madame de Montreuil's visit.

and contradiction. Like all the acts of destruction at the Reformation, as distinct from those in the civil wars at a later period, it was probably carried out in the presence of the Royal Commissioners with all formality and order. The jewels—so we may infer from the analogy of the like event at Durham—were first carefully picked out by a goldsmith in attendance, and then the iron chest of the shrine broken open with a sledge-hammer.[1] The bones within—as far as we can judge from the conflicting evidence[2]—were either scattered to the winds, or mingled indiscriminately with others; in this respect, sharing a different fate from that of most of the disinterred saints, who, after the destruction of their shrines, were buried with decency and care near the places where the shrines had stood.[3] . . . The reputed skull in the golden " Head " was treated as an imposture, from its being so much larger than the portion that was found in the Shrine with the rest of the bones,[4] and was burnt to ashes as such. . . . The jewels and gold of the Shrine were carried off in two strong coffers, on the shoulders of seven or eight men ;[5] for the removal of the rest of the spoils, six and twenty carts are said to have waited at the church door.[6] . . . The jewels, no doubt, went into the royal stores ; the "Regale of France," the glory of the Shrine, was long worn by Henry himself in the ring which after the manner of those times encircled his enormous thumb : the last time that it appears in history is among the " diamonds " of the golden " collar " of his daughter Queen Mary.[7] . . . The blood with which the water of the Canterbury bottles was discoloured was examined by a commission appointed for that very purpose, at the request of Cranmer, who suspected that it was red ochre.[8] . . . The healing virtues of the well, it was observed, instantly

---

[1] See Raine's Durham, p. 55.
[2] It was a dispute afterwards, whether the bones had been burnt or not, the Roman Catholics maintaining that they had been, the Protestants vehemently denying it. This shows a certain consciousness on the part of the latter that there had been excessive violence used. See Declaration of Faith, 1539, (in Nichols' Erasmus, 236 ; Collier, Appendix, No. xlvii.), and William Thomas, 1566, (Note C.)
[3] See Raine's Durham, pp. 56, 57.
[4] Declaration of Faith, 1539.
[5] Stow's Annals, 1538.
[6] Sanders in Wilkins' Conc., iii. 836.
[7] Nichols' Erasmus, p. 224.
[8] Jenkyns' Cranmer, i. 262.

disappeared.[1] . . . Finally, a proclamation was issued on the 16th of November, setting forth the cause and mode of Becket's death, in a statement which displays considerable ability, by fixing on those points in the ancient narratives which unquestionably reveal the violent temper and language of the so-called Martyr.[2] " For these, and for other great and urgent reasons, long to recite, the King's Majesty, by the advice of his council, hath thought expedient to declare to his loving subjects, that notwithstanding the said canonisation, there appeareth nothing in his life and exterior conversation whereby he should be called a Saint ; but rather esteemed a rebel and traitor to his prince. Therefore his Grace straightly chargeth and commandeth, that henceforth the said Thomas Becket shall not be esteemed, named, reputed, nor called a Saint, but ' Bishop Becket,' and that his images and pictures throughout the whole realm shall be put down and avoided out of all churches and chapels, and other places ; and that from henceforth the days used to be festivals in his name, shall not be observed—nor the service, office, antiphonies, collects and prayers in his name read, but rased and put out of all books."[3]

Most rigidly was this proclamation carried out. Not more carefully is the name of Geta erased by his rival brother on every monument of the Roman Empire, from Britain to Egypt, than that of the contumacious Primate by the triumphant King. Not only has every statue and picture of the "Traitor" been swept away, but there is hardly an illuminated psalter or missal, hardly a copy of any historical or legal document, from which the pen or the knife of the eraser, has not effaced the once honoured name and figure of St. Thomas wherever it occurs. At Canterbury the arms of the city and cathedral were altered. Within the church some fragments of painted glass, and the

---

[1] William Thomas. (Note C.)

[2] " His death, which they untruly called martyrdom, happened upon a rescue by him made ; and that, as it is written, he gave opprobrious names to the gentlemen which then counselled him to leave his stubbornness, and to avoid the commotion of the people risen up for that rescue. And he not only called one of them 'bawde,' but also took Tracy by the bosom, and violently shook and plucked him, in such a manner as he had almost overthrown him to the pavement of the church ; so that upon this fray, one of their company perceiving the same, struck him, and so in the throng Becket was slain." See Wilk. Con. iii. 848.   [3] Ibid.

defaced picture at the head of Henry IV.'s tomb, are his only memorials. Even in the second year of Edward VI. the obnoxious name was still hunted down; and Cranmer, in his Articles of Visitation for that year, enquires,— "Whether they have put out of their church books the name and service of Thomas Becket?" The site of his original tomb in the crypt was a few months after the fall of the Shrine annexed by Order in Council to the house of the first canon of the newly erected Chapter, and retained almost to our own time as his cellar for wine and faggots. Every record of the Shrine was so completely destroyed, that the Cathedral archives throw hardly the slightest light, either on its existence or its removal.[1] And its site has remained, from that day to this, a vacant space, with the marks of the violence of the destruction even yet visible on the broken pavement.

Round it still lie the tombs of King, and Prince, and Archbishop ; the worn marks on the stones show the reverence of former ages. But the place itself is vacant, and the lessons which that vacancy has to teach us must now take the place of the lessons of the ancient Shrine.

There are very few probably at the present time, in whom, as they look round on the desolate pavement, the first feeling that arises is not one of disappointment and regret, that a monument of past times so costly and curious should have been thus entirely obliterated. There is probably no one, who, if the Shrine were now standing, would dream of removing it. One such tomb, as has been said, still remains in Westminster Abbey : the very notion of destroying it would call out a general outcry from all educated men throughout the kingdom. Why is it that this feeling, so familiar and so natural to us, should then have been so completely over-ruled ? The answer to this question is doubly instructive. First, it reveals to us one great difference between our age, and the age—not only of the Reformation, but of many ages which have gone before us. In our time, there has sprung up, to a degree hitherto unprecedented, a love of what is old, of what is beautiful,- of what is venerable —

[1] See Appendix.

a desire to cherish the memorials of the past, and to keep before our eyes the vestiges of times, which are brought so vividly before us in no other way. It is, as it were, God's compensation to the world for its advancing years. Earlier ages care but little for these relics of antiquity; one is swept away after another to make room for what is yet to come ; precious works of art, precious recollections, are trampled under foot; the very abundance in which they exist seems to beget an indifference towards them. But in proportion as they become fewer and fewer, the affection for them grows stronger and stronger ; and the further we recede from the past, the more eager now seems our craving to attach ourselves to it by every link that remains. Such a feeling it is which most of us would entertain towards this ancient Shrine—such a feeling as, in the mass of men, hardly existed at the time of its destruction. We are so far richer by at least one step than were our fathers ; other gifts they had, which we have not : this gift of insight into the past, of loving it for its own sake, of retaining around us as much as we can of its grace and beauty—we have, as they had not. It is true that reverence for the dead ought never to stand in the way of the living—that when any great evil is avoided, or any great good attained, by destroying old recollections, no historical or antiquarian tenderness can be pleaded for their preservation : but where no such reason exists let us keep them as best we can, and as we stand on the vacant space of Becket's Shrine, let us be thankful that we have retained what we have, and cherish it accordingly.

It is impossible, however to read the signs of the fifteenth and sixteenth centuries without perceiving that the Shrine of St. Thomas fell not simply from a love of destruction, or a desire of plunder, but before a sense of overwhelming necessity. Had the Reformers been ever so anxious to retain it, they would probably have found it impossible to do so. However much the rapacity of Henry VIII. may have prompted him to appropriate the treasures to himself, and however much we may lament the wholesale plunder of riches, which would have endowed all the public institutions in the country ; yet the destruction of the Shrine was justified on general reasons, and those reasons commended themselves to the common sense and feeling of the nation and the age. The mode in which it was destroyed may appear violent ; but it was the violence, partly characteristic of a barbarous and revolutionary epoch, partly such as always is produced by the long growth of some great abuse. A striking proof of this fact, which is also itself one of the most surprising parts of the whole transaction, is the apathy with which the clergy and the people acquiesced in the act of the government. When a similar destruction was effected in France, at the time of the great Revolution, although the horrors perpetrated were even greater, yet there were loyal hands to save some relic at least from the general ruin ; and when the Abbey of St. Denis was again opened after the Restoration, the ashes of the sovereigns, the fragments of the royal tombs, were still preserved sufficiently to fill again the vacant spaces. Yet of Becket's shrine hardly a shred or particle has ever been traced ; the storm had long been gathering, yet it burst at last with hardly an effort to arrest it, and the desecration was executed by officers, and sanctioned by ecclesiastics, who, in name at least, still belonged to the ancient faith. At Rome, indeed, it was made one of the special grounds of the bull of excommunication issued by the Pope in the December of that year. But in England hardly a murmur transpires. Only one complaint has reached our time : Cranmer wrote to Cromwell in the following year, to tell him that a drunken man had been heard to say[1] that "it was a pity and naughtily done to put down the Pope and St. Thomas." Something of this silence may doubtless be ascribed to the reign of terror which more or less characterises the administration of justice in the time of Henry VIII. But it cannot be so explained altogether. No Thomas More was found to die for Becket, as there had been for the Pope's supremacy. And during the five years of the restored Roman Catholic religion in the reign of Mary, no attempt was made to revive the worship of Becket ; and the Queen

[1] Jenkyns' Cranmer, i. 278.

206 HISTORICAL MEMORIALS OF CANTERBURY.

herself, though usually so eager for the restitution of the
treasures which her father had taken from the churches
and convents, did not scruple, as we have seen, to wear
in her necklace the choicest jewel of the shrine. The
account of Erasmus' visit, as already given, is in fact
sufficient to show how completely the system of relic-
worship and of pilgrimage had worked its own ruin—how
deep was the disgust which it awakened in the minds
of intelligent men, unwilling though they might be to
disturb the established forms of religion. By the time
that the catastrophe was accomplished, Colet had already
been laid to rest in the choir of St. Paul's; the tomb
had already closed over Erasmus in his beloved retirement
at Basle. But we cannot doubt that could they have
lived to see the completion of the overthrow which their
sagacious minds clearly foresaw, as they knelt before
the shrine a few years before, the one would have received
the tidings with undisguised exultation, the other with a
sigh indeed, yet with a full sense of the justice of the act.

It is therefore a satisfaction, as we look on the broken
pavement, to feel that, here as elsewhere, no great institution perishes without good cause. Had Stephen Langton
been asked which was most likely to endure, the Magna
Charta which he won from John, or the Shrine which, five
years afterwards, he consecrated in the presence of
Henry III., he would, beyond all question, have said, the
Shrine of St. Thomas. But we see what he could not see
—we see that the Charter has lasted, because it was
founded on the eternal laws of truth, and justice, and
freedom ; the Shrine has vanished away, because it was
founded on the passing opinion of the day ; because it
rested on ignorance, which was gradually dissolving ;
because it was entangled with exaggerated superstitions,
which were condemned by the wise and good even of those
very times. But the vacant space is more than this ;
it is not only a sign of the violent convulsion through
which the Reformation was effected, but it is a sign also,
if we could so take it, of what the Reformation has effected
for us, and what duties it has laid upon us. If one of the
ancient pilgrims were to rise again, and look in vain for

the object of his long devotion, he would think that we were men without religion. So, in like manner, when the Gentile conqueror entered the Holy of Holies and looked round, and saw that there was no graven image or likeness of anything on earth or in heaven, he marvelled at the "vacant sanctuary," [1] as of a worship without a God. Yet Pompey in the Temple of Jerusalem, and the ancient pilgrim in Canterbury Cathedral, would be alike mistaken. It is true that a void has been created—that the Reformation often left, as here in the old sanctuary of the Cathedral, so on a wider scale in the hearts of men, a vacancy and a coldness which it is useless to deny, though easy to explain, and, to a certain point, defend. But this vacancy—this natural result of every great convulsion of the human mind—is one which it is our own fault if we do not fill up, in the only way in which it can be filled up—not by rebuilding what the Reformers justly destroyed, nor yet by disparaging the better qualities of the old saints and pilgrims, but by a higher worship of God, by a more faithful service of man, than was then thought possible. In proportion to our thankfulness that ancient superstitions are destroyed, should be our anxiety that new light, and increased zeal, and more active goodness should take their place. Our pilgrimage cannot be Geoffrey Chaucer's, but it may be John Bunyan's. In that true "Pilgrim's Way" to a better country, we have all of us to toil over many a rugged hill, over many a dreary plain, by many opposite and devious paths, cheering each other by all means, grave and gay, till we see the distant towers. In that pilgrimage and progress towards all things good, and wise, and holy, Canterbury Cathedral, we may humbly trust, may still have a part to play: although it is no longer the end in the long journey, it may still be a stage in our advance ; it may still enlighten, elevate, sanctify, those who come within its reach ; it may still, if it be true to its high purpose, win for itself, in the generations which are to come after us, a glory more humble, but not less excellent, than when a hundred thousand worshippers lay prostrate before the shrine of its ancient hero.

[1] " Vacuam sedem, inania arcana." (Tacit. Hist. v. 9.)

APPENDIX TO THE "SHRINE OF BECKET."

NOTE A.

[The following extracts are from a MS. History of Canterbury Cathedral, in Norman French, entitled, "Polistoire," in the Harleian MSS. in the British Museum. My attention was called to this curious document by Mr. Bond, to whom I would here beg to express my thanks for his constant courtesy whenever I have had occasion to consult him.]

THE WELL OF ST. THOMAS.

(See p. 185.)

Harl. MS. 636, f. 143 b., col. 1, line 6, ab imâ.

(1.) Si fust la place apres tost balee, et la poudre coylee de coste le eglise gettue en vn lyu dunt auaunt nout parlaunce; mes en fest le poer Deu tauntost habundaunt par uirtue tregraciouse de queu merite le martyr estoyt a tute gent nout tost estre conu. Dunt en le lyu auaunt dist ou ne gweres en sa ariere moysture ny apparust mes euwe hi auoyt tut fust ele petite, sa colur naturele quant la poudre ressu auoit tost chaunga, cest a sauoir vne foiz en let et quatre foyz la colour de saunc reprist. E puys en sa nature demeyne returna. Si comensa aboylir de source habundaunte et demurt funtayne plentyuuse. Dunt puys plusurs greues de diuers maladies graciousement en sunt garys.

Ibid. fol. 150, col. 1.

(2.) [*King Henry II. after his penance*] . . . . Puis le matyn kaunt le iur cler apparust messe requist et la oyst deuoutement et puis del ewe Seint Thomas bust a la funtaine auaunt nomee, ke de saunc et let la colur prist, et puys en sa nature returna, et vne ampulle de cele ewe pleyne oue ly prist, cum en signe de pelryn, et ioyous de Caunterbur departist cel samady.

THE TRANSLATION OF THE RELICS OF ST. THOMAS IN 1220.

(See p. 16.)

Ibid. fol. 202 b., col. 2, l. 15, ab imâ.

Ausi memes cel an la none de Jun a Caunterbire fust Seint Thomas le martir translate. Le an de sun martyrement l. per lerseueske Estephene auaunt nome de Canterbire. Coment ceste sollempnete estoyt feste a tote gent uoil estre conu, et me a forceray de cele la manere brevement parcunter. Lerseueske Estephene de Langetone del hure ke cele dignete out ressu, apres ceo ke en Engletere fust ariue et le couent del exil reuenu estoyt, se purpensa totes hures coment les reliqes sun predecessur Seint Thomas le glorious martyr poeyt honurer par la translatiun fere, et la pur-ueaunce des choses nessessaries largement fist, cum ia mustre en fest serra. Dunt cum del iur certein ke cele translatiun sollempne fere uoloyt, au puple parmye la tere out la notificatiun fest, tauns des grauns hi sunt venuz, et puple cum sauns numbre, ke la cite de Caunterbire ne la suburbe, ne les menues uiles enuiroun, a cele yoingnauntes procheynes, le puple taunt uenu ne poeyent en lurs mesuns resceyure. Le Roy ausi Henry le iij. a la requeste ler-seueske de Caunterbire uenu hi estoit. Si demora oue lerseueske et ansemble oue ly tuz les grauns ke venus estoyent la ueile et le iur de la translatiun en tuz custages. Estre ceo en les entrees de la cite a chescune porte en my la rue les toneaus de vin en foylis fist cocher lerseueske et ces mynistres mettre pur largement au puple doner en la chalyne sauns paer accune moneye. E ausi en quatre lyus dediens la cite en les quarfoucs en memes la manere fist les toneaus mettre pur seruir a la mene gent. E defendre fist en les iiij. celers de vin ke riens ny fust au puple estraunge uendu, si nun pleynement a ces custages, et ceo par sureuwe de ces gens a ceo assignes. Quar nestoyt lors dediens la cite en plus de lyus uin troue a uendre. En teu manere les choses dehors ordines, ler-seueske Estephene et Gauter le priur ansemble oue tut le couent del eglise Jhu Crist en la nuyt procheyne deuaunt le iur de la trans-latiun en due furme de deuociun au sepulcre del martyr appro-cherent. E ilukes au comencement en lurs orisuns se donerent tuz taunt cum la brefte de la nuyt le poeyt suffrir. Puys sunt les peres de la tumbe sauns blemysement remues per les meyns des moygnes a ceo ordines, et se leuerent les autres tuz si aprocherent et cel martyr de ioye regardauns ne se poeyent des lermes tenir. E puys autrefoyz as orisuns se unt dones tuz en comune hors pris accuns des moygnes ke de seinte vie especiaument elu furent a cel tresor precious hors de sepulcre remuer. Les queus le unt leue et en une chace de fust honeste a ceo appareylee le unt mys. La quele de fer bien yert asseurie si la fermerent queyntement par clous de fer, et puys en lyu honeste et priue le porterent tannt ke lendemeyn le iur de la translatiun sollempnement a celebrer. Puys le matyn en cele mere eglise se assemblerent les prelats tuz, cest a sauoyr, Pandulf auaunt nome de la seinte eglise de rome legat, et Esteuene erseueske de Caunterbire oue les autres eueskes ces suffragans tuz uenuz hors pris troys, des queus lun mort estoyt et les deus par maladie furent escuses. Ceus en la presence le Roy Dengletere auaunt nome

P

Henry le iij. au lyu ou le martyr glorious fust demore tost alerent, et la chace pristrent les prelats a ceo ordines sur lurs espaules, si la porterent deuoutement en quer deuaunt lauter de la Trinite ke est en le orient del see patriarchal.   Ilukes desuz un autre chace de fust trerichement de oer et des peres preciouses appareylee en tote reuerence honurablement cele mistrent.   Si demurt par plate de oer tote part couerte et richement garnye.

MARRIAGE OF EDWARD I. AT CANTERBURY.
(See p. 188.)

Ibid. fol. 225, *col.* 1, *line* 4.

Pus sur cele ordinaunce vint en Engletere le auauntdiste Margarete, et la v. Ide de Septembre lerceueske de Caunterbyre Robert les esposailes celebra entre le Eduuard auauntdist et cele Margarete en le hus del eglise de Caunterbyre deuers len cloistre de coste le hus del martirement Seynt Thomas.   Kar le roy hors de la chaumbre le priur vint, et Margarete hors du paleys lerceueske ou lurs hosteaus pris estoient.   E sur ceo lerceueske auaunt nome Robert la messe des esposayles celebra al auter del fertre Seynt Thomas le martir. E le drap ke outre le roy et la royne fust estendu en tens de la benisun plusurs chalengerent.   Cest a sauoyr lerceueske par la resun de sun office, le priur par la resun de la mere eglise, en la quele vnkes accun riens ne ressust ne ne auoyt de fee, par la resun de office ke en cele feist, pur ceo ke leglise de Caunterbyre ne est une chapele lerceueske, mes mere eglise de totes les eglises et chapeles de tute la prouince de Caunterbyre.   Le clerc ausi ke la croyz lerceueske porta le auauntdist drap chalanga.   E les clers ausi de la chapele le roy cel memes drap chalengerent.   Dunt pur ceo ke en teu manere taunt de diuers chalenges sur cel drap hy estoyent et certein vnkore nestoit a ki de droit demorer deuoyt, comaunda le roy cel drap au Cunte de Nichole liurer, ausi cum en owele meyn, taunt ke la discussiun se preist, ky de droyt le deueroyt auoyr.   Si fust cel drap negeres apres de par le roy au fertre Seynt Thomas maunde. Le samaday procheyn suyaunt la auauntdiste royne Margarete sa messe en la chapele lerceueske dediens le paleys oyst, la quele celebra le eueske de Couentre.   Si offrist ilukes la royne a la manere de autres femmes sun cirge a les meins del eveske chauntaunt.   E fust cel cirge tauntost au ferte Seint Thomas porte.

NOTE B.

[In 1446 a Bohemian noble, Leo von Rotzmital, was sent on an embassy to England. His travels are related in two curious narratives : one by a Bohemian, Schassek, now only known through a Latin translation; the other, a German, Tetzel of Nuremberg. They were published in 1847 by Professor Hye, in the University of Ghent, and were first introduced to the notice of the English public in an able and instructive article in the "Quarterly Review," of March, 1852, ascribed to Mr. Ford. To his courtesy I am indebted for the volume from which the following extracts are made.]

JOURNEY OF THE BOHEMIAN AMBASSADOR TO CANTERBURY.

(See pp. 165, 177, 183, 187.)

(1.) Post eum casum die tertia, rursus navim conscendentes, in Angliam cursum tenuimus. Cumque appropinquaremus, conspeximus montes excelsos calce plenos, quam igne urere opus non est.

Ii montes e longinquo nivibus operti videntur. Iis arx adjacet, a Cacodaemonibus extructa, adeo valida et munita, ut in nulla Christianorum provincia par ei reperiri queat. Montes illos arcemque praetervecti Sandvico urbi appulimus ; ea mari adjacet, unde multae regiones navibus adiri possunt. Haec prima urbium Angliae in eo littore occurrit.

Ibi primum conspexi navigia maritima, Naves, Galeones, et Cochas. Navis dicitur, quae ventis et solis agitur. Galeon est, qui remigio ducitur : eorum aliqui ultra ducentos remiges habent. Id navigii genus est magnitudine et longitudine praecellenti, quo et secundis et adversis ventis navigari potest. Eo, ut plurimum, bella maritima geri consuevere, utpote quod aliquot centenos homines simul capere possit. Tertium genus est Cocha, quam dicunt, et ea satis magna. Sed nullam rem magis demirabar, quam nautas malum ascendentes, et ventorum adventum distantiamque praedicentes, et quae vela intendi, quaeve demi debeant, praecipientes. Inter eos unum nautam ita agilem vidi, ut vix cum eo quisquam comparari possit.

Sandvici consuetudo est, ut totam noctem cum fidicinibus et tubicinibus obambulent, clamantes, et quis eo tempore ventus flet, annunciantes. Eo audito negociatores, si ventus sibi commodus flare nunciatur, egressi naves conscendunt et ad patrias suas cursum dirigunt.

Sandvico Cantuariam octo milliarium iter est. Ea urbs est Archiepiscopo Angliae subjecta, qui ibi domicilium suum habet. Coenobium ibi visitur tanta elegantia, ut ei vix in ulla Christianorum

provincia par inveniatur, sicut hac in re omnes peregrinatores con-
sentiunt. Id templum triplici contignatione fornicata constat, ita
ut tria templa, unum supra alterum, censeri possint : desuper stanno
totum contegitur.

In eo templo occisus est Divus Thomas Cantuariensis Archiepiscopus, ideo quod iniquis legibus, quas Rex Henricus contra
Ecclesiae Catholicae libertatem rogabat, sese constanter opposuit.
Qui primum in exilium pulsus est, deinde cum revocatus esset,
in templo sub vespertinis precibus a nefariis hominibus, qui
regi impio gratificari cupiebant, Deum et sanctos invocans, capite
truncatus est.

Ibi vidimus sepulchrum et caput ipsius. Sepulchrum ex puro
auro conflatum est, et gemmis adornatum, tamque magnificis donariis
ditatum, ut par ei nesciam. Inter alias res preciosas spectatur in
eo et carbunculus gemma, qui noctu splendere solet, dimidi ovi
gallinacei magnitudine. Illud enim sepulchrum a multis Regibus,
Principibus, mercatoribus opulentis, aliisque piis hominibus munifice
locupletatum est. Ibi omnes reliquiae nobis monstratae sunt :
primum caput Divi Thomae Archiepiscopi, rasuraque vel calvities
ejusdem ; deinde columna ante sacellum Genitricis Dei, juxta quam
orare, et colloquio Beatae virginis (quod a multis visum et auditum
esse nobis certo affirmabatur) perfrui solitus est. Sed ex eo tempore, quo haec facta fuerant, jam anni trecenti elapsi sunt. Divus
autem ipse non statim pro sancto habitus est, verum post annos
demum ducentos, cum ingentibus miraculis inclaresceret, in
numerum divorum relatus est.

Fons est in eo coenobio, cujus aquae quinquies in sanguinem, et
semel in lac commutatae fuerant, idque non multo ante, quam nos
eo venissemus, factum esse dicitur.

Caeteras sacras reliquias, quas ibi conspeximus, omnes annotavi,
quae hae sunt : primum vidimus redimiculum Beatae virginis,
frustum de veste Christi, tresque spinas de corona ejusdem.

Deinde contemplati sumus sancti Thomae subuculam, et cerebrum
ejus, et divorum Thomae Iohannisque Apostolorum sanguinem.
Spectavimus etiam gladium, quo decollatus est sanctus Thomas
Cantuariensis, et crines matris Dei, et portionem de sepulchro
ejusdem. Monstrabatur quoque nobis pars humeri Divi Simeonis,
ejus, qui Christum in ulnis gestaverat, Beatae Lustrabenae caput,
crus unum S. Georgii, frustum corporis et ossa S. Laurentii, crus
S. Romani Episcopi, crus Ricordiae virginis, calix Beati Thomae,
quo in administratione Missae Cantuariae uti fuerat solitus, crus
Mildae virginis, crus Euduardae virginis. Aspeximus quoque
dentem Johannis Baptistae, portionem crucis Petri et Andreae
Apostolorum, ossa Philippi et Jacobi Apostolorum, dentem et
digitum Stephani Martyris, ossa Catharinae virginis, oleumque de
sepulchro ejus, quod ad hanc usque diem inde manare fertur ; crines

Beatae Mariae Magdalenae, dentem divi Benedicti, digitum sancti Urbani, labia unius infantium ab Herode occisorum, ossa beati Clementis, ossa divi Vincentii. Et alia plurima nobis monstrabantur, quae hoc loco a me annotata non sunt.

Cantuaria digressi per noctem substitimus Rochestriae, urbe viginti milliaribus inde distante. Rochesteria Londinum, viginti quatuor milliarium itinere confecto, progressi sumus. Ea est urbs ampla et magnifica, arces habet duas. Earum alteram, quae in extremo urbis sita, sinu maris alluitur, Rex Angliae incolit, quem ibi offendimus. Ille sinus (Thamesis fl.) ponte lapideo longo, super quem per totam ejus longitudinem aedes sunt extructae, sternitur. Nullibi tantum milvorum numerum vidi, quam ibi, quos laedere capitale est.

Londini cum essemus, deducti sumus in id templum, in quo vivus Thomas natus esse fertur; ibi matris et sororis ipsius sepulchra disuntur; deinde et in alterum ubi S. Keuhardus sepultus est.

(2.) Do fuoren wir mit grossem ungewitter in ein stat, heisst Kanterburg.

Meinem herrn und andern gesellen thet das mer so we, das sie auf dem schiff lagen, als wæren sie tot.

Kanterburg ist in Engellant und gehort dem kunig von Engellant zu. Do leit der lieb herr sant Thomas. In der selben stat ist gar ein kostlicher sarch im münster, wann es ist ein bistum da und gar ein hübsche kirchen. Der sarch, darinne sant Thomas leit, ist das geringst daran gold, und ist lang und weit, das ein mitlein person darin ligen mag; aber mit perlein und edelgestein so ist er gar seer kostlich geziert, das man meint, das kein kostlicher sarch sey in der christenheit, und da auch so gross wunderzeichen geschehen als da.

Item zu einen zeiten, da het sich ein kunig von Frankreich in einem veldstreit dahin gelobt; also gesigt der kunig seinen veinden ob und kam zu dem münster und zu dem heiligen herrn sant Thomas, und kniet für den sarch und sprach sein gebet und het einen ring an seiner hand, darin was ser ein kostlicher stein. Also het der bischof des selben münster Kanterburg den kunig gebeten, er sol den ring mitsamt dem stein an den sarch geben. Der kunig saget, der stein wær jm zu vast lieb und hett grossen glauben : was er anfieng, so er den ring an der hand hett, das jm nit mocht mislingen. Aber er wolt jm an den sarch geben, domit er aber desder basser geziert wurd, hunderttausend gulden. Der biscof was ser fro und dankt dem kunig. Sobald der kunig die wort het geredet und dem bischof den ring het versagt, von stund an springt der stein auss dem ring und mitten in den sarch als hett en ein goldschmid hinein gemacht. Do das miracul der kunig sach, do bat er den lieben herrn sant Thomas und den bischof, das er jm sein sünd vergeb, und gab darnach den ring und etwan vil ob hunderdt tausend gulden an den sarch. Niemand kan gewissen wass stein das ist. Er hat ser einen hellen liechten schein und brinnt als ein liecht, das kein gesicht erleiden mag, jn so stark anzusehen, domit man jm sein varb erkennen möcht. Man meint, das er an seiner, güet so kostlich sey : so ein kunig von Engellant gefangen wurd, so möcht mam jn damit lösen ; wann er sey kostlicher, dann das ganz Engelland. Und unter dem sarch ist die stat, do der lieb herr sant Thomas enthaubtet worden ist, und ob dem sarch hecht ein grob härein hemd, das er angetragen hatt, und auf der linken seiten, so man hinein geet, do ist einn brunn, darauss hat sant Thomas altag trunken. Der hat sich zu sant Thomas zeiten funfmal verwandelt in milch und blut. Darauss trank meinn herr Herr Lew und all sein diener. Und darnach geet man in ein kleine grufft als in ein cappellen, da man sant Thomas gemartert hat. Da zeiget man uns das schwert, damit man jm den kopf abgeschlagen hat. Da weiset man auch ein merklich stuck des heiligen creuzes, auch der nägel einen und den rechten arm des lieben herrn Ritter sant Görgen und etlich dorn in einer mostranzen von der dürren kron.

Auss der cappellen get man herfur zu einem steinen stul, da ist unser Frawen bild, das gar oft mit sant Thomas geredet hat. Das selbig bild stet iezunt im kor und hat ser von kostlichem gestein und perlein ein kron auf, die man umb gross gut schätzt. Da sahen wir gar kostlich cantores meinem herrn zu eren ein schons salve singen. In unser sprach heisst man den sant Thomas von Kandelberg ; aber er heisst sant Thomas von Kanterburg.

NOTE C.

[The following extract is from a work of William Thomas, Clerk of the Privy Council in the reign of Edward VI., who was executed in the reign of Mary, for an alleged share in Wyat's conspiracy. Amongst other works, he left a "Defence of King Henry VIII.," entitled, "Il Pelerino Inglese," which is couched in the form of a dialogue with some Italian gentlemen, who ask him numerous questions as to the common charges against the King, to which he replies. The work is in the Cotton MSS. in the British Museum.]

THE WELL AND THE SHRINE OF BECKET.

(See pp. 185, 200.)

—◆—

Cotton MS., Vespasian D. xviii., p. 61.

" ' These wordes were marked of them that wayted on the table, in such wise that without more adoe, iij of those gentylmen waiters considered together, and streyght wayes toke their iourney to

Canturbury where tarrying there tyme, on an euening fyndyng this Byshop in the common cloyster, after they had asked hym certayne questions, whereunto he most arrogantly made answere, they slew hym. And here began the holynes, for incontinently as these gentylmen were departed, the monkes of that monastery locked up the church doores, and perswaded the people that the bells fell on ryngyng by them selves, and here was crying of 'miracles, miracles,' so earnestly that the deuilish monks, to nourish the supersticion of this new martired saynt, having the place longe tyme seperate unto them selves, *quia propter sanguinem suspenduntur sacra,* corrupted the fresh water of a well thereby, with a certayne mixture; that many tymes it appeared bloudy, which they perswaded should procede by myracle of the holy marterdome : and the water merveylously cured all maner of infirmities, insomuch that the ignoraunt multitude came runnyng together of all handes, specyally after the false miracles were confermed by the popes canonisacion, which folowed within a few yeres after as sone as the Romayne See had ratified this saintes glory in heaven : yea, and more, these fayned miracles had such credit at length, that the poore kynge hymselfe was perswaded to beleve them, and in effect came in person to visett the holy place with greate repentaunce of his passed euil doyng, and for satisfaction of his synnes gave many greate and fayre possessions to the monasterye of the foresayde religious : and thus finally was this holy martir sanctified on all handes. Butt the kynges maiestie that now is dead fyndyng the maner of the saints lyfe to agree evil with the proportion of a very sainte, and merveylyng at the vertue of this water that healed all infirmities, as the blynde world determined, to see the substanciall profe of this thinge, in effect found these miracles to be utterly false, for when supersticion was taken away from the ignoraunt multitudes, then ceassed all the vertue of this water, which now remayneth playne water, as all other waters do : so that the kyng moved of necessitie, could no lesse do then deface the shryne that was author of so much ydolatry. Whether the doyng thereof hath bene the undoyng of the canonised saint, or not, I cannot tell. But this is true, that his bones are spred amongest the bones of so many dead men, that without some greate miracle they wyll not be founde agayne.' 'By my trouth' (sayde one of the gentylmen) 'in this your kynge dyd as I wold have done.' 'What' (quoth myne adversary) 'do ye credit hym ?' 'Within a litle,' sayd that other, 'for his tale is sensible : and I have knowen of the lyke false miracles here in Italye, proved before my face.' "

THE PILGRIMS' WAY OR PATH TOWARDS THE SHRINE OF ST. THOMAS OF CANTERBURY.

THE evidence of local tradition in several places in Surrey and Kent appears to favour the supposition that a line of road, tracked out possibly in very early times, even before the coming of the Romans, and running along the south flank of the north Downs, which traverse Surrey from Farnham westward into Kent, and thence towards Canterbury, had been subsequently frequented by pilgrims in their progress from Southampton, as also from the west through Winchester, to the Shrine of St. Thomas. It has been supposed, with much probability, that Henry II., when he landed at Southampton, July 8, 1174, and made his pilgrimage to Becket's tomb, may have approached Canterbury by this route.

It may be assumed that foreign devotees from Brittany, Anjou, the western parts of Normandy, and the adjacent provinces of France, would choose the more convenient transit from the mouth of the Seine, or other French ports, to the ancient haven of Hanton, or Southampton. That place, from the earliest times, was greatly frequented on account of the facilities which it presented to commercial intercourse with the continent, and its vicinity to the ancient capital of the Heptarchy, the city of Winchester, where our earlier sovereigns constantly resided. This course would obviously be more commodious to many, who were attracted to our shores by the important ecclesiastical establishments which surrounded the shrine of St. Swithin at Winchester, and still more by the extended celebrity of the reliques of St. Thomas ; whilst pilgrims from the more northern parts of France, or from Flanders, would prefer the more frequented passage by Seaford, Dovor, or Sandwich.

On leaving Southampton, the pilgrims—unless their course lay by Winchester—would probably take the most secure and direct line of communication towards Farnham, crossing the Itchen at Stoneham, and thence in the direction of Bishop's Waltham, Alton, and Froyle. It is, however, by no means evident that the line would pass through those places, and it must be left to the local observation of those who may care to investigate the ancient trackways of Hampshire, whether the course of the pilgrims may not have passed from Southampton, in the direction of Durley, to Upham, and rather north of Bishop's Waltham, falling into the " Salt Lane," a name often serving to indicate the trace of an early line of communication, and so either by Cheriton and Alresford, or by Ropley into the old road from Winchester to Farnham, or else over Millbarrow and Kilmison downs, towards Farnham. Or the track may have passed by Beacon hill, west of Warnford, joining the present road from Fareham to Alton, at about nine miles south of the latter. Near this line of road, moreover, a little west of it, and about three miles from Alton, a trace of the course of the "Pilgrims' Path" seems to be found in the name of a farm or dwelling near Rotherfield Park and East Tisted, still known as "Pilgrims' Place."

At Farnham, the abrupt termination of the Surrey downs presents itself, in the remarkable ridge known as the "Hog's Back." Thence there are two communications towards Guildford, diverging at a place called "Whiteway's End," one being the main turnpike-road along the ridge, the other—and probably the more ancient —running under that height towards the tumulus and adjoining eminence south of Guildford, known as St. Catharine's hill, where it seems to have crossed the river Wey, at a ferry towards Shalford. The name of "Conduit Farm," near this line, situate on the south flank of the Hog's Back, may possibly be worth observation. Eastward of Guildford, the way doubtless proceeded along the flank of the downs, by or near St. Martha's Chapel, situate on a remarkable eminence, insulated from the adjacent downs.

One of the county historians gives the following observation under Albury: "The ancient path called the Pilgrims' Way, which led from the city of Winchester to Canterbury, crosses this parish and is said to have been much used in former times."[1] From Albury the line of the way, running east, is in many places discernible on the side of the Surrey downs, sometimes still used as an occupation road or bridle-way, its course indicated frequently by yew trees at intervals, which are to be seen also occasionally left standing in the arable fields, where ancient enclosures have been thrown down and the plough has effaced every other vestige of this ancient track. The line, for the most part, it would seem, took its course about midway down the hill-side, and on the northern verge of the older cultivation of these chalk-downs. The course of the way would doubtless have been marked more distinctly, had not the progress of modern improvements often extended the line of cultivation upwards, and converted from time to time further portions of the hill-side into arable. Under the picturesque height of Boxhill several yews of large size remain in ploughed land, reliques no doubt of this ancient way, and a row more or less continuous marks its progress as it leads towards Reigate, passing to the north of Brockham and Betchworth.

It may be worth inquiry whether Reigate (Saxon, Rige-gate, the Ridge-road), originally called Cherchefelle, may not have received its later name from its proximity to such a line of communication east

[1] Brayley's Hist. of Surrey, vol. v., p. 168.

and west along the Downs, rather than from the supposed ancient ascent northward[1] over the ridge to Gatton, and so towards London.

It must be noticed, in connection with the transit of pilgrims along the way, at no great distance north of Reigate, towards the Shrine of St. Thomas, that when they descended to that little town to seek lodging or provisions, they there found a little chapel dedicated to the Saint, midway in their journeying from Southampton or Winchester towards Canterbury. The site is now occupied by the town-hall or court-house, built about 1708, when the chapel had been demolished. In 1801, when an enlargement of the prison, here used at Quarter Sessions, was made, some portion of the foundations of this chapel of St. Thomas was brought to view.[2]

Proceeding eastward from Reigate, the way traversed the parish of Merstham. The county history states, that "a lane in the parish retains the name of Pilgrims' Lane. It runs in the direction of the chalk-hills, and was the course taken by pilgrims from the west, who resorted (as indeed from all parts) to Canterbury, to pay their devotions at the Shrine of St. Thomas à Becket. It remains perfect in Titsey, a parish to the east of this."[3]

The way may have proceeded by Barrow Green, and the remarkable tumulus there situated, in the parish of Oxtead, and although the traces are obscure, owing to the progress of cultivation along the flank of the downs, positive vestiges of the line occur at intervals. Thus, in the parish of Tatsfield the county historian relates, that Sir John Gresham built his new house "at the bottom of the hill near the Pilgrim Road (so called from the passage of pilgrims to the Shrine of Thomas à Becket, at Canterbury), which is now perfect, not nine feet wide, still used as a road. It commences at the village of Titsey, and passes on close at the foot of the hill, through this parish, into Kent." A more recent writer, Brayley, describing this Pilgrims' road in the parish of Tatsfield, says, that the measurement stated to be "not nine feet," is incorrect. "It is in fact about fifteen feet in width, and without any appearance of having been widened."[4] Mr. Leveson Gower, of Titsey-place, has a farm adjacent to it, and known as the "Pilgrims-way Farm." At no great distance from the course of the way, near Titsey, there is a small unenclosed green on the ridge of the downs, bearing the designation of "Cold Harbour," a name constantly found near lines of ancient road.

---

[1] This supposition has been sometimes advanced. See Manning and Bray, i. 271. It is there conjectured that a branch of the Stone-street turned off from Ockley by Newdigate to Reigate, and so over the Ridge.

[2] Manning and Bray, History of Surrey, vol. i. pp. 288, 289.
[3] *Ibid.*, vol. ii. p. 253. Gent. Mag. xcvii. ii. p. 414.
[4] Manning and Bray, vol. ii. p. 408; Brayley's Hist., vol. iv. p. 198.

Not far from Tatsfield the Pilgrims' Way entered the county of Kent, and its course appears plainly indicated towards Chevening Park. From thence it seems to have traversed the pastures and the opening in the hills, serving as the passage for the river Darent, and it is found again skirting the chain of downs beyond for several miles, rarely, if ever, passing through the villages or hamlets, but pursuing a solitary course about a quarter of a mile more or less to the northward of them. This observation applies generally to this ancient track. It is to be traced passing thus above Kemsing, Wrotham, Trottescliffe, and a few small hamlets, till it approaches the Medway. From Otford towards the East to Halling, the track appears to be well known, as I am informed by the Rev. W. Pearson, of Canterbury, as "the Pilgrims' Road." He describes this portion as a narrow way, much like an ordinary parish road, and much used as a line of direct communication along the side of the Downs. The name is generally recognised in that part of the county, and the tradition is that pilgrims used, in old times, to ride along that road towards Canterbury. In the maps given in Hasted's History of Kent, this line is marked as the Pilgrims' Road, near Otford, as also near Halling. Here, doubtless, a branch of the original ancient track proceeded along the high ground on the west of the river Medway, towards Strood and the Watling Street. This might have been indeed, it were reasonable to suppose, the more convenient mode of pursuing the remainder of the journey to Canterbury. It is, however, more probable that the Pilgrims' Way crossed the pastures and the Medway, either at Snodland or Lower Halling, and regained the hills on the opposite side, along the flank of which it ran as before, near Kits Coty House, leaving Boxley Abbey to the south at no great distance, and slightly diverging towards the south-east, by Deptling, Thurnham, and the hamlet of Broad Street, progressed past Hollingbourn, Harrietsham, and Lenham, towards Charing,[1] where the lane passing about half a mile to the north of that place is still known, as Mr. Pearson informs me, by the name of the Pilgrims' Road. The remarkable feature of its course is invariable, since it does not pass through any of these places, but near them, namely from a quarter to half a mile to the north of them.

From Charing the ancient British track may have continued towards the sea by Wye, near another "Cold Harbour," situate at the part of the continuation of the hilly chain, east of Wye, and so by Stouting, across the Roman Stone Street, to the coast. The pilgrims, it may be conjectured, directed their course from Charing through the woodland district, either by Chilham and along the north bank of the river Stour, thus approaching Canterbury by an ancient deep road, still strikingly marked on the flank of the hill,

---

[1] At Charing, a remarkable relique was shown, the block on which St. John the Baptist was beheaded. It was brought to England by Richard I. Philipot, p. 100.

not far from Harbledown. Another course from Charing may, however, have been taken rather more north of the present road from that place to Canterbury; and such a line may be traced by Snode Street, Beacon Hill, Stone Stile, and Fisher's Street, names indicative of an ancient track, and so by Hatch Green and Bigberry Wood, straight into the deep way already mentioned, at Harbledown, which falls nearly in a straight line with the last half mile of the great road from London entering into Canterbury at St. Dunstan's Church. It must, however, be remarked, that the hill-side lane proceeds in a direct line towards the S.E. beyond Charing, and although it presented a more circuitous course towards Canterbury, it may, especially in earlier times, have been frequented in preference to any shorter path across the woodland district. The line indeed is distinct, passing north of Westwell and Eastwell; and I am here again indebted to the local knowledge of my obliging informant, the Rev. W. Pearson, who states that an ancient track, still known as the Pilgrims' Road, exists, running above the Ashford and Canterbury turnpike road and parallel with it. It is a bridle-way, taking its course near the villages of Boughton Alph and Godmersham, towards Canterbury.

There can be no doubt that frequent vestiges of the "Pilgrims' Path" might be traced by actual examination of the localities along the course here tracked out, chiefly by aid of the Ordnance Survey. The careful investigation of this remarkable ancient track might throw light upon the earlier occupation of the south-eastern parts of England; although there are no indications of its having been formed by the Romans, there can be little doubt that it was used by them, as evinced by numerous vestiges of villas and other remains of the Roman age near its course. It is difficult to explain the preference shown, as it would appear, by the pilgrims of later times for a route which avoided the towns, villages, and more populous districts, whilst a road for the most part is found at no great distance, pursuing its course through them parallel to that of the secluded Pilgrims' Path. Our thoughts naturally recur to times of less favoured social conditions than our own, times of misrule or distrust, when, to repeat the apposite passage of Holy Writ cited in a former part of this volume, as "in the days of Shamgar, the son of Anath, in the days of Jael, the highways were unoccupied, and the travellers walked through by-ways." [1]

It may be here observed that the principal route to Walsingham, by Newmarket, Brandon and Fakenham, was known as the "Palmers' Way," or "Walsingham Green Way."

A. W.

[1] Judges, v. 6.

NOTE E.

VISIT OF JOHN, KING OF FRANCE, TO THE SHRINE OF ST. THOMAS, IN 1360.

(See pp. 109, 110, 188.)

On two memorable occasions was the Shrine of St. Thomas visited by a King of France; the first being the solemn pilgrimage made in 1179, by Louis VII., to whom, according to the relation of Brompton, the saint had thrice appeared in a vision. No French King previously to that time, as it is observed by a contemporary chronicler, had set foot on English ground. The King came in the habit of a pilgrim; amongst his rich oblations were the celebrated gem, the *"lapis regalis,"* and the grant to the convent of a hundred *modii* of wine, for ever. We are indebted to the Historical Society of France for the publication of certain particulars regarding another royal visit to Canterbury, namely that made by John, King of France, on his return from captivity in England, after the Treaty of Bretigny. John, with Philip, his youngest son, had been taken prisoners at the field of Poitiers, September 20th, 1356, and they were brought to England by the Black Prince, in May following. Their route to London lay, according to the relation of Froissart, by Canterbury and Rochester, and he states that the captives rested for a day to make their offerings to St. Thomas.

The document which has supplied the following particulars of the visit on their quitting England, is the account by the King's chaplain and notary of the expenditure during the last year of his captivity, from July 1st, 1359, to July 8th, 1360, when John landed at Calais.[1]

On the last day of June, 1360, John took his departure from the Tower of London and proceeded to Eltham Palace, where a grand farewell entertainment had been prepared by Queen Philippa; on the next day, July 1st, after dinner, the King took his leave, and passed the night at Dartford. It may suffice to observe that five days were occupied in his journey to Canterbury, where he arrived on July 4th, remained one night, and proceeded on the following day, being Sunday, to Dovor. The journal records the frequent offerings and alms dispensed liberally by the King at various places along his route from Eltham,—to the friars at Dartford, the master and brothers of the Ostel Dieu, at Ospring, where he lodged for the night, to four *" maladeries,"* or hospitals for lepers, and to " Messire

---

[1] Comptes de l'Argenterie des Rois de France au XIV.e siècle, edited by L. Douët-d'Arcq for the Société de l'Histoire de France. Paris, 1851. The Journal of King John's expenses in England commences at p. 194, and it is followed by an Itinerary of the King's captivity in England, pp. 278—284. This curious Journal is preserved in the Imperial Library at Paris.

Richart Lexden, chevalier anglois qui est hermite lez Stiborne," (Sittingbourn). The knightly anchorite received no less than twenty nobles, valued at 6*l.* 13*s.* 4*d.* As John passed Harbledown, ten *escuz,* or 23*s.* 4*d.*, were given by the King's command as alms to the "nonains de Helbadonne lez Cantorberie."

The following entries record the offerings of the King and of Philip, his son, afterwards Duke of Burgundy, the companion of his captivity. "Le Roy, offerande faicte par li en 3 lieux de l'église de St. Thomas de Cantorbérie, sans les joyaux qu'il y donna, 10 nobles, valent 33*l.* 6*s.* 8*d.* Monseigneur Philippe, pour samblable, en ce lieu, 16 royaux, 3*s.* pièce."[1] The three places at which the King's offerings were made, may probably have been the Shrine, the altar *ad punctum ensis* in the Martyrdom, and the head of the saint, described by Erasmus as shown in the crypt.[2] The jewels presented by John on this occasion are not described, but they were probably of a costly character, since his offering in money amounted only to ten nobles, whereas at St. Augustine's, where he heard mass on the Sunday morning before his departure for the coast, his offering was seventy-five nobles.[3] These *joyaux* may have been precious objects of ornament which the King had about his person at the moment, and they were accordingly not entered by the chaplain amongst current expenses. The offerings at the Shrine were usually, it is well known, rings, brooches or *firmacula,* and the like. The precious regal of France appears to have been actually worn by Louis VII. at the time of his pilgrimage, when he offered that jewel to the saint.

On the 5th of July, John reached Dovor and took up his lodging with the brothers of the Maison Dieu, where travellers and pilgrims were constantly entertained. On the morrow he dined with the Prince of Wales at the Castle, and set sail for Calais after dinner on the following day (July 6th) with the shipping provided by Edward III. for his accommodation. He made an offering to St. Nicholas for the vessel in which he crossed the channel, and reached Calais safely on July 8th. Edward sent as a parting gift to his royal captive a chess-board (" j. instrument appellé l'eschequier "),

[1] Journal de la depense du Roi Jean, p. 272.

[2] In the Household Accounts of 25, 26 Edward III., the oblations of Queen Philippa are thus recorded :—At the Shrine, 40*s.* '; at the *punctum ensis,* 5*s.* ; and in alms, 12*d.* Edmund of Woodstock offered at the same time 12*d.* at the Shrine ; the like amount at the image of the Virgin in the crypt (*in volta*), at the *punctum ensis,* and at the head of St. Thomas. Battely, p. 20. Edward I. appears to have presented annually a *firmaculum* of gold, value 5*l.*, at the Shrine and at the image of the Virgin *in vouta,* and ornaments of the same value were offered in the names of his Queen and of Prince Edward. Liber Garderobe Edw. I.

[3] The alms of the King of France were distributed with no niggardly hand on this occasion. To the Friars preachers in Canterbury he gave 20 nobles, as also to the Cordeliers and the Augustinians, and smaller sums to the *nonains* of Northgate and of St. Augustine, the women of the Hospital of Our Lady, &c. Journal, p. 273.

which must have been of considerable value, since twenty nobles were given to the maker, who brought it to the King. He presented also a more appropriate gift, the *gobelet* in which he was accustomed to drink, in return for which John sent "le propre henap à quoy il buvoit, qui fu monseigneur St. Loys." [1]   A. W.

<hr>

NOTE F.

DOCUMENTS PRESERVED AMONGST THE RECORDS IN THE TREASURY AT CANTERBURY.

—•—

I.—*Grant of the Manor of Doccombe by William de Tracy.*

(See p. 83.)

AMONGST the possessions of the monastery of Christ Church, Canterbury, enumerated in the list of the "Donationes Maneriorum et Ecclesiarum," published by Somner, and given in the Monasticon, the grant of Doccombe is recorded.[2] "Willielmus Tracy dedit Doccombe tempore Henrici secundi, idem donum confirmantis." The manor of Doccombe, Daccombe, or Dockham, in the parish of Moreton Hampstead, Devonshire, still forms part of the possessions of the church of Canterbury.

The grant by William de Tracy has not, as far as I can ascertain, been printed; nor, with the exception of a note appended to Lord Lyttelton's "Life of Henry II.," have I found mention of the existence of such a document, with the seal described as that of Tracy appended, preserved in the Treasury at Canterbury. There can be no doubt that the grantor was the identical William de Tracy who took so prominent a part in the murder of Thomas à Becket. Lord Lyttelton supposed that it might be his grandson.[3] The document is not dated, but there is evidence that the grant was made within a short period after that event, which took place on December 29, 1170.

The confirmation by Henry II. of Tracy's grant at Doccombe is tested at Westminster, the regnal year not being stated. Amongst the witnesses, however, occur "R. Electo Winton, R. Electo Hereford, Johanne Decano Sarum." Richard Toclive was elected Bishop of Winchester May 1, 1173; confirmed and consecrated in October, 1174. Robert Foliot was elected Bishop of Hereford in 1173, and

---

[1] Ducange, in his notes on Joinville, mentions this cup of gold which had been used by St. Louis and was preserved as a sacred relique, and for a long time it was not used, through respect to the saint. It is described in the time of Louis X. as "la coupe d'or S. Loys, où l'on ne boit point."

[2] Somner, Antiquities of Canterbury, Appendix, p. 40; Monast. Angl., Caley', edition, vol. i., p. 98. In the Valor, 26 Hen. VIII., the manor of Doccombe, part of the possessions of Christ Church, is valued at 6l. 6s. 8d. per annum.

[3] Lord Lyttelton's Life of Henry II., vol. iv., p. 284.

consecrated in October, 1174. John de Oxeneford was Dean of Sarum from 1165 until he was raised to the see of Norwich in 1175. It was only on July 8, 1174, that Henry II. returned to England after a lengthened absence amongst his French possessions; he crossed to Southampton, and forthwith proceeded to Canterbury, to perform his memorable humiliation at the Shrine of St. Thomas. The date of his confirmation of Tracy's gift is thus ascertained to be between July and October, 1174, and probably immediately on the King's arrival at Westminster after his pilgrimage to Canterbury.[1]

Tracy's gift had, moreover, as it appears, been regarded by the monks of Christ Church as an oblation to make some amends for his crime. In one of the registers of the monastery, a transcript of a letter has been preserved, addressed by Prior Henry de Estria to Hugh de Courtenay.[2] It bears date July 4, 1322, and reminds Sir Hugh, doubtless the second baron of Okehampton of that name, and subsequently created Earl of Devon by Edward III., that the charter of William de Tracy, with the confirmation by Henry II., had been shown to him, as evidence regarding "la petite terre qe le dit William dona a nostre esglise et a nous a Dockumbe, en pure et perpetuele almoigne, pur la mort Saint Thomas." The prior requests accordingly his orders to his "ministres" at that place to leave the tenants of the monastery in peaceable possession.

(Original Charter, Canterbury Treasury, D. 20.)

Willelmus de Traci omnibus hominibus suis tam Francis quam Anglis, et amicis, et ballivis, et ministris, et omnibus ad quos littere iste pervenerint, Salutem. Dono et concedo Capitulo Cantuar' pro amore dei et salute anime mee, predecessorum meorum, et amore beati Thome Archipresulis et Martiris memorie venerande, in puram et perpetuam elemosinam, Centum solidatas terre in Mortuna, scilicet Documbam cum pertinentiis et cum terris affinioribus, ita quod ex Documba et aliis terris proximis perficiantur centum ille solidate terre. Hoc autem dono ad monachum unum vestiendum et pascendum omnibus diebus secul'[3] in domo illa, qui ibi divina celebret pro salute vivorum et requie defunctorum. Ut hoc autem firmum sit et ratum et inconcussum et stabile sigilli mei munimine et Carta mea confirmo. His testibus, Abbate de Eufemia, Magistro Radulfo de Hospitali, Pagano de Tirn', Willelmo clerico, Stephano de Pirforde, Pagano de Acforde, Rogero Anglico, Godefrido Ribaldo et aliis.

To this document is appended a seal of white wax, the form pointed oval, the design rudely executed, representing a female figure with very long sleeves reaching nearly to her feet. Some traces of letters may be discerned around the margin of the seal, but

---

[1] This confirmation by Henry II. may be found in the Registers, 2, fol. 400, and 8, fol. 26, *verso.*

[2] Register K. 12, fol. 129, *verso.*

[3] Probably, *seculi,* for ever; in place of the ordinary phrase *imperpetuum.*

too much worn away to be deciphered. It must be observed that notwithstanding the expression "sigilli mei munimine," it can scarcely be supposed that this seal was actually that customarily used by Tracy. The pointed oval form was almost exclusively appropriated to seals of ladies, ecclesiastics, and conventual establishments. The figure, *à manches mal taillés*, is a device seemingly most inappropriate to the knightly Tracy. It is probable, and not inconsistent with the ancient practice of sealing, that having no seal of his own at hand, he had borrowed one for the occasion. The first of the witnesses is described as Abbot of Eufemia.[1] This may have been the monastery of some note on the western shores of the Calabria, near the town and gulf of Santa Eufemia, and about sixty miles north of the Straits of Messina. It is remarkable that this place is not far distant from Cosenza, where, according to one dreadful tale of the fate of Becket's murderers, Tracy, having been sentenced, with his accomplices, by Pope Alexander III. to expiate their crime in the Holy Land, had miserably died on his way thither, after confession to the Bishop of the place.[2]

In regard to the other witnesses, I can only observe that Roger de Acford occurs in the Red Book of the Exchequer, as holding part of a knight's fee in the Honor of Barnstaple under William Tracy. Payn may have been his son or kinsman. Pirforde may have been the place now known as Parford, near Moreton Hampstead. The correct reading of the name *de Tirn'* may possibly be Tirun. The family de Turonibus, settled in early times at Dartington, Devon, were connected by marriage with the Tracys.

The fact that Tracy actually set forth on pilgrimage to the Holy Land, which some have seemed to question, is proved by the following curious letter in one of the Canterbury registers:—

Qualiter Amicia uxor Willelmi Thaun post mortem viri sui terram quam vir ejus dedit Sancto Thome ipsa postea dedit.

(*Register in the Canterbury Treasury, 2, fol. 400.*)

Viro venerabili et amico in Christo, karissimo domino Johanni filio Galfridi, Anselmus Crassus Thesaurarius Exoniensis[3] salutem et paratam ad obsequia cum devocione voluntatem. Noverit quod quadam die, cum dominam Amiciam de la More mortuo viro suo Everardo Chole in manerio de Moreth'[4] visitassimus, dixit nobis

---

[1] The conjecture seems not altogether inadmissible, that this seal may have been that of the Abbot, or of some member of the congregation of St. Eufemia, and that the figure may have represented the Virgin Martyr of Chalcedon, a saint greatly venerated in the Eastern church. The reliques of St. Eufemia were transferred into the church of St. Sophia at Constantinople.

[2] Cosenza is situated about eighteen miles north of Santa Eufemia.

[3] Anselm Crassus, or Le Gros, was treasurer of Exeter in 1205, and in 1230 was made Bishop of St. David's. Le Neve's Fasti, ed. by Hardy, vol. i., p.414.

[4] Probably Morthoe, where the Tracys had estates and their residence. The

quod quidam nomine Willelmus Thaun vir ejus qui eam duxit in uxorem, cum iter arriperet cum domino suo Willelmo de Traci versus terram sanctam, eam fecit jurare tactis sacrosanctis quod totam terram ipsius cum pertinentiis suis, quam dominus ejus Willelmus de Tracy ipsi Willelmo Thaun dedit pro homagio et servicio suo, beato Thome Martiri et Conventui ecclesie Christi Cantuariensis assignaret in perpetuum possidendam : defuncto autem predicto Willelmo Thaun in peregrinacione terre sancte eadem Amicia alium virum accepit, videlicet Everarddum Chole, per quem impedita voluntatem et votum primi viri sui Willelmi Thaun minime complevit. Volens autem dicta Amicia saluti anime sue providere in manum nostram totam terram Willelmi Thaun resignavit, et Conventum Ecclesie Christi Cantuariensis per nos pilliolo suo seisiavit. Nos vero, conventus dicte ecclesie utilitati secundum testamentum dicti Willelmi Thaun solicite providere curantes, seisinam dicte terre loco ipsius Conventus Cantuariensis benigne admisimus, et ejusdem terre instrumenta omnia a dicta Amicia nobis commissa eidem Conventui Cantuariensi restituimus. In cujus rei testimonium fieri fecimus presentes literas et sigillo nostro sigillari.

I have not been able to ascertain who was the " Dominus Johannes filius Galfridi" to whom the Treasurer of Exeter addressed this communication. If the supposition be correct that the transaction relates to certain lands in the parish of Morthoe, where the Tracys had considerable property, and where William de Tracy is supposed to have resided, at Wollacombe Tracy, the presence of the Treasurer of Exeter and his visit to the lady Amicia de la More are in some measure explained, since the advowson of Morthoe was part of the possessions of the church of Exeter. Amicia de la More, as it appears, was the wife of a certain William Thaun, who held land under William de Tracy, and had gone with him to the Holy Land.[1] Before his departure, however, Thaun had caused his wife to swear upon the Gospels, foreseeing doubtless the uncertainty of his return, that she would duly assign over to St. Thomas and the Convent of Christ Church the land abovementioned. On his decease in the course of his journey, Amicia espoused Everard Chole, by whose persuasion she neglected to fulfil her oath and the will of her deceased husband. On Everard's death, however, it appears that she was seized with remorse, and took the occasion of the Treasurer's visit to make full confession, and to resign into his hands the land held by William Thaun, giving the Convent of Christ Church seisin in

word seems to be written "Morech'," but the letter t is often so formed as to be scarcely distinguishable from a c.

[1] Sir W. Pole gives " More, of de la More" in his Alphabet of Arms of the old Devonshire Gentry. The ancient family of de la Moore, named in later times At Moore, had their dwelling at Moorehays, in the Parish of Columpton.—Pole's Collections, p. 186.

the person of the Treasurer, by delivery of her cap (*pilliolum*), being the object probably most conveniently at hand. By the foregoing letters under his seal, Anselm Crassus acknowledges seisin of the land for the use of the Convent of Canterbury, and restores to them all *instrumenta* or documents of title entrusted to him on their behalf.

II.—*The " Corona beati Thome."*

(See p. 181.)

In searching the ancient accounts for any evidence regarding the Shrine, or those parts of the church of Canterbury where the reliques of the Saint were chiefly venerated, a few particulars have been noticed which suggest the reconsideration of the origin and true significance of the term *Corona*, " Becket's Crown," as applied to the round chapel and tower, terminating the eastern part of the church.

It had been concluded by several writers that this part of the fabric, the construction of which commenced, as we learn from Gervase, in 1180, had received this designation from the circumstance that the head of the Saint had been placed there, eastward of his Shrine. Matthew Parker, in his " Antiquitates Britannicæ Ecclesiæ," at the close of his Life of Becket, observes, that at first St. Thomas was placed less ostentatiously in the crypt:—
" Deinde sublimiori et excelso ac sumptuoso delubro conditus fuerit, in quo caput ejus seorsim a cadavere situm, Thomæ Martyris *Corona* appellabatur, ad quod peregrinantes undique confluerent, muneraque preciosa deferrent," &c. Battely, Gostling, Ducarel, and Dart, speak of " Becket's Crown," and appear to have connected the name with the supposed depository of the head of the Saint, or of the portion of the skull cut off by the murderers.[1]

Professor Willis, whose authority must be regarded with the greatest respect, rejects this supposition. " The notion (he remarks) that this round chapel was called Becket's Crown, because part of his skull was preserved here as a relic, appears wholly untenable." He considers the term *corona* as signifying the principal apse of a church, referring to a document relating to the church of La Charité on the Loire, in which the *Corona Ecclesie* is mentioned.[2] Mr. John

---

[1] Gostling observes (p. 123), "At the east end of the chapel of the Holy Trinity, another very handsome one was added, called Becket's Crown ; some suppose from its figure being circular, and the ribs of the arched roof meeting in a centre, as those of the crown royal do ; others on account of part of his skull being preserved here as a relic."

[2] Architectural History of Canterbury Cathedral, p. 56, note. The learned Pro-

fessor observes, that "at all events it was a general term, and not peculiar to the church of Canterbury." He cites, however, no other evidence of its use, except that above mentioned, given amongst the additions made by the Benedictines to Ducange's Glossary. " *Corona Ecclesiæ*, f. Pars Templi choro postica, quod ea pars fere desinat in circulum. Charta anni 1170, in Tabulario B. Mariæ de Charitate : *Duo altaria in Corona Ecclesiæ.*" In

Gough Nichols has likewise sought to refute as a "popular error, into which many writers have fallen," the misconception which was as old, he remarks, as Archbishop Parker, that the head of St. Thomas was preserved in that part of the Cathedral called Becket's Crown.[1]

The earliest mention of the *Corona*, as I believe, is in Registers of Henry de Estria, Prior of Canterbury, in the enumeration of the "Nova Opera in Ecclesia" in his times. Under the year 1314 is the entry—"Pro *corona* sancti Thome auro et argento et lapidibus preciosis ornanda, cxv. li. xij. s." In the same year the Prior provided a new crest of gold for the Shrine.[2] The same record comprises a list of the relics in the cathedral, amongst which are mentioned—"Corpus Sancti Odonis, in feretro, *ad coronam* versus austrum.—Corpus Sancti Wilfridi, in feretro, *ad coronam* versus aquilonem." It seems improbable that this large expenditure in precious metals and gems[3] should relate to the apsidal chapel, according to Professor Willis's explanation of the term *Corona*, no portion of the building being specified to which such costly decoration was applied. The expression would rather imply, as I conceive, the enrichment of some precious object, such as a *phylacterium*, *scrinium*, feretory, or the like, described as "Corona sancti Thome." The phrase "*ad* coronam," moreover, in the list of relics, can scarcely, I would submit, signify that the bodies of St. Odo and St. Wilfrid were placed *in* a building or chapel called *Corona*, but rather implies that they were placed adjacent to some object known as *Corona*, at its north and south sides, respectively; thus also in the context we find other reliques placed "*ad* altare," whilst others are described as "*in* navi Ecclesie," &c.

The *Corona*, like the shrine, the *martirium* and *tumba*, was in charge of a special officer, called the "Custos Corone beati Thome," and mention also occurs of the "Magister Corone," apparently the same official. In a "Book of Accounts" of one of the officers of the Monastery, preserved in the Chapter Library, the following entries occur under the head of "Oblaciones cum obvencionibus."

"De Custode Corone beati Thome, xl.s.

"Denarii recepti pro vino conventus. — Item, de Custodibus Feretri Sancti Thome, xxx.s. Item, de Custode Corone Sancti Thome, xx.s. Item, de Custode Tumbe beati Thome, iij.s. iiij.d.

---

an additional note, the Professor says :— "The *Corona* may also mean the aisle which often circumscribes the east end of an apsidal church, and which, with its radiating chapels, may be said to crown its eastern extremity." (p. 141.)

[1] Pilgrimages to Walsingham and Canterbury, p. 119. Mr. John Nichols, in his Royal Wills, p. 70. adopted the popular opinion. The altar where the Saint's head was, he remarks, "was probably in that part of the Cathedral called Becket's Crown."

[2] Register I. 11, fol. 212, Canterbury Treasury ; Register of Prior Henry, Cott. MS., Galba E. IV. 14, fol. 103.

[3] Dart, Appendix, p. xlii.

Item de Custode Martirii Sancti Thome, iij.s. iiij.d. Item, de Custode beate Marie in cryptis," &c. 30 Henr. VI. (1451).[1]

There were, it appears, three objects of especial veneration, the *feretrum* in the chapel of the Holy Trinity, the *punctum ensis* in the Martyrdom, and the *caput beati Thome.* At each there was an altar. The Black Prince bequeathed tapestry to three altars, besides the High Altar, namely, " l'autier la ou Mons'r Saint Thomas gist,— l'autier la ou la teste est—l'autier la ou la poynte de l'espie est."

The authority of Erasmus seems conclusive that the *caput* was shown in the crypt. After inspecting the *cuspis gladii* in the Martyrdom, Erasmus says :—" Hinc digressi subimus cryptoporticum : ea habet suos mystagogos : illic primum exhibetur calvaria martyris perforata ; reliqua tecta sunt argento, summa cranii pars nuda patet osculo."

I have been induced to offer these notices, from the conviction that the apsidal chapel, called Becket's Crown, received that name from some precious object connected with the *cultus* of St. Thomas of Canterbury, or from some peculiar feature of its decorations. The notion obviously suggests itself, that such an object may have been a reliquary in which the *corona,*[2] or upper portion of the cranium, cut off by the savage stroke of Richard le Breton, was placed apart from the skull itself. This supposition, however, seems to be set aside by the inscription accompanying the drawing in Cotton. MS. Tib. E. VIII. fol. 286, b., of which an accurate copy has been given in this volume. The MS. suffered from fire in 1731, and the following words only are now legible. " This chest of iron cont . . . . . bones of Thomas Becket . . . . . all with the wounde . . . . and the pece cut . . . . ." Thus rendered on Vaughan's plate, engraved from this drawing when it was in a more perfect state (Dugdale, Monast. Angl., vol. i. p. 18, orig. edit., printed in 1655).—" Loculus ille, quem vides ferreum, ossa Tho: Becketti cum calvaria necnon rupta illa cranii parte quæ mortem inferebat complectebatur."[3]

---

[1] MSS. in the Chapter Library, volume marked E. 6, fol. 33. Amongst the few evidences of this nature which have escaped destruction may be mentioned a curious Book of Accounts of William Inggram, Custos of the Martirium, MS. C. 11. It contains much information regarding the books in the library of the Monastery, and other matters.

[2] *Corona* properly designated the circle of hair left on the priest's head by the tonsure. "Fit corona ex rasura in summitate capitis, et tonsione capillorum in parte capitis inferiore, et sic circulus capillorum proprie dicitur corona."— Lyndwood. "The hair was shorn from the top of the head, more or less wide,

according as the wearer happened to be high or low in order."—Dr. Rock's Church of our Fathers, vol. i., p. 187. The word is used in the accounts of Becket's murder to describe the upper part of the skull, or brain-pan. Thus Fitzstephen says, "Corona capitis tota ei amputata est ;" and he describes the savage act of Hugh de Horsea—"a concavitate coronæ amputatæ cum mucrone cruorem et cerebrum extrahebat."—Ed. Sparkes, p. 87. Diceto states that Becket received his death-wound "in corona capitis."—Ang. Sacra, ii., p. 691.

[3] On comparing this drawing with Stow's account of the removal of Becket's shrine, it seems almost certain that

It has been questioned whether any altar existed in Becket's Crown. The original stones still remaining on the raised platform at this extreme East end of the church still present traces of some arrangement which does not appear to indicate the position of an altar, but rather of some railing, or *clausura*, which may have protected the object of veneration there displayed. No clue appears to direct the enquiry as to its character, with the exception of the brief notice of Erasmus, who seems to allude to Becket's Crown when speaking of the upper church behind the high altar:— " Illic in sacello quodam ostenditur tota facies optimi viri inaurata, multisque gemmis insignita." May not this have been an image of St. Thomas, or one of those gorgeously enriched busts, of life size, covered with precious metals and richly jewelled, a class of reliquaries, of which remarkable examples still exist in many Continental churches? Such a reliquary existed in 1295 at St. Paul's, London, and is described in an Inventory given by Dugdale as " Capud S. Athelberti Regis in capsa argentea deaurata, facta ad modum capitis Regis cum corona continente in circulo xvi. lapides majores," &c.

In conclusion I will only invite attention to the probability that a *capsa* of this description, highly suitable to receive so remarkable a relique as the *corona* of Becket's skull, separate from the other remains of the saint, may have been displayed in the apsidal chapel thence designated " Becket's Crown." If it be sought to controvert such a supposition by the conflicting evidence of the Cotton MS., of Erasmus' Colloquy, or of the account given in Stow's Annals (cited in the note, *infra*), it can only be said that it is as impracticable to reconcile such discrepancies, as to explain the triple heads of St. John the Baptist. The declaration by royal authority, in 1539, records that Becket's "head almost hole was found with the rest of the bones closed within the shryne, and that there was in that church a great scull of another head, but much greater by the three-quarter parts than that part which was lacking in the head closed within the shryne."

III.—*Miraculous Cures at the Shrine of St. Thomas.*

(See pp. 153, 202.)

The relations of contemporary biographers, Gervase and Fitzstephen, are diffuse in the enumeration of the dreadful maladies for which an efficacious remedy was sought by multitudes from the reliques

this *loculus ferreus*, shown with the shrine in the Cotton MS., was the "chest of yron conteyning the bones of Thomas Becket, scull and all, with the wounde of his death, and the peece cut out of his scull layde in the same wound." This chest is distinctly said by Stow to have been within the shrine.

of St. Thomas, and the miracles effected—" Domino operante, et fide christiana, cui omnia possibilia sunt, suffragante." Even the dead are said to have been restored to life, the blind received their sight, and lepers were healed. Gervase states that two volumes of such miracles were extant at Canterbury.

Having been favoured with unusual facilities of access to the ancient Registers and evidences preserved in the Treasury,[1] in searching for materials which might throw light upon the subjects to which this volume relates, I have been surprised at the extreme paucity of information regarding Becket, or any part of the church specially connected with the veneration shown towards him. Scarcely is an item to be found in the various Rolls of Account making mention of St. Thomas, and where his name occurred, it has for the most part been carefully erased. With the exception of certain Papal Bulls, and some communications regarding Canterbury Jubilees, the name is scarcely to be found in the long series of Registers. We seek in vain for any schedule of the accumulated wealth which surrounded his shrine : even in the long inventory of plate and vestments left in 1540 by the Commissioners after the surrender, "till the king's pleasure be further declared," and subscribed by Cranmer's own hand, the words, " Storye of Thomas Beket," in the description of a piece of embroidered velvet, are blotted out. It is remarkable to notice the pains bestowed on the destruction of everything which might revive any memory of the Saint.

The following extracts from the Registers have appeared to claim attention, because they are the only records of their class which have been found. A Royal letter is not without interest, whatever may be its subject, and it is remarkable to find Richard II. congratulating the Primate on the good influence anticipated from a fresh miracle at the Shrine of Becket, in counteracting the doctrine of Wycklyffe, or the perilous growth of Lollardism. The subject of the miracle appears to have been a foreigner, probably of distinction ; but I found no clue to identify who the person may have been.

The second of these documents appears to be a kind of encyclical certificate of a noted cure miraculously effected in the person of a young Scotchman, Alexander, son of Stephen, of Aberdeen; and it is remarkable as showing the widely spread credence in the efficacy of a pilgrimage to St. Thomas, and the singular formality with which it was thought expedient to authenticate and publish the miracle.

---

[1] It is with much gratification that I would record the acknowledgment of the kindness of the Very Rev. the Dean, the Ven. Archdeacon Harrison, and of other members of the Chapter, in the liberal permission to prosecute my investigation of these valuable materials for local and general history.

This document moreover states, that St. Thomas having (with the succour of Divine clemency) restored to the said Alexander the use of his feet, he proceeded, in pursuance of his vow, to the Holy Blood of Wilsnake, and returned safe and sound to the shrine of the Martyr. I am not aware that mention has been made by English writers of the celebrated relique formerly preserved at Wilsnake, in Prussia; and, although not connected with Canterbury, a brief account of the origin of this pilgrimage, which appears to have been much in vogue in our own country, may not be inadmissible in these Notes. I am indebted to the learned biographer of Alfred, M. Pauli, for directing my attention to Wilsnake and the curious legend of the Holy Blood.

Wilsnack, or Wilsnake, is a small town in the north parts of the Mark of Brandenburg.[1] In times of popular commotion, in 1383, the town, with its church, was burnt. The priest, Crantzius relates, having been recalled by a vision to perform mass in the ruined fabric, found the altar standing, the candles upon it, and between them, in a napkin or corporal, three consecrated hosts, united into one and stained with blood. Another account states, that, searching amongst the ashes near the altar, he discovered the bleeding wafers. The priest hastened to his diocesan the Bishop of Havelberg; he came with his clergy and certified this miracle, which was forthwith proclaimed far and near. Before the close of the century, innumerable pilgrims visited the place, kings and princes sent costly gifts, and Pope Urban VI. promulgated indulgences to the faithful who repaired thither.[2] From all quarters, says Crantzius, votaries came in crowds—from Hungary, France, England, Scotland, Denmark, Sweden, Norway. The fame of the relique may have quickly spread to our own island, as M. Pauli observes, through the numerous English knights who, about that time, traversed the north of Europe to join the Teutonic Knights in Prussia.

The miracle, it is alleged, soon engrossed so much attention that neighbouring churches where noted reliques were preserved became neglected. Enquiry was instituted, and the Archbishop of Prague sent a deputy to investigate the matter, no less a person than John Huss, who, with the fearless spirit of the Reformer, exposed the abuses practised at Wilsnake. He wrote a remarkable treatise on superstitions of the same nature in various places.[3] In 1400, the

[1] An account of Wilsnack is given by Stenzel, in his "Geschichte des Preussischen Staats," tom. i. p. 175.

[2] Leaden signs, or *signacula*, representing the bleeding wafers, were distributed to pilgrims, in like manner as the *ampullæ* of St. Thomas, or the mitred heads, tokens of their journey to Canterbury, as mentioned in this volume, pp.

184, 186. Several signs of St. Thomas are represented in Mr. Roach Smith's Collectanea, vol. i. p. 83; vol. ii. pp. 46—49.

[3] The "Holy Blood" of our Lord was believed to exist in several places, of which Mantua was the most celebrated. M. Paris relates that Henry III. presented to the monks of Westminster in

learned Wunschebergius also assailed the feigned miracles of Wilsnake, and an eminent canon of Magdeburg put forth a philippic against the prelate who tolerated such pious frauds for lucre's sake. It was, however, of no avail; the Bishop of Havelberg sustained his suit at Rome with energy; the Papal approbation was renewed; the credit of the Holy Blood was confirmed by the Councils of Constance and Basle.

In the sixteenth century, Matthew Ludecus, Dean of Havelberg, compiled the history of this superstition. There was, he relates, a large balance suspended in the church of Wilsnake. In one scale it was usual to place the pilgrim who sought remission of his offences; in the other were piled his oblations, bread and flesh, perhaps cheese, or other homely offerings. If the visitor seemed wealthy, no impression was made on the beam; the priest affirming that indeed he must be a grievous offender, whose crimes could not be expiated without more valuable oblations. At length, by some secret contrivance, the scale was permitted to fall.[1]

Huss has narrated a characteristic anecdote of the miraculous fallacies of Wilsnake. A citizen of Prague, Petrziko de Ach, afflicted with a withered arm, offered a silver hand, and desiring to discover what the priests would put forth concerning his costly gift, he tarried till the third day and repaired unnoticed to the church. As it chanced, the priest was in the pulpit, declaiming to the assembled votaries, " Audite pueri miraculum ! "—" Behold, a citizen of Prague has been healed by the Holy Blood, and see here how he hath offered a silver hand in testimony of his cure ! " But the sufferer, standing up with arm upraised, exclaimed, " Oh, priest, what falsehood is this ! Behold my hand, still withered as before." " Of this," observes Huss, " his friends and kinsmen at Prague are witnesses to this day."

It was only in 1551 that Joachim Elfeldt, becoming pastor of the church, being imbued with the Reformed faith, put an end to the superstition, and committed the wafers to the flames. The canons of Havelberg, indignant that their gains were gone, threw him into prison and sought to bring him to the stake, but he was rescued by the Elector of Brandenburg.   A. W.

1247 some of the blood shed at the Crucifixion, which he had received from the Master of the Templars. The Earl of Cornwall gave a portion to Hayles Abbey, a relique much celebrated, and to which allusion is made by Chaucer. He gave other portions to the Bons Hommes, Ashridge, and to Berkhampstead.

[1] A curious woodcut representing this proceeding, is given by Wolfius, in his "Lectiones Memorabiles, p. 619."

Litera domini Regis graciosa missa domino archiepiscopo, regraciando sibi de novo miraculo Sancti Thome Martiris sibi denunciato.[1] (*Circa* A.D. 1393, *temp.* Rich. II.)

(*Register of Christ Church, Canterbury,* R. 19, *fol.* 15.)

Tresreverent piere en dieu et nostre trescher Cosyn, nous vous saloioms tresovent denter coer, vous ensauntz savoir qe a la fesaunce de cestes noz lettres nous estoioms en bone sancte, merciez ent soit nostre seignour, et avoms · tresgraunt desyr de trestout nostre coer davoir de vous sovent novelles semblables, des quex vous priomos (*sic*) cherement qacercer nous vuillez de temps en temps au pluis sovent qe vous purrez bonement pur nostre graunt confort et singuler plesaunce. Si vous mercioms trescher Cosyn tresperfitement de coer de voz lettres, et avons presentement envoyez, et par especial qen si bref nous avetz certefiez du miracle quore tarde avint en vostre esglise au seynt feretre du glorious martir Seint Thomas, et avoms, ce nous est avis, tresgrant et excellente cause et nous et vous de ent mercier lui haut soverayn mostre (?) des miracles, qui ceste miracle ad pleu monstrer en noz temps, et en une persone estraunge, sicome pur extendre as parties estraungez et lointeines la gloriouse deisoñ[2] verray martyr susdit. Nous semble parmi ce qe nous sumes treshautemens tenuz de luy loer et ent rendre merciz et gracez, et si le voiloms faire parmi sa grace de nostre enter poer sauntz feintise ; especialment vous enpriauntz qe paraillement de vostre fait le vuillez faire a honour de luy de qui sourde tout bien et honour, et au bone example de touz noz subgestez. Et verramient treschier Cosyn nous avoms tresperfit espiraunce qen temps de nous et de vous serront noz noblez et seyntes predescessours pluis glorifiez qe devant longe temps nont estez, dont le cause verisemblable qe nous moeve est celle qen noz temps, ceste assavoir de present, noz foie et creaunce ount plusours enemys qe de temps hors de memorie navoient, les quex par la mercie de mercie (*sic*) de Jhesu Crist et ces gloriousez miracles serount a ce qe nous creouns de lour erroure convertyz a voie de salue ; celui dieu de sa haute puissaunce lottroie a la glorie de luy et de toutz seyntz, et la salvacioun de soen poeple universele. Trescher Cosyn de vous vouellez, et de tout quamque vous vorrez auxi devers vous nous certefiez pur nostre amour, sachauntz qe nous vorroms tresvolunters faire tout ce qa honour vous purra tourner et plesir. Et le seynt esprit vou eit en sa garde. Done souz nostre signet, a nostre Chastelle de Corf', le vij. jour daugst.

---

[1] This letter was written, as may be supposed from the place in which it is found in the Register, and the dates of documents accompanying it, about A.D. 1393. If this conjecture be correct, it was addressed by Richard II. to William Courtenay, Archbishop of Canterbury from 1381 to 1396.

[2] This passage is apparently incomplete, or incorrectly copied into the Register. The sense may, however, be easily gathered from the context.

De quodam miraculo ostenso ad feretrum beati Thome Cantuariensis. Litera Testimonialis (A.D. 1445).

(*Register of Christ Church, Canterbury*, R. 19, *fol.* 163.)

Universis sancte matris ecclesie filiis ad quos presentes litere nostre pervenerint, Johannes permissione divina prior Ecclesie Christi Cantuariensis,[1] et ejusdem loci Capitulum, Salutem et semper in domino gloriari. Cum fidelis quilibet Christicola divine majestatis cultor de mirifica Dei clemencia gloriari et mente extolli tenetur, apostolica sic dictante sententia, "Qui gloriatur in domino glorietur,"[2] in Dei laudis magnificenciam ore et mente undique provocamur, tum immensis operibus suis operator est semper Deus mirabilis et in sanctorum suorum miraculis coruscans gloriosus. Unde, cum nuper in nostra sancta tocius Anglie metropoli novum et stupendum per divine operacionis clemenciam in meritis sancti martiris Thome Cantuariensis experti sumus miraculum, Deum laudare et ejus potenciam glorificare obligamur, quam totus orbis terrarum ympnis et laudibus devote laudare non cessat. Nam cum Allexander Stephani filius in Scocia, de Aberdyn oppido natus, pedibus contractus vigintiquatuor annis ab ortu suo penaliter laborabat,[3] ad instanciam cujusdam matrone votum ad Feretrum sancti Thome emittens, per grandia laborum vehicula cum ceterorum impotencium instrumentis, supra genua debilia ad feretrum predictum pervenit, ibique beatus Thomas, divina opitulante clemencia, secundo die mensis Maii proximi ante datum presentium, bases et plantas eidem Allexandro ilico restituit. Et in voti sui deinde complementum ad sanguinem sanctum de Wilsnake, divino permittente auxilio, sanus et firmus adiit, et in martiris sui Thome merito ad feretrum illius prospere revenit. Nos igitur, divine majestatis gloriam sub ignorancie tenebris latitare nolentes, sed super fidei tectum predicare affectantes, ut Christi cunctis fidelibus valeat undique coruscare, ea que de jure ad probacionem requirentur miraculi, sub sacramento dicti Allexandri necnon aliorum fide dignorum de oppido predicto, videlicet Allexander Arat generosi, Robertique filii David, et Johannis Thome filii, legitime comprobato, in nostra sancta Cantuariensi ecclesia fecimus solempniter publicari. Unde universitati supplicamus literas per presentes quatinus dignetis Deum laudare de (?) sancto martire ejus Thoma Cantuariensi, in cujus meritis ecclesiam suam unicam sibi sponsam in extirpacionem heresum et errorum variis miraculis pluribus decursis temporibus mirifice hucusque decoravit. In cujus rei testimonium, &c. Dat' Cantuaria in domo nostra Capitulari, xxvij^mo. die Mensis Julii, Anno Domini Millesimo cccc^mo. xlv^to.

---

[1] John Salisbury, who became Prior in 1437, and died in 1446.

[2] 1 Corinth. i. 31.

[3] Amongst the miraculous cures obtained by pilgrims, Fitzstephen specially mentions, "contractis membrorum lineamenta extensa et directa sunt."—Vita S. Thome, ed. Sparkes, p. 90.

NOTE G.

THE CRESCENT IN THE ROOF OF CANTERBURY CATHEDRAL.

(See p. 182.)

The Crescent in the roof of Canterbury Cathedral, above the Shrine of Becket, has given rise to much perplexity. An obvious but untenable conjecture has often been offered that it was placed there in relation to the story of Becket's Saracen mother. That legend, however, is now known to be later than the period of the erection of the shrine, and it is, besides, exceedingly improbable that such an allusion should have been commemorated by this symbol, in such a place. It is much more likely that it was placed there by the Crusaders in reference to the well-known title of Becket, "St. Thomas of *Acre*," and to the success which his intercession was supposed to have achieved in driving the Saracens out of that fortress. If so, it possesses more than a local interest, as a proof that the Crescent was already the emblem of the Seljukian Turks, long before the capture of Constantinople, which is assigned by Von Hammer as the date of the assumption of the Crescent by the Turkish power.

In confirmation of this view I subjoin the following interesting remarks of Mr. George Austin, founded on actual inspection of the materials and accompaniments of the crescent :—

" Much difficulty has been found in attempting to account for the presence of this crescent in the roof of the Trinity Chapel. Even if the legend of Becket's mother had obtained credence at that early period, the monks would not appear to have been at that time proud of the mother of their saint having been an infidel, as no reference is made to the legend in the painted windows around, and they would scarcely have neglected a subject capable of so much pictorial effect; but if so placed, why should it have been carved of foreign material?

" I have always believed it to have been one of a number of trophies which, in accordance with a well-known custom of the time, once adorned this part of the Cathedral, and I have been governed by the following reasons : First, that more than one fresco painting of encounters with the Eastern infidels formerly ornamented the walls, (the last traces of which were removed during the restoration of the Cathedral under Dean Percy, now Bishop of Carlisle), and in one of which the green Crescent flag of the enemy seems borne away by English archers. Might not these frescoes have depicted the fights in which these trophies were won? Secondly, that when the groined roof was relieved of the long accumulated coats of white-wash and repaired, some six-and-thirty years since, the Crescent was taken down and re-gilt. It was found to be made of a foreign wood, somewhat like in grain to the Eastern wood known by the name of iron-wood. It had been fastened to the groining by a large nail of very singular shape, with a large square head, apparently of foreign manufacture.

"In the hollows of the groining which radiate from the Crescent were a number of slight iron staples (the eyes of which were about 1½ inches in diameter) driven into the ceiling, and about 12 inches farther from the crescent were a number of other staples about the same diameter, but projecting 4 or 5 inches from the ceiling; many of these had been removed, and all bore traces of violence. Now if the use of these staples could be accurately defined, it would, I think, demonstrate the origin of the crescent. They could only have been used, I think, either to attach to the ceiling the cords by which the wood canopy of the shrine was raised, or suspend the lamps which doubtless were hung around the shrine below, or else to suspend trophies of which the crescent was the centre. But I believe there is little doubt that the shrine was not placed immediately beneath the centre of these rings of staples but more to the westward. But if not so placed, the canopy was doubtless raised by a pulley attached to the ceiling by *one* cord, and not by a web of upwards of twenty, and in addition to this, the staples were attached so slightly to the roof that they would not even have borne the weight of a cord alone, of the length sufficient to reach the pavement. And it does not seem likely that small lamps singly suspended from the groining would have been arranged in two small concentric circles, the inner only 2½ feet in diameter, and the exterior but 4½. Had this form been desired the ancient form of chandelier would have been adopted.

"These staples then could not have been used for those purposes, but it will be seen that they are singularly well adapted for displaying

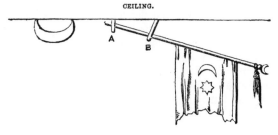

CEILING.

some such trophy as a flag or spear, for which no great strength was requisite, and the position and peculiar form of the staples favours the supposition, as the diagram shows, A being the short staple and B the long one.

"According to this view, the crescent would have formed the appropriate centre of a circle of flags, horsetails, &c., in the manner attempted to be shown in the following sketch.

"GEORGE AUSTIN."

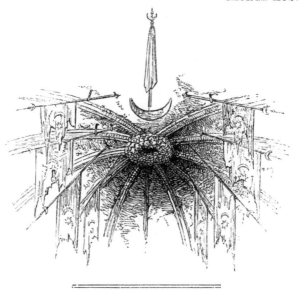

NOTE H.

THE MIRACLES OF BECKET, AS REPRESENTED IN THE PAINTED WINDOWS OF THE TRINITY CHAPEL IN CANTERBURY CATHEDRAL.

(See pp. 152, 162.)

"The space left between the slender groups of pillars round the Trinity Chapel has been so entirely filled with windows, that it appears like a single zone of light, and the effect must have been magnificent when every window was filled with painted glass.

"Of these, unfortunately, but three remain, but they are sufficient to attest their rare beauty; and for excellence of drawing, harmony of colouring, and purity of design, are justly considered unequalled. The skill with which the minute figures are represented cannot even at this day be surpassed; it is extraordinary to see how every feeling of joy or sorrow, pain and enjoyment, is expressed both in feature and position; and even in the representation of the innumerable ills and diseases which were cured at the Martyr's Shrine, in no single case do we meet with any offence against good taste, by which the eye is so frequently shocked in the cathedrals of

Bourges, Troyes, and Chartres. But in nothing is the superiority of these windows shown more than the beautiful scrolls and borders which surround the windows, and gracefully connect the groups of medallions.

"Unfortunately, the windows throughout the Cathedral, besides the effects of the decree of Henry VIII., (mentioned in p. 203,) were, during the troubles of the Civil Wars, destroyed as high as a man could reach up with a pike, at which time every figure of a priest or bishop was relentlessly broken. These windows, like everything else around, seem to have aided in paying homage to the Saint, upon whose shrine their tinted shadows fell. They were filled with illustrations of the miracles said to have been performed by the Saint after his death. Three, as has been said, still remain, and fragments of others are scattered through the building.[1]

"As these windows were very similar in arrangement, it will be sufficient to describe one of them, that towards the east on the north of the Shrine.

"The space of this window has been divided into geometric patterns, each pattern consisting of a group of nine medallions, and each of these groups has contained the illustration of one or more of the most important miracles said to have been performed at the Shrine of the Saint.

"This window has at some time been taken down, and the lights or medallions replaced without the slightest regard to their proper position, and the groups of subjects are separated and intermixed throughout the windows.

"The lower group of medallions has been filled by illustrations of a miracle, described by Benedict,[2] where a child is miraculously restored to life by means of the Saint's blood mixed with water, after having been drowned in the Medway—the body having been hours in the water. Unfortunately, but three of these medallions have escaped. In the first medallion, the boys are seen upon the bank of the Medway pelting the frogs in the sedges along the stream with stones and sticks, whilst the son is falling into the stream. In the next, his companions are shown relating the accident, with hurried gestures, to his parents at the door of their house. And in the third, we are again taken to the banks of the stream, where the parents stand gazing in violent grief upon the body of their son, which is being extracted from the water by a servant. The landscape in these medallions is exceedingly well rendered; the trees are depicted with great grace.

In the next group was pourtrayed a miracle, or rather succession of miracles. The story which is graphically told by Benedict,

---

[1] A group representing the Martyrdom remains in one of the windows of Christ Church, Oxford.—A. P. S.

[2] *Benedicti de Miraculis S. Thomæ Cantuar*, iii. c. 61. See pp. 40, 152.

is as follows:—The household of a distinguished knight, Jordan, son of Eisulf, was struck with sickness. Amongst others died first the nurse of his son, and then the son himself, a boy of ten years old. Mass was said—the body laid out—the parents were in hopeless grief. It so happened that there arrived, that day, a band of twenty pilgrims from Canterbury, whom Jordan hospitably lodged, from old affection's sake of the Martyr, whom he had intimately known. The arrival of the pilgrims recalled this friendship,—and 'his heart,' he said, 'assured him so positively of the Martyr's repugnance to the death of his son,' that he would not allow the body to be buried. . From the pilgrims he borrowed some of the diluted water so often mentioned, and bade the priest pour it into the boy's mouth. This was done without effort. He then himself uncovered the body, raised the head, forced open the teeth with a knife, and poured in a small draught. A small spot of red showed itself on the left cheek of the boy. A third draught was poured down the throat. The boy opened one eye and said, 'Why are you weeping, father?—Why are you crying, lady?—The blessed martyr Thomas has restored me to you.' He was then speechless till evening. The father put into his hands four pieces of silver, to be an offering to the Martyr before Midlent, and the parents sate and watched him. At evening, he sate up, ate, talked, and was restored.

"But the vow was forgotten, and on this a second series of wonders occurred. A leper three miles off was roused from his slumber by a voice calling him by name, 'Guirp, why sleepest thou?' He rose, asked who called him—was told that it was Thomas Archbishop of Canterbury, and that he must go and warn the knight Jordan, son of Eisulf, of the evils that would befall him unless he instantly fulfilled his vow. The leper after some delay and repetitions of the vision, sent for the priest—the priest refused to convey so idle a tale—St. Thomas appeared again—and ordered the leper to send his daughter for the knight and his wife. They came, heard, wondered, and fixed the last week in Lent for the performance of the vow. Unfortunately a visit from the Lord Warden put it out of their heads. On the last day of the last week—that is, on Easter-eve, they were suddenly startled by the illness of the eldest son which terminated fatally on the Friday after Easter. The parents fell sick at the same time, and no less than twenty of the household. The knight and his wife were determined at all hazard to accomplish their vow. By a violent effort—aided by the sacred water—they set off; the servants by a like exertion dragging themselves to the gate to see them depart. The lady fell into a swoon no less than seven times from the fatigue of the first day—but at the view of the towers of Canterbury Cathedral she dismounted, and with her husband and son, barefoot, walked for the remaining three miles into Canterbury, and then the vow was discharged.

[This story, Benedict says, he received in a private letter from the priest.[1]—A. P. S.]

"In the first compartment we see the funeral of the nurse. The body, covered by a large yellow pall, is borne on a bier carried by four men. At the head walks the priest, clothed in a white close fitting robe, adorned with a crimson chasuble, bearing in his right hand a book, and in his left the brush for sprinkling holy water. He is followed by a second priest, in a green dress, bearing a huge lighted taper; the legend at foot runs this, '*Nutricis funus reliquis sui flacra minatur.*' The next medallion represents the son at the point of death stretched on a bier. The priest at the head anoints the body with holy water, and on the forehead of the child is the Viaticum or Sacred Wafer. On a raised bench at the side sits the mother absorbed in deep grief, and by her side the father, wringing his hands and gazing sorrowfully at his expiring child; the legend attached is, '*percutitur puer moritur planctus geminatur.*' In the next compartment of the group, the mother stands at the head of the bier raising and supporting her son's head, whilst the father pours between the clenched lips the wonder-working blood and water of St. Thomas. A short distance from the bier stand the pilgrims, reverently gazing upon the scene, each with his pilgrim's staff and bottle of 'water of St. Thomas;' the legend at foot runs, '*Vox patris—vis martiris ut restituatur.*' The vow so fatally delayed forms the subject of the next medallion. The boy, still reclining on the bier; the mother, caressing her son with one hand, whilst with the other outstretched she gives to the father the 'Quatuor argenteos,' which he demands, and vows to the Saint.

"The neighbouring compartment shows the son upon a couch fast recovering, feeding himself with a spoon and bason. The parents are placed at each end of the couch in an attitude of thanksgiving. The following cartoon shows the old man struck with leprosy and bedridden. The Martyr, dressed in full robes, stands at the bedside, and charges him with the warning to the parents of the child not to neglect the performance of the vow. In the next portion of the group the leper is represented in bed conveying to the parents, who stand in deep attention at the bedside, the warning with which he has been charged by St. Thomas. The leprosy of the sick man is very curiously shown; the legend, '*Credulus accedis . . . vot . . . fert nec obedit.*' And now forming the central medallion of the group, and the most important, is depicted the vengeance of the Saint for the slighted vow and neglected warning. In the centre of a large apartment stands a bier, on which is stretched the victim of the Saint's wrath. At the head and feet of the corpse, leaning on large chairs

---

[1] Benedict, iii. 62.

R

or thrones, are the father and mother distracted with grief, the latter with uncovered head and naked feet gazing in deep despondency on her dead child.   Behind the bier are seen several figures in unusually violent attitudes expressive of grief, from which circumstance they are probably professional mourners.   Whilst unseen by the persons beneath, the figure of St. Thomas in full pontificals is appearing through the ceiling.   He bears in his right hand *a sword*, and points with his left to the dead body of the victim upon the bier.   It is singular that Becket is always represented in full episcopal costume, when appearing in dreams or visions, in these windows.   The legend attached to this light is, ' *Vindicte moles—Domus egra—mortua proles.'*

" The last medallion of the group represents the final accomplish‑ ment of the vow.   The father is seen bending reverently before the altar of the Saint, offering to the attendant priest a large bowl, filled with broad gold and silver pieces.   Near him is the mother, holding by the hand the son miraculously recalled to life.   In token of their pilgrimage, both the mother and son hold the usual staves. The expression of the various figures in the above compartments, both in gesture and feature, is rendered with great skill.   In the execution of this story, the points which doubtless the artists of the monastery were chiefly anxious to impress upon the minds of the devotees who thronged to the Shrine are prominently brought out: the extreme danger of delaying the performance of a vow, under whatever circumstances made, the expiation sternly required by the Saint, and the satisfaction with which the Martyr viewed money offerings made at his Shrine.

" The fullness with which the last group has been described, will render it less necessary to speak at length of the rest of the window, as similar miracles described by Benedict are in the same minute manner represented.

" The group above should consist of two miracles, the first described by Benedict,[1] wherein Robert, a smith from the Isle of Thanet, is miraculously cured of blindness.   In a dream, he is directed by Becket to repair to Canterbury, where a monk should anoint his eyes and restore his sight; and he is seen stretched in prayer at the priest's feet in front of the altar.   In another medallion the priest anoints his eyes with the miraculous blood, and his sight is restored. In another, Robert is seen offering at the altar a large bowl of golden pieces, in gratitude for the Saint's interference.

" The next group proves that not only offerings and prayers were made at the Shrine, but also severe penances were performed.   In one compartment, a kneeling female figure is bowing herself to the ground before the priest at the altar, who is receiving a large candle

---

[1] Benedict, i. c. 36.

PRODIRE FERETRO

REPRESENTATION OF BECKET'S
WINDOW IN CANTERBURY

SHRINE IN A PAINTED
CATHEDRAL. (Page 243.)

G. A. del.

apparently offered by her, holding a book in his left hand, whilst two men, armed with long rods, stand by. In the next medallion, the female figure is being violently beaten by the two men with the rods, one of whom stands on either side of her.

"In the third, though the woman is falling fainting to the ground, one of the figures is still striking her with the scourge. The other figure is addressing the priest, who is sitting unmoved by the scene reading from the book; a figure is standing by with a pilgrim's staff, looking at the flagellation, much concerned. A legend is attached, ' Stat modo jocunda lapsa jacet moribunda.'

"This window is undergoing a thorough repair, which has been very much needed for years past.

"In the other two windows may be traced many of the multifarious miracles described by Benedict, and by him thus summed up : [1]— ' Quæ est enim in Ecclesia conditio, quis sexus vel ætas, quis gradus vel ordo, qui non in hoc thesauro nostro aliquid sibi utile inveniat? Administratur huic schismaticis lumen veritatis, pastoribus timidis confidentia, sanitas ægrotantibus, et pænitentibus veniat ejus meritis cœci vident, claudi ambulabunt, leprosi mundantur, surdi audiunt, mortui resurgunt, loquuntur muti, pauperes evangelizantur, paralytici convalescunt, detumescunt hydropici, sensui redonantur amentes, curantur epileptici, febricitantes evadunt, et ut breviter concludatur, omnimoda curatur infirmitas.'

"G. A."

NOTE I.

REPRESENTATION OF BECKET'S SHRINE IN ONE OF THE PAINTED WINDOWS IN CANTERBURY CATHEDRAL.

(See p. 180.)

"The accompanying view of the Shrine of Becket is engraved from a portion of a painted glass window, of the 13th century, on the north side of the Trinity Chapel in Canterbury Cathedral. It is one of a group of medallions representing a vision described by Benedict[2] as having been seen by himself. Becket is here shown issuing from his shrine in full pontificals to go to the altar as if to celebrate mass. The monk to whom the vision appears is lying in the foreground on a couch. The shrine by a slight anachronism is represented as that erected subsequently to the vision; and this representation is the more valuable as being the only one known to

---

[1] Benedict, i. 2.   [2] Ibid.

exist; for there can be little doubt that the drawing in the Cottonian MS. does not attempt to represent the *Shrine*, but only the outside covering or case. The medallion is the more interesting, from being an undoubted work of the 13th century; and having been designed for a position immediately opposite to and within a few yards of the Shrine itself, and, occupying the place of honour in the largest and most important window, without doubt represents the main features of the Shrine faithfully.

"The view will be found to tally in a singular manner with the *description*, though not with the sketch in the Cottonian MS., given p. 180.

"In the drawing upon the glass cartoon, the Shrine, shaped like an ark, was placed upon a stone or marble platform which rested upon arches supported by six pillars—three on either side. The space between these pillars was open, and it was between them that crippled and diseased pilgrims were allowed to place themselves for closer approximation to the martyr's body, as mentioned by Benedict. This could not have been the case had the Cottonian drawing been correct, as no spaces are there given, but only a few very small openings. But in the glass painting it is clearly delineated, as the pillar of the architectural background, passing behind the Shrine, is again shown in the open space below. This platform was finished at the upper edge by a highly ornamented cornice, and upon this cornice the wooden cover of the Shrine rested.

"The Shrine was built of wood, the sides and sloping roof of it being ornamented with raised bands, or ribs, forming quatrefoils in the middle, and smaller half circles along the edges. This mode of ornamentation was not uncommon at that date, as is shown upon works of the kind yet remaining.

"Inside the quatrefoils and semicircles so formed were raised, in like manner, ornaments resembling leaves of three and five lobes, the then usual ornament. The wooden boards and raised bands and ornaments were then covered with plates of gold, and on the raised bands and ornamented leaves were set the most valuable of the gems. The wondrous carbuncle, or Regale of France, was doubtless set as a central ornament of one of the quatrefoils.

"The plain golden surface left between the quatrefoils and semi-circles then required some ornament to break the bright monotonous surface, and it was apparently covered with a diagonal trellis-work of golden wire, cramped at its intersections to the golden plates, as shown in the engraving. It was to this wire trellis-work that the loose jewels and pearls, rings, brooches, angels, images, and other ornaments offered at the Shrine, were attached.

"In the interior rested the body of Becket, which was exposed to view by opening a highly ornamented door or window at the ends. The saint is emerging through one of these in the view.

"These windows were occasionally opened, to allow pilgrims, probably of the highest orders, who were blind or deaf, to insert their heads.

"The ridge, or upper part of the roof, was adorned with large groups of golden leaves.

"On a comparison of the engraving, as thus explained, with the *description* given in the Cottonian MS., no discrepancy will be found, but the drawing appears to be only a simple outline approximating to the general form, or perhaps only of the wooden cover, but even that must have been ornamented in some degree.

"G. A."

The treatise of Benedict, to which allusion is made in these notes, has already been referred to in p. 152. It is a document of considerable interest, both as containing a contemporary and detailed account of these strange miracles, and also as highly illustrative of the manners of the time. On some future occasion I may return to it at length. I will here confine myself to a few particulars, which ought to have been incorporated into the body of the work.

The earlier shrine in the crypt has nowhere been so fully described. It was first opened to the public gaze on April 2nd, 1171.[1]

The body of the Saint reposed in the marble sarcophagus in which it had been deposited on the day after the murder. Round the sarcophagus, for the sake of security, was built a wall of large hewn stones, compacted with cement, iron, and lead. The wall rose to the height of a foot above the coffin, and the whole was covered by a large marble slab. In each side of the wall were two windows, to enable pilgrims to look in and kiss the tomb itself. In one of these windows it was, that Henry laid his head during his flagellation. It was a work of difficulty—sometimes an occasion for miraculous interference—to thrust the head, still more the body, through these apertures. Some adventurous pilgrims crawled entirely through, and laid themselves at full length in the space intervening between the top of the sarcophagus and the superincumbent slab; and on one occasion, the monks were in considerable apprehension, lest the intruder should be unable to creep out again.[2]

The tomb—probably the marble covering—was stuck all over with tapers, the offerings of pilgrims, like that of S. Radegonde at Poitiers; and, in the darkness of the crypt and the draughts from the open windows, it was a matter of curiosity and importance to see which kept burning for the longest time.[3] Votive memorials of waxen legs, feet, arms, anchors, hung round.[4] A monk always sate beside the tomb, to receive the gifts, and to distribute the sacred water.[5]

[1] Benedict, i. 30.
[2] *Idem.* i. 40, 41, 53, 54, 55.
[3] *Idem*, ii. 13.
[4] *Idem*, i. 77; ii. 7, 44.
[5] *Idem*, iii. 41, 58.

The "water of Canterbury," or "the water of S. Thomas," as it was called,[1] was originally contained in small earthenware pots, which were carried away in the pouches of the pilgrims. But the Saint played so many freaks with his devotees (I use the language of Benedict himself[2]), by causing all manner of strange cracks, leaks, and breakages in these pots, that a young plumber at Canterbury conceived the bold design of checking the inconvenience by furnishing the pilgrims with leaden or tin bottles instead. This was the commencement of the "ampulles" of Canterbury, and the "miracles of confraction" ceased.[3]

The water was used partly for washing, but chiefly (and this was peculiar[4] to the Canterbury pilgrims) drunk as a medicine. The effect is described as almost always that of a violent emetic.[5]

I take this opportunity of stating a doubt, which has been pointed out to me with regard to the Black Prince's visit to Canterbury on his return from France (p. 110). It appears from a letter in Rymer's "Fœdera," that he was expected to land at Plymouth; it is stated by Knyghton that he actually did so. The question, therefore, arises, whether Froissart's detailed account of his arrival at Sandwich, and of his subsequent journey to Canterbury, can be reconciled with those intimations, or, if not, which authority must give way? I would also add to the account of the battle of Poitiers the curious dispatch addressed by the Black Prince to the Bishop of Worcester a month after the engagement (Archæologia, i. 213.) It winds up with a list of prisoners, drawn up, probably by some aide-de-camp, who finishes thus :—

"Et sont pris, &c., des gentz d'armes M.IX^c.XXXIII.— Gaudete in Domino !

"Et outre sont mortz MMCCCCXXVI. Iterum dico Gaudete !"

It is remarkable that he notices that he had set out on his expedition the eve of the Translation of St. Thomas.—A. P. S.

---

[1] Benedict, i. 42, 43.
[2] Jucundum quoddam miraculum, i. 43; Ludus Martyris, i. 43 ; Jucunditatis Miracula, i. 46.
[3] Benedict, ii. 35.
[4] Idem, i. 13.
[5] Idem, i. 33, 34, 84 ; ii. 30 ; iii. 69.

INDEX.

Aberbrothock, 154

Alfege, St., tomb of, 45, 152

Argenton, 87

Augustine, St., mission of, 11; landing at Ebbe's fleet, 12—14; interview with Ethelbert, 15—17; arrival at Canterbury, 18; Stable-gate, 18; baptism of Ethelbert, 19; worship at St. Pancras, 20; monastery, library, &c., of, 24; foundation of Sees of Rochester and London, 25; death, 26; effects of his mission, 28; character, 33

Augustine's, St., Abbey, 24, 50, 148, 156, 175

Avranches, cathedral of, 88

Becket. Sources of information, 39, 40; return from France, 41; controversy with Archbishop of York, 42; parting with Abbot of St. Albans, 43; insults from Brocs of Saltwood, 44; scene in Cathedral on Christmas day, 45; the fatal Tuesday, 51; appearance of Becket, 54; interview with knights, 54, 57; retreats to Cathedral, 60; miracle of lock, 60; scene in Cathedral, 62; entrance of knights, "The Martyrdom," 63, 68, 69; watching over his dead body, 71, 72; discovery of hair shirt, 73; unwrapping his body, 75; burial, 76; canonisation, 78; effect of martyrdom and spread of his worship, 153—156, 245; shrine erected, 157; translation in 1220, 161; well, 185, 212, 214; abolition of festival, 196; trial, 198; destruction of shrine, 200, 214, 230

Benedict, 40, 152, 245

Bertha, 14, 26

Black Prince, birth of, 102; qualities, *ib.*; education at Queen's College, 103; name given, 107; visits Canterbury, 110, 246; well at Harbledown, 111; marriage, 112; chantry in crypt, *ib.*; Spanish campaign, *ib.*; return—illness, 113; appears in parliament, *ib.*; death-bed, 114; exorcism by Bishop of Bangor, 115; death, 116; mourning, 117; funeral, 118, 119, 140; tomb, 120; effect of life, 122, 123, 142; Ordinance of Chantries, 127; Will, 132, 138

Bohemian embassy, 164, 178, 183, 187, 211

Bret, or *Brito*, 48, 81, 154

Broc family, 44, 45, 62, 74

Canterbury Cathedral, first endowment of, 21; primacy, 28, 41, 42; scene in, 45; at the time of the murder, 65; desecration and re-consecration of, 77; King Henry's penance in, 92; historical lessons of, 100; tombs in, 101; Black Prince's visit to, 110; insignificance before murder of Becket, 148; Pilgrims' entrance to, 171; crypt, 178; Shrine, 181, 199, 200

Chaucer's Canterbury Tales, 166, 170

Chequers' Inn, 174

Colet, Dean, 191, 195

Cranmer, 197, 201

Crescent, 182, 236

Cressy, battle of, 104, 106

Crown, Becket's, 181, 226

Ebbe's Fleet, 12—14, 35

Edward I., 188, 210

Erasmus, 191, 195

Ethelbert, King, 14; interview with Augustine, 15—17; baptism of, 19; death of, 27

Fawkes Hall, 112
Fitzranulph, $\Big\}$ 48, 63, 88
Fitzurse,

Gorham in Normandy, 88
Gregory the Great, character, 5, 7; dialogue with Anglo-Saxon slaves, 7, 10; effects on English church, 29—31

Harbledown, 90, 171, 193, 222; Black Prince's well at, 111
Harrow, Becket parts with Abbot of St. Alban's at, 43; vicar excommunicated, 45, 46
Henry II., fury, 48; remorse, 86; penance, 88—92, 245; death, 162
Henry III., 161
Henry IV., 120
Henry VIII., 195, 198, 199
Hermansole, 32

Inns for Pilgrims, 174
Isabella, Queen, 188

John, King of England, 47, 157
John, King of France, 109, 111, 188, 221
Jubilees, 172, 189, 194

Langton, 101, 162, 164, 206
Limoges, siege of, 123
Lollards, 189, 230
London, See of, 25, 28, 42; *pilgrims approach from*, 166; *worship of Becket in*, 155
Louis VII., 183, 221
Lyons, Chapel of St. Thomas at, 153

Malling, South, turning-table at, 79
Martin's, St., Church, 14, 34
Mary, Queen, 200, 206

Montreuil, visit of Madame de, 200
Moreville, Hugh de, 48, 81, 154

Pancras, St., church of, 20
Pilgrims, 164, 187, 242, 245
Pilgrims' road, 165, 216
Pilgrims' signs, 186, 246
Poitiers, battle of, 108, 109, 126, 246

Queen's College, Oxford, 103

Reculver, 21, 27
Regale of France, 157, 183, 201, 206
Richard II., 231
Richborough, 17, 35
Rochester, foundation of See of, 25

Saltwood Castle, 44, 50
Sandwich, 41, 164, 211
Sens, 153, 158
Southampton, King Henry arrives at, 90; pilgrims approach from, 165
Stable-gate, 18
Sudbury, Simon of, 101, 119, 190

Tabard Inn, 169
Tracy, 48, 54, 82, 83, 223

Verona, Church of St. Thomas at, 153

William the Englishman and *of Sens*, 158, 159
William Thomas, 215
William the Lion, 93, 154
Wilsnake, 232
Wycliffe, 104

York, controversy with Archbishop of, 41, 42

THE END.

LONDON:
BRADBURY AND EVANS, PRINTERS, WHITEFRIARS.

For EU product safety concerns, contact us at Calle de José Abascal, 56–1°, 28003 Madrid, Spain or eugpsr@cambridge.org.

www.ingramcontent.com/pod-product-compliance
Ingram Content Group UK Ltd.
Pitfield, Milton Keynes, MK11 3LW, UK
UKHW010345140625
459647UK00010B/836